JOHN NICHOLS and SON, Printers,
Red Lion Passage, Fleet Street, London.

# TO MRS. MOORE.

*London, July* 4, 1809.

MY DEAR AND HONOURED MOTHER,

To you I dedicate this account of the late Campaign in Spain; where your eldest Son quitted life in the manner he had always aspired to.

Being unable to write what was worthy of him, I have collected the facts, and arranged the materials, to enable Historians to do him justice.

Should they enter into his private character, they ought to represent him as a man who felt for his Father and Mother filial piety; and for his Sister and Brothers fraternal affection : who was faithful in friendship, and in his intercourse with the world was guided by honour.

When they shall display those qualities and actions which properly belong to the province of History, if truth be observed, he must be described as exercising his genius in the profession of Arms for the service of his Country, to which he had devoted his life. Finally, he must be shewn leading on to victory a British army, which he had preserved by his wisdom, and falling gloriously in the front of battle !

The contemplation of what he was, is your chief consolation ; and to assist in disclosing his achievements is the highest ambition of one of his Brothers, and

Your affectionate Son,

JAMES MOORE.

v

# PREFACE.

----------

THERE is here presented to the Public, perhaps, the most authentic fragment of History on record : for Sir John Moore kept a journal of his proceedings ; and, with an exactness unusual in a military man, preserved every official paper, or letter of importance, which he received, together with copies of those which he wrote.

All these documents the author has in his possession ; and he has, besides, had the opportunity of acquiring full information respecting the events. He could not misrepresent them, had he been so inclined, without being exposed to immediate detection ; but he is under no temptation either to disguise or to conceal any part of the conduct of the person in whom he is most deeply interested. His only wish has been to make a full disclosure ; and with this view he has, as much as possible, made every individual concerned explain himself by his own letters; which, together with other documents, are selected and arranged in the order adapted to elucidate the facts.

There is also given a connecting narrative; and such reflections are added as naturally arose out of the transactions.

The intermingling of a multitude of letters with the narration, though not the most concise, is certainly the most candid mode of describing the Campaign ; for, if a false inference be drawn, the reader can immediately discover it.

One disagreeable consequence, however, is likely to be produced by so open an explanation : it may irritate those whose conduct cannot bear investigation. The love of tranquillity, his professional avocations, and his private interest, would have hindered the Author from undertaking so laborious a work, and engaging in such vexatious hostility, had he not been urged forward by an impulse superior to these combined motives. He could not remain passive when his Brother's memory was assailed by ungenerous attacks and dark insinuations. The sufferers from this publication ought to bear in recollection, that the Author only acts defensively; and they should point their indignation against the first assailants, who are the original cause of any mortification they may endure.

Although the reason for composing this work is of a private nature, yet it cannot fail being of public utility both to Spain and Great Britain; for success in future operations is more likely to be obtained, when there is a competent knowledge of the past.

As many original documents are incorporated with the narrative, as were considered requisite to explain clearly the transactions, without embarrassing the reader with repetitions.

The whole correspondence with Mr. Frere is given, except two useless letters from him, which were never received by the General, and which on that account were considered as improper to be published.

All Sir John Moore's dispatches to the Secretary of State are placed in the Appendix; the omissions, which are very few, and quite immaterial to the. publick, are marked by blank spaces.

The Spanish Documents in their own language, and Translations of the French letters, are also given in the Appendix.

# INDEX

## TO THE

## *LETTERS AND PAPERS.*

———————

| | Page. |
|---|---|
| Sir John Moore to Lord William Bentinck, dated Salamanca, 13th Nov. 1808, | 21 |
| Sir John Moore to the Right Hon. J. H. Frere, Almeida, 10th November, | 29 |
| Mr. Frere to Sir John Moore, Aranjuez, 13th November, | 31 |
| Sir John Moore to Mr. Frere, Salamanca, 16th November, | 33 |
| The same to the same, Salamanca, 19th November, | 38 |
| General Leith to Sir John Moore, Renedo, 15th November, | 40 |
| Sir David Baird to Sir John Moore, ———, 23rd November, | 48 |
| Mr. Frere to Sir John Moore, Aranjuez, 25th November, | 53 |
| Mr. Frere à S. E. Mr. de Garay, Aranjuez, 23rd November, | 56 |
|    Translation of Ditto, | 310 |
| Mr. de Garay to Mr. Frere, Aranjuez, 24th November, | 60 |
| Sir John Moore to Mr. Frere, Salamanca, 27th November, | 63 |
| Sir John Moore to Charles Stuart, Esq. Salamanca, 27th November, | 65 |
| Sir John Moore to Sir David Baird, Salamanca, 28th November, | 69 |
| Sir John Moore to Lieutenant-General Hope, Salamanca, 28th November, | 70 |
| Sir John Moore to Charles Stuart, Esq. Salamanca, 29th November, | 73 |
| Sir John Moore to Charles Stuart, Esq. Salamanca, 1st December, | 74 |
| Charles Stuart, Esq. to Sir John Moore, Madrid, 30th November, | 77 |
| Mr. Frere to Sir John Moore, Aranjuez, 30th November, | 79 |
| The same to the same, Aranjuez, the same day, | 80 |
| Mr. de Garay to Sir John Moore, Aranjuez, 28th November, | 85 |
| Prince of Castelfranco and Don T. Morla to Sir John Moore, Madrid, 2nd Dec. | 87 |

|  | Page. |
|---|---|
| Mr. Frere to Sir John Moore, dated Talavera, 3rd December, | 88 |
| Sir John Moore to Sir David Baird, Salamanca, 5th December, | 91 |
| The same to the same, Salamanca, 6th December, | 92 |
| Sir John Moore to the Marquis la Romana, Salamanca, 6th December, | 93 |
| Mr. Frere to Sir John Moore, 3rd December, | 95 |
| Sir John Moore to Mr. Frere, Salamanca, 6th December, | 97 |
| The same to the same, Salamanca, the same day, | 100 |
| Sir John Moore to the Duke of Castelfranco and Mr. de Morla, Salamanca, 6th December, | 101 |
| The Junta of Toledo to H. E. Sir John Moore, Toledo, 5th December, | 104 |
| Sir John Moore to their Excellencies the Junta of Toledo, Salamanca, 7th December, | 105 |
| Don Ventura Escalante to Sir John Moore, La Calzada de Banos, 7th Dec. | 109 |
| Sir John Moore à Le Marquis la Romana, Salamanca, 8th December, | 110 |
| Translation of Ditto | 313 |
| Sir John Moore to Sir David Baird, Salamanca, 8th December, | 111 |
| Colonel Graham to Sir John Moore, Talavera de la Reina, 7th and 8th Dec. | 112 |
| Sir John Moore to Sir David Baird, Salamanca, 12th December, | 116 |
| Sir John Moore to Mr. Frere, Salamanca, 12th December, | 118 |
| Marquis la Romana à Sir John Moore, Leon, 11th December, | 120 |
| Translation of Ditto, | 314 |
| Le Prince de Neuchatel au Duc de Dalmatie, Chamartin, 10th December, | 121 |
| Translation of Ditto, | 314 |
| Sir John Moore to Sir David Baird, Head Quarters, Alaejos, 14th December | 125 |
| Sir John Moore to Mr. Frere, Toro, 15th December, | 127 |
| Lieutenant-Colonel Symes to Sir David Baird, Leon, 14th December, | 128 |
| Marquis la Romana à Sir John Moore, Leon, 14th December, | 132 |
| Translation of Ditto, | 316 |
| Don Martin de Garay to Mr. Frere, Truxillo, 8th December, | 134 |
| Mr. Frere to Sir John Moore, Truxillo, 8th December, | 138 |
| Sir John Moore to the Marquis la Romana, Castro Nuevo, 18th December, | 141 |
| Marquis la Romana à Sir John Moore, Leon, 19th December, | 144 |
| Translation of Ditto, | 318 |
| Duc de l'Infantado à S. E. J. H. Frere, Cuença, 13th December, | 147 |
| Translation of Ditto | 320 |
| Mr. Frere to Sir John Moore, Merida, 14th December, | 149 |
| The same to the same, Las Santos, 16th December, | 154 |

|  |  | Page. |
|---|---|---|
| Sir John Moore to the Marquis la Romana, dated Sahagun, 22nd December, | | 156 |
| Marquis la Romana à Sir John Moore, Leon, 21st December, | - | 157 |
| Translation of Ditto | - | 321 |
| Sir John Moore to the Marquis la Romana, Sahagun, 23rd December, | - | 159 |
| Sir John Moore to Mr. Frere, Sahagun, 23rd December, | - | 160 |
| Marquis la Romana à Sir John Moore, Leon, 22nd December, | - | 162 |
| Translation of Ditto | - | 323 |
| Marquis la Romana à Sir John Moore, Mansilla, 23rd December, | - | 163 |
| Translation of Ditto, | - | 323 |
| Sir John Moore to the Marquis la Romana, Sahagun, 23rd December, | - | 163 |
| The same to the same, Sahagun, 24th December, | - | 166 |
| The same to the same, Sahagun, the same day, | - | 170 |
| Colonel Symes to Sir John Moore, Mansilla, 25th December, | - | 171 |
| Sir John Moore to the Marquis la Romana, Benavente, 27th December, | | 176 |
| Mr. Frere to Sir John Moore, Seville, 28th December, | - | 200 |
| The same to the same, Seville, 2nd January, 1809, | - | 208 |
| General Orders by the Commander in Chief, | - | 225 |
| Sir David Baird to Lord Castlereagh, His Majesty's Ship Ville de Paris, at Sea, 18th January, | - | 227 |
| Lieutenant-General Hope to Sir David Baird, His Majesty's Ship Audacious, off Corunna, 18th January, | - | 228 |

## APPENDIX.

| A. | Lord Castlereagh to Sir John Moore, Downing Street, 25th Sept. 1808, | 237 |
|---|---|---|
| B. | Lord Castlereagh to Lord William Bentinck, London, 30th September, | 241 |
| C. | Sir John Moore to Lord Castlereagh, Lisbon, 9th October, | 243 |
| D. | The same to the same, Lisbon, the same day, | 245 |
| E. | The same to the same, Lisbon, 18th October, | 246 |
| F. | The same to the same, Lisbon, the same day, | 248 |
| G. | The same to the same, Lisbon, 27th October, | 250 |
| H. | Resolution of a Council of War of the Spanish Generals, Tudela, 5th November, | 252 |
| I. | Don Pedro Cevallos to Charles Stuart, Esq. Aranjuez, 6th November, | 253 |
| K. | Lord Castlereagh to Sir John Moore, Downing Street, 14th November, | 254 |
| L. | Sir John Moore to Lord Castlereagh, Salamanca, 24th November, | 257 |
| | The same to the same, Salamanca, the same day, | 260 |

Page.

M. Sir John Moore to Lord Castlereagh, dated Salamanca, 25th November, 264

N. The same to the same, Salamanca, 25th November, - - - 265

O. The same to the same, Salamanca, 26th November, - - 267

P. The same to the same, Salamanca, 29th November, - - 268

Q. Marquis la Romana to Sir John Moore, Leon, 30th November, - 269

R. Sir John Moore to Lord Castlereagh, Salamanca, 5th December, 270

S. The same to the same, Salamanca, the same day, - - 273

T. Mr. de Garay to Sir John Moore, Aranjuez, 28th November, - 274

V. El Principe de Castelfranco and Don Thomas Morla to Sir John Moore, Madrid, 2nd December, - - - - - 275

U. Thirteenth Bulletin of the French Army in Spain, Madrid, 2nd and 4th December, - - - - - 276

Fourteenth Ditto, Madrid, 5th December, - - - 277

W. Mr. de Garay to Mr. Frere, Truxillo, 8th December, - - 283

X. Junta of Toledo to Sir John Moore, Toledo, 5th December, - 286

Y. Number of Effective Soldiers who marched from Portugal under Sir John Moore, - - - - - - - 287

Number of Effective Soldiers who marched from Corunna under Sir David Baird, - - - - - - 288

Z. Sir John Moore to Lord Castlereagh, Salamanca, 8th December - 289

A A. The same to the same, Salamanca, 10th December, - - 291

B B. The same to the same, Salamanca, 12th December, - - 293

C C. Don Ventura Escalante to Sir John Moore, Calzada de Banos, 7th Dec. 296

D D. Sir John Moore to Lord Castlereagh, Toro, 16th December, - 297

E E. The same to the same, Benavente, 28th December, - - 300

The same to the same, Benavente, the same day, - - 303

The same to the same, Astorga, 31st December, - - 303

F F. The same to the same, Corunna, 13th January, 1809, - 306

Translations of Letters in the French Language, - - - 310

# AN ACCOUNT

OF

## THE LATE CAMPAIGN

OF THE

# BRITISH ARMY IN SPAIN,

COMMANDED BY

HIS EXCELLENCY

*LIEUT.-GENERAL SIR JOHN MOORE, K. B.*

&c. &c. &c.

---

ALTHOUGH The King and the British Nation have proclaimed their admiration of Sir John Moore as loudly as of any of the most distinguished military characters that preceded him: yet, like the Great and Good of every age, he has not escaped the insinuations of Envy, even after terminating an illustrious career by a most glorious death. The effects of Calumny against so noble a character can be of no long duration; but during that period the Relatives and Friends suffer, and the uninformed part of the Publick remain, in some degree, in suspence. It is, therefore, incumbent on a Brother by unfolding the truth to prove to all, that the pretended facts upon which the malignant representations were founded, are utterly false.

This plain narrative, extracted from his own Journal, authenticated by original documents, official records, and the reports of Staff Officers, will give to his beloved countrymen some faint idea of the zeal, valour, and skill, with which he served them.

B

Few private men have risen to so conspicuous a station as that filled by Sir John Moore with fewer enemies. This was chiefly owing to his modest and unassuming manners, to firmness tempered with kindness towards those under his command, and to a conduct to all scrupulously just. He spent his life in the army; and his popularity, both among Officers and Soldiers, never was exceeded. But universal approbation never was attained by Man : and it must be admitted that with Politicians he was not sufficiently pliant to be always equally approved of by them.

The mystery in which the transactions in Sweden were involved, gave the lovers of detraction an opportunity too tempting to be neglected.

Should it become necessary, the conduct of Sir John Moore at that Court can be most satisfactorily explained. But all that shall at present be communicated is, that, in the month of May 1808, he was entrusted with the command of ten thousand men to assist Sweden against a combined attack from Russia, France, and Denmark.

On the 17th of May this army reached Gottenburgh; and it was soon intimated that the troops were not to be permitted to land ; the soldiers and horses, consequently, remained tossing on board the crowded transports. Sir John Moore prudently suppressed the feelings excited by so inhospitable a reception, so opposite from what he had been led to expect : and he repaired to Stockholm to communicate his orders, and to concert measures for the security of Sweden. He there found to his surprise, that, although the Swedish army was quite inadequate even for defensive operations, His Majesty's thoughts were entirely bent on conquest.

It was first proposed that the British should remain in their ships, till some Swedish regiments were collected at Gottenburgh ; and that the combined forces should land and conquer Zealand.

Upon an examination of this plan, it was acknowledged, that the Island of Zealand, besides containing several strong fortresses, was filled with a far superior regular force to any that could be assembled. And also that the Island of Funen was full of French and Spanish troops, which could not be hindered from crossing over in small bodies. Sir John Moore, in the mildest and most respectful manner, represented, that these difficulties seemed too great to be surmounted by the bravest troops.

It was next proposed, that the British alone should land in Russian Finland; storm a fortress, and take a position there.

This notion was still more preposterous than the former: and Sir John Moore endeavoured to prove that ten thousand British were insufficient to encounter the principal force of the Russian Empire, which could quickly be brought against them at a point so near Petersburgh.

The objections which he was obliged to make to these, and to another scheme equally impracticable, drew upon him the resentment of his Swedish Majesty, who arrested him in his Capital. He, however, with considerable address, withdrew from the thraldom of Sweden without committing his Government: and, conformably to his instructions, brought back the army to England.

At his return, he was honoured with the approbation of the Ministers and of his Sovereign: indeed, there is no doubt, that, with a General possessed of less good sense and political firmness, the Army would have been exposed to inevitable destruction.

After having acted both in the Mediterranean and in Sweden as Commander in Chief, Sir John Moore was now superseded by Sir Harry Burrard; and he received the Secretary of State's Orders to serve in Portugal, as Third in Command.

There are few Generals in the British service who would not have resigned upon such treatment. But, superior to modern military etiquette, he possessed a large portion of the antient Roman spirit : for he has been heard to declare, that he would never refuse serving his Country while he was able; and that if The King commanded him to act as an Ensign, he would obey.

In conformity to this patriotic principle, after resigning his command at Portsmouth to Sir Harry Burrard, he sailed in the fleet to Portugal on the 31st of May.

Two Generals so circumstanced, seldom live very amicably together: but Sir John Moore, instead of behaving with dry reserve towards the person who was thus placed over him, evinced to Sir Harry the deference due to his Commanding Officer; and behaved with so much good humour, that they lived together in perfect harmony.

This army did not arrive in Portugal till after the battle of Vimeira, and the subsequent armistice. These transactions, therefore, do not come within the scope of this narrative. Yet it is proper to mention that Sir John Moore, upon learning the particulars of the action, bestowed warm praises upon Sir Arthur Wellesley. He declared to Sir Hew Dalrymple, the new Commander, that he wished to wave all pretensions derived from his seniority; that as Sir Arthur had done so much, it was fair he should take the lead in the operations against Lisbon; and, if the good of the service required it, he would execute any part that was allotted to him, without interfering with Sir Arthur.

No opportunity, however, of this kind presented itself; as a Convention was agreed upon between the British and French Commanders, for the evacuation of Portugal by the French troops.

While this was carrying into effect, Sir Arthur Wellesley applied for leave of absence, and soon returned to England; and several General Officers followed his example.

Sir Hew Dalrymple was next recalled, and the Command devolved upon Sir Harry Burrard. But this General, from bad health and other causes, requested leave to resign.

It was not thought advisable by the Cabinet again to supersede Sir John Moore : accordingly, on the 6th of October * dispatches arrived from London, conferring upon him the chief command of an army to be employed in Spain.

It appears, by various Government dispatches, that the design of sending an army into Galicia was communicated to Sir Hew Dalrymple in August. But the necessity of transporting the army of Junot to France occasioned this measure to be deferred. It was now resolved that it should be carried into execution.

Sir John was ordered to send the Cavalry by land; and it was left to his discretion to move the Infantry and Artillery either by sea or land.

It was also communicated to him, that fifteen thousand men were ordered to Corunna; and he was directed to give such orders to Sir David Baird, their Commander, as would most speedily effect a junction of the whole force.

From the moment that Sir John Moore obtained this command, he exerted the utmost activity to fulfil the instructions; and received essential assistance from Sir Harry Burrard, who forwarded the expedition with the greatest zeal. Before this time nothing had been begun for the equipment of the troops, or for their advance: all was to be done, and all was accomplished with celerity; for the greatest part of the troops were in motion in eight days.

Soon after the General entered upon his command, he published the following Order to his troops.

* Vide Appendix A. and B.

" General Orders. *Lisbon, 9th October*, 1808.

" THE Troops under Lieut.-General Sir John Moore will hold
" themselves in readiness to move on the shortest notice.

" The Lieut.-General trusts that the General Officers will lose
" no time in ascertaining, that the Regiments under their command
" are in good order and complete in every equipment to enable
" them to keep the field.

" Lieut.-General Sir John Moore will take an early opportunity of
" inspecting the several corps of the army.

" All the heavy baggage will be left in Lisbon, and directions
" will be given hereafter respecting it.

" The General Officers will communicate with the Commanding
" Officers of corps, upon the situation and fitness of the stores
" for their heavy baggage, and report thereupon for the information
" of Lieut.-General Sir J. Moore.

" Directions will be given with respect to the sick. The Lieut.-
" General sees with much concern the great number of this descrip-
" tion, and that it daily increases. The General assures the troops,
" that it is owing to their own intemperance, that so many of them
" are rendered incapable of marching against the Enemy: and having
" stated this, he feels confident that he need say no more to British
" soldiers to insure their sobriety."

This Order was understood to have been relished by the soldiers,
and had some effect upon them. And previous to their setting
off, another Order was issued to instruct them in their conduct
towards the Spaniards.

" G. O.                                     *Head Quarters,*
                                    *Lisbon, 15th October,* 1808.

" THE Commander of the Forces trusts, that on the troops enter-
" ing Spain, they will feel with him how much it is for their honour
" and advantage to maintain the high opinion, and cherish the good-
" will, which that brave and high-spirited people entertain towards
" the British Nation.

" The troops will generally be received by the inhabitants. The
" Spaniards are a grave, orderly people, extremely sober; but gene-
" rous and warm in their temper, and easily offended by any insult
" or disrespect which is offered them; they are grateful to the
" English, and will receive the troops with kindness and cordiality.

" This the General hopes will be returned with equal kindness
" on the part of the soldiers, and that they will endeavour to ac-
" commodate themselves to their manners, be orderly in their
" quarters, and not shock, by intemperance, a people worthy of
" their attachment, and whose efforts they are come to support
" in the most glorious of causes—to free themselves from French
" bondage, and to establish their national liberty and independence.

" Upon entering Spain, in compliment to the Spanish nation,
" the Army will wear the Red Cockade in addition to their own."

It is proper to remark here, that British armies are little experienced in the business of a long campaign on shore. Our warfare
has usually been carried on by maritime expeditions: and we are
extremely defective in the organization of the departments which
are requisite for the field; the Commissariat particularly is inferior
to that of France. But no part of military affairs was unknown
to the General; he was capable of forming, in some degree, what

was deficient; and, though he complains of the inexperience of some of the departments, he writes with approbation of their zeal and exertions. The directions of Government were, that the Cavalry should be sent by land*; but a discretionary power was given to the Commander to move the Infantry, by sea or land, as he judged best. Upon an examination of the subject, there was found to be no choice; for, independently of the uncertainty and danger of a coasting voyage in winter, which, even when prosperous, unhinges the whole machinery of an army, it was ascertained that, at Corunna, there were hardly the means of equipping and forwarding the corps commanded by Sir David Baird †.—The Spanish Government deputed Colonel Lopez, a Spanish officer, who was well acquainted with the roads and resources of the country, to assist the British army on its march, to establish magazines, and to make the necessary arrangements with Sir John Moore. He confirmed the former intelligence, and pressed him in the name of the Junta, to march by land; assuring him, that if he went by sea, one half of the army could never leave the coast for want of necessaries.

The next question was, whether they should proceed in a northerly direction, through Portugal to Almeida; or should take the great Eastern road to Elvas, and thence march through Estremadura. Necessity decided this question likewise; for it was found that the whole could not be subsisted on the road by Elvas; no magazines having been formed for such a body of troops. When the Spanish Commissary General was consulted on this subject, and when the quantity of meat required by the British army was explained to him, he computed, that were they to be supplied with the rations specified, in three months all the oxen would be consumed, and very few hogs would be left in the country.

* Vide Appendix A.       † Appendix C. D. E. F.

Strict enquiry was then made respecting the roads through the North of Portugal, where there was known to be abundance of food.

He found the Portuguese at Lisbon incredibly ignorant of the state of the roads of their own country; but all agreed that cannon could not be transported over the mountains, which form the northern boundary between Spain and Portugal. Even British Officers, who had been sent to examine the roads, confirmed the Portuguese intelligence.

As equipments could not be procured at Corunna, as food could not be supplied on the road by Elvas, and as the artillery could not be drawn over the Portuguese mountains, it became absolutely necessary to divide the Army.

This distressing measure was not adopted but from necessity. In an absolute Government, like France, where the Ruler is skilled in military operations, and possesses power to bring forth all the means and resources of the country, such difficulties vanish; but in Spain and Portugal few obstructions can ever be removed by the Government; they can only be evaded.

It was then determined to send five brigades of artillery to accompany the cavalry through Spain; and four regiments of infantry were added for their protection.

This important corps of six thousand men were entrusted to Lieut.-General Hope, and directed to march by Elvas on the Madrid road, to Badajos and Espinar. And two brigades under General Paget moved by Elvas and Alcantara.

The rest of the army moved through Portugal.

Two brigades under General Beresford went by Coimbra and Almeida.

Three brigades under General Fraser, by Abrantes and Almeida.

Sir John Moore thinking it of very great importance that some

c

artillery should accompany these corps, ordered one light brigade of six pounders, under Captain Wilmot, to proceed through Portugal; and he trusted to this Officer's activity to transport the guns over the mountains by dint of labour.

The different regiments of each division followed each other in succession to facilitate the march; Sir John Moore intending, that the whole of the troops coming from Portugal should unite at Salamanca; and that Sir David Baird and General Hope should either join them there, or at Valladolid.

The several divisions having moved off, Sir John left Lisbon on the 27th of October *. And I shall here introduce some remarks on the state of Spain, and on the plan of the Campaign decided on by the British Government.

Towards the end of summer, after the surrender of Dupont, the French Army retired from Madrid, and repassed the Ebro. Their force in this direction consisted of above 45,000 men concentrated in Navarre and Biscay; their right at Bilboa, and their left at Aybar. They had besides garrisons in Barcelona, Figueras, and other fortresses in Catalonia, amounting to fully 15,000 men more.

In these positions they quietly waited for reinforcements. And every foreign journal announced, that vast bodies of troops of every description were hastening through Germany and France to Bayonne.

During this period the Spanish and English newspapers were reporting the enthusiastic patriotism of the Spaniards; that all ranks, young and old, had taken up arms, were eager to rush upon their enemies, and determined to die rather than submit to a treacherous, cruel, and impious Invader. Such was the spirit of the proclamations

* Vide Appendix G.

of the provincial Juntas,—all vying with each other in magna-
nimous expressions.

But the British Government, not trusting to such authorities, sent
Officers and Agents into various parts of Spain, who rivalled each
other in reporting the universal ardour of the country. Full credit
appears to have been given to this description of the state of Spain;
and the British Army was dispatched into Leon to participate in
the glory of expelling the French from the Peninsula.

The Spanish Government recommended Burgos as the point of
union for the British troops, and Madrid and Valladolid were the
places appointed for magazines. And Government communicated
to Sir John Moore, through Lord William Bentinck, that it was
expected he would find between sixty and seventy thousand men,
assembled under Blake and Romana, in the Asturias and Galicia*.
These were independent of the armies on the front and left flank
of the French position. The latter was conceived to be the most
numerous of any, and placed under the command of the Marquis
de Castanos.

The conviction of the universal enthusiasm of the Spaniards was,
at this time, so prevalent in the British Cabinet, that, in a memorial
transmitted for the information of Sir John Moore by the Secretary
of State, it is stated, that the French Armies could not enter the
defiles of the Asturias without exposing themselves to be destroyed,
even by the armed peasants.

But the strongest proof of the misinformation upon the state of
Spanish affairs is this, that in the month of September it was considered most probable, that the Spaniards alone would soon drive
the French out of the Peninsula. This conviction was so strong,
that enquiries were directed to be made by Lord William Bentinck

* Vide Appendix B.

respecting the intentions of the Spanish Government upon the expulsion of the French. And directions were given, under particular circumstances, to urge the invasion of the South of France with a combined British and Spanish Army.

Had these relations been well founded, and had the general fervour really existed, there could have been no objections to sending the British Army by the nearest roads to join such numerous and intrepid allies. For the most timid could entertain no apprehensions, if the French were to be assaulted by such superior numbers.

Such was the flattering picture of affairs that was presented to the view of Sir John Moore, before he commenced his march, and was enabled to judge for himself.

In passing through the Portuguese territory the troops behaved with order and regularity, which formed a striking contrast to the cruelty and rapine that of late years disgrace the French armies. The people were civil; but considerable difficulties occurred respecting provisioning the troops. Saltero, a contractor at Lisbon, had agreed to supply the divisions with rations on the march through Portugal. But this man failed in his contract; and the divisions of General Fraser and Beresford were obliged to be halted; and, had it not been for the great exertions of the Generals, the troops would have been long delayed.

There was also a great want of money, from which excessive inconveniences resulted. It had been supposed that Government bills would have been accepted. But promissary notes do not obtain credit in Spain and Portugal, as in England. At Guarda, the Chief Magistrate refused to procure provisions without regular payments, and the peasantry had a dread of paper money. These difficulties were, however, surmounted, but not without great expence.

The Commander of the Forces was usually entertained with politeness at the houses of the nobility. He saw little appearance of a French party, but was surprised to observe the slight interest the Portuguese took in public affairs. They were generally well inclined, but luke-warm.

As Sir John Moore was approaching the scene of action, he gradually acquired just notions of Spanish affairs; for he was in close correspondence with men of candour and discernment, who resided on the spot. Little was written by them of Spanish ardour and enthusiasm: their letters, on the contrary, were filled with details of the weakness and tardiness of the Central Junta.

This assembly consisted of thirty-four persons with equal powers. So numerous an executive body was ill calculated for prompt decisions. Self-interest, mutual jealousy and discord, distracted their councils. There was no predominant leader to give uniformity to their acts, no animating passions to elevate their minds. By cold languor, and foggy dullness, they chilled and damped the spirits of the nation.

The love of independence and hatred of a tyrant so instantaneously excite all the energies of Britons, that they can hardly credit the sluggish indifference that pervaded the Spanish nation, when menaced by the rapid approach of the victorious armies of Buonaparte.

Judging what he could do, by what Spaniards were capable of, they thought it almost impossible for his army to traverse the Pyrennees in winter. But should the French have the temerity to effect such a passage, it was believed they would soon be famished. These notions were applicable to the resources formerly possessed by France. But the magnitude of the military preparations of their present enemy, and the celerity of his movements, confounded all such calculations.

Lord William Bentinck saw clearly the error committed by the Spaniards. In a dispatch about the beginning of October he observes, with a melancholy presage, " I am every moment more and more " convinced, that a blind confidence in their own strength, and na- " tural slowness, are the rocks upon which this good ship runs the " risk of being wrecked."

It was wondered at in England, why the bold patriots, who were believed to be swarming in Spain, did not charge the discomfited remains of the French armies lurking behind the Ebro: Why are they not exterminated before they are reinforced?

The Marquis de Castanos and General Blake could have answered these enquiries very satisfactorily to all intelligent military men. For it is clear from existing documents, that the Spanish armies were so weak in numbers, and so wretchedly equipped, as to be incapable of encountering the French, even before their reinforcements arrived. This deplorable deficiency was carefully concealed, to prevent its sinking the nation into despair.

Notwithstanding the extensive correspondence which Sir John Moore carried on, he could obtain no certain accounts of the numbers or condition of the Spanish forces, before the arrival of Buonaparte. But after that event, when they had assembled all their new levies, it was found that the Armies of the Centre and Right united, under the Generals Castanos and Palafox, only formed a force of 40,000 men. And the following extract from the Resolutions of a Council of War composed of the principal Spanish Generals, which was held at Tudela on the 5th of November, exposes part of the distresses of these armies. At this period General Blake's army, called the Army of the Left, was known to be in the utmost danger; yet the Council came to this resolution:

"Attention being had to the actual state of penury and want, "which the Army of the Centre, destitute of the most necessary "means, is suffering; considering also that this effective force is "much less than had been supposed; it is agreed that in the present "moment it cannot be of assistance to the Army of the Left, not- "withstanding the conviction of the urgency of such assistance," &c. *

* Vide Appendix H.

To give a further view of the state of the principal Spanish Army, I shall extract a short passage from the Marquis of Castanos's dispatches to the Secretary of the Central Junta, Nov. 25, 1808.

" I leave to your Excellency to conceive the critical situation of an " army immoveable from its few resources, and the greatest part " of which was composed of new levies, badly clothed, and badly " provisioned."

This was the language of the Spaniards. And I shall give an extract of a Letter from Captain Whittingham to Lord William Bentinck, which will shew the impression that the appearance of part of their army made upon an English officer.

*Head Quarters, Calahorra,*
*28th Oct.* 1808.

" On the 25th General Castanos left this place for Logrono. We " arrived about four in the evening. The army of Castile was drawn " up to receive the General. Its strength about 11,000 men. But " to form any idea of its composition, it is absolutely necessary to " have seen it. It is a complete mass of miserable peasantry, with- " out clothing, without organization, and with few Officers that de- " serve the name.

" The General and principal Officers have not the least confidence " in their troops; and, what is yet worse, the men have no con- " fidence in themselves.

" This is not an exaggerated picture; it is a true portrait," &c. &c.

Such was the condition and amount of the troops under Castanos and Palafox towards November, after all were collected that could be raised. But in August and September they were, doubtless, much fewer. Castanos found it dangerous to approach the French posts. The Spaniards sometimes engaged in skirmishes; but were so much worsted, that they found it prudent to keep at a distance, and wait for reinforcements.

A similar reason accounts for the inactivity of General Blake during these important months. The disposition to exaggeration in Spain is such, that it is difficult even now to ascertain what was the number of this army. But it certainly could never have been considerable; for after the arrival of Romana's corps, of upwards of 8000 men, and every exertion that was made, it appears from Captain Carrol's dispatches that the actual number that fought the French did not amount to 17,000 men. And the want of Officers, of food, of clothing, and of every species of warlike equipment, was lamentable. Instead of General Blake being culpable for not attacking the French, his error undoubtedly was extreme rashness.

Sir John Moore, by the close correspondence he carried on with Lord William Bentinck, Mr. Stuart, Colonel Graham and others, gradually penetrated the disguises with which the Spanish Government enveloped their affairs. It is self-evident, that a judicious plan of a campaign can only be formed by reflecting upon the actual state of things: and must necessarily be ill-contrived, and probably unsuccessful, if drawn up on false intelligence. Yet the Spanish Juntas exerted all their finesse to deceive, not their enemy, but their ally; and succeeded so perfectly, as to lead them to execute a plan adapted to a state of circumstances the reverse of their real condition. Their high-sounding proclamations, exaggerated numbers, invented victories, and vaunted enthusiasm, could not deceive him whom it was useful to deceive. Buonaparte possessed ample means of obtaining exact information. There were traitors, even among the loudest seeming patriots; who enabled him to calculate, with perfect accuracy, the precise portion of patriotism scattered through Spain.

Yet there are some facts that would lead one almost to suspect, that the Spanish Juntas, from excess of presumption, ignorance, and a heated imagination, were so blinded, as to have misled the British Cabinet unintentionally. For it is a well-known fact, that at first they considered Spain as more than a match for France. They applied to us for arms and money, but said they wanted no men: believing they could raise more soldiers, than they required. How long this infatuation continued, I cannot pretend to say; but they appear to have acquiesced in the offer of British auxiliaries on the 26th of September.

It happened that accounts were brought to the Junta at Aranjuez, Oct. 4th, of " a Letter having been intercepted, addressed by " the Governor of Bayonne to Marshal Jourdan (the French Com- " mander in Chief) wherein it is stated, that between the 16th of " October and the 16th of November reinforcements to the amount of " 66,000 infantry and from 5 to 7000 cavalry might be expected to " enter Spain.

" Mr. Stuart will tell you that this news is credited."

That this news was correct, I have no doubt. Buonaparte, though he constantly attempts to deceive the world by his public proclamations, has too much political wisdom to deceive his own Generals. Nor could he have thrown this letter purposely in the way of the Spaniards, as he could not wish to rouse them from their lethargy.

This intelligence threw the Central Junta into great alarm; they began to think the business was serious; Castanos was ordered to his post, and such levies as they could collect were sent forward to the Ebro.

Urgent and alarming as was the situation of affairs, the dilatoriness of the Spanish Government could not be corrected. So that when Sir David Baird arrived at Corunna, Oct. 13th, the Junta of Galicia refused him permission to land the troops. Sir David was astonished,

Vide Appendix, E.

D

and sent off expresses to Madrid and to Lisbon. He at last obtained leave to land, but his reception was so cold, and there was such a total want of all exertion to assist him in equipping the army for its advance, that he wrote to Sir John Moore to know if he had the sanction of the Supreme Junta for the admission of British troops into Spain.

He was at last satisfied as to this point; but he found, that whatever was necessary either for the sustenance or movement of the troops must be procured solely by his own exertions; and by paying a high price to those whom he came to assist.

Sir John Moore marched on rapidly, and reached Atalaia Nov. 5th. Here it was discovered, contrary to the information received at Lisbon, that the roads though very bad were practicable for Artillery. But the ignorance of the Portuguese respecting their own country is such, that the road was only found out from stage to stage by the British officers. This was now a subject of serious regret; for had the road, bad as it was, been known at first, General Hope's division could have marched with the rest of the army.

Dispatches were now sent to meet him at Truxillo, to desire he would not trust to report, but send forward officers to examine if there were a nearer road practicable for the guns, without going round by Madrid.

Letters were here received from Lord William Bentinck, acquainting Sir John Moore that the French reinforcements were entering Biscay, and that Castanos was making some movements which might bring on an action: and also that the Central Junta referred Sir John to concert his movements with General Castanos.

The General arrived at Almeida Nov. 8th: it rained incessantly; the troops however moved on in spite of the weather, and behaved extremely well: but it is painful to be obliged to make an exception of some soldiers who had committed many daring crimes. The Commander in Chief determined to put a stop to such disorders. One of the soldiers who was detected in marauding and robbing, was tried by a General Court Martial, found guilty, and sentenced to death. Sir John Moore then issued the following order.

    " General Orders.                 " *November 11th*, 1808.

    " NOTHING could be more pleasing to the Commander of the " Forces, than to shew mercy to a soldier of good character under his " command, who had been led inadvertently to commit a crime ; but " he should consider himself neglectful of his duty, if, from ill-judged " lenity, he pardoned deliberate villainy.

    " The crime committed by the prisoner now under sentence, " is of this nature, and there is nothing in his private character or " conduct which could give the least hope of his amendment, were " he pardoned ; he must therefore suffer the awful punishment to " which he has been condemned.

    " The Commander of the Forces trusts that the troops he commands " will seldom oblige him to resort to punishments of this kind : " and such is his opinion of British soldiers, that he is convinced " they will not, if the Officers do their duty, and pay them proper " attention.

    " He however takes this opportunity to declare to the Army, that " he is determined to shew no mercy to plunderers and marauders, " or, in other words, to thieves and villains.

    " The Army is sent by England to aid and support the Spanish " nation, not to plunder and rob its inhabitants. And soldiers who " so far forget what is due to their own honour, and the honour " of their country, as to commit such acts, shall be delivered over to " justice : the military law must take its course, and the punishment " it awards shall be inflicted."

On the 11th of November the advanced guard crossed a rivulet which divides Spain from Portugal, and marched to Cividad Roderigo. The Governor of this town met Sir John two miles off; a salute was fired from the ramparts, and he was conducted to the principal house of the town; and hospitably entertained.

The appearance of the country, and the manners of the people, change most remarkably, immediately on crossing the boundary between Spain and Portugal; and the advantage is entirely in favour of Spain. We were received, on approaching Cividad Roderigo, with shouts of " Viva los Ingleses."

This agreeable reception was gratifying; and the General proceeded next day to San Martin, a village seven leagues distant, where he lodged at the house of the Curate, a sensible, respectable man, who, in the course of conversation, told him, that on the same day the preceding year he had lodged the French General Loison, on his march to Portugal; and that Junot and the other French Generals had slept there in succession.

On the 13th of November, Sir John arrived with his advanced guard at Salamanca, where he halted, intending to assemble there all the troops which were coming from Portugal. But before he entered the town, he learnt the fate of what was called, the Army of Estramadura.

This Spanish corps, consisting of about 12,000 raw recruits, commanded by a very young man, the Count Belvedere, had advanced without support to Burgos, an open town, in the front of the French Army. So extraordinary a manœuvre was followed by a natural result. They were attacked by a superior force, and completely routed.

A few hours after Sir John arrived at Salamanca, he wrote to Lord William Bentinck at Madrid, who was acting as Minister from the British Court.

*Sir John Moore to Lord William Bentinck.*

"MY DEAR LORD,

"*Salamanca,* 13*th November,* 1808.

"I ARRIVED here early in the afternoon. I am not
"only jaded by my journey, but also by the different people I have
"been obliged to speak to; and only that I am anxious to send
"a Courier to you as soon as possible, I should have delayed writing
"to you until morning. I received upon the road your two letters
"of the 8th, and that of the 9th with the enclosures, some of which
"shall be returned to you by the next courier.

"I am sorry to say, from Sir David Baird, I hear nothing but
"complaints of the Junta of Corunna, who afford him no assist-
"ance. They promise every thing, but give nothing; and, after
"waiting day after day for carts, which they had promised to pro-
"cure for the carriage of stores, his Commissary was at last obliged
"to contract for them at an exorbitant price, and then got them.
"This is really a sort of conduct quite intolerable to troops that
"the Spanish Government have asked for, and for whose ad-
"vance they are daily pressing.

"On my arrival here, and telling Colonel O'Lowler that I wished
"to have supplies immediately provided on the road from Astorga to
"this place, for the march of the troops from Corunna, he began
"by telling me that a power which he should have got, and which
"it was promised should be sent after him from Madrid, had not
"been sent; that he had thus no authority, and had hitherto been
"acting upon his own credit. Part of this was an Irish trick—*pour*
"*se faire valoir;* it tended only, however, to shew me, that he was

" not the man who should have been selected for us; but, if selected,
" he should have been furnished with every authority to make him
" useful. I run over all this to you, though, perhaps, it should pro-
" perly be addressed to Mr. Frere; but to you I can state it with
" more ease, and I shall thank you to speak to Frere upon it; when
" I hope he will have some serious communication with the Spanish
" Ministers, and plainly tell them, if they expect the advance of
" the British Army, they must pay somewhat more attention to
" its wants. Proper Officers must be sent to me, vested with full
" powers to call forth the resources of the country when they are
" wanted, and without delay; the same as is done, I presume, for
" the Spanish Armies; we shall pay, but they are not to allow us
" to be imposed upon, but to tell us what is paid by the Spanish
" Government in such cases. We find no difficulty with the people;
" they receive us every where well. But the authorities are back-
" ward, and not like those of a country who wish our assistance.

" The Officer you mention to have been sent to Sir David Baird,
" travelled by slow journies, as if in profound peace, and consequently
" arrived too late, and when little wanted. The head of Baird's
" column is this day at Astorga; but had they waited for the said
" Officer, it would have been still at Corunna. The Spaniards seem
" to think that every body should fly but themselves. The troops
" from Lisbon begin to march in here to-morrow, and will continue
" to arrive by corps daily until the 23d, when the whole will be
" assembled. I have directed Baird also to continue the march of
" his troops on Benevente, as soon as supplies permit it; and by
" the time the head reaches Benevente, I shall probably direct it to
" proceed on to Zamora, and close the whole as near to me at this
" place, as cover will admit; probably by the 23d instant the rear
" of Baird's will be about Zamora, but it will depend on the aid and
" activity of the Authorities of the country; if they are slow, it is

" impossible for me to be quick. All this, however, is upon the sup-
" position that the French do not disturb us; and I suppose you
" know they are at Burgos. At Cividad Rodrigo, I received a letter
" by express from El Conde de Belvedere, from Burgos, dated the
" 9th, stating that he expected to be attacked by superior numbers,
" and begging that I would hasten to his assistance. I wrote to him
" that I had been marching for some time with all the haste I could;
" but if he was to be attacked so soon, it was impossible for me to
" render him any assistance; and he should report his situation to
" Madrid. Upon my arrival here, I was informed by the Marquis
" de Cinalbo, that the Spanish troops had been forced to retire from
" Burgos, and the French were in possession of it. I hope the letter
" I wrote to General Castanos will draw from him some explanation
" of his views, by which I may regulate my motions. But his move-
" ments, and those of the army under General Blake, require some
" explanation in order to be understood; for, though they know that
" a British force is marching from different parts, in order to unite,
" they have marched away from the point of assembly, and have
" left us exposed to be attacked and interrupted before our junction;
" but if we were united, he can hardly expect that, with my force,
" I should march forward and place myself within reach of attack
" from such superior numbers, whilst his and Blake's armies are
" removed at such a distance as to be able to render me no assistance :
" but all this I expect will be made plain, when I hear from General
" Castanos. With respect to magazines, it is impossible for me to
" say where they ought to be made, whilst I am so much in the
" dark as to the movements which are likely to occur; but if the
" country is abundant, as is said, we cannot want. But I must have
" persons of an authority attached to me, who are acquainted with
" the resources, and who, knowing the interior government, customs,
" and manners of Spain, can call them forth for me and the British

" troops, in the same manner as they are called forth for those of
" Spain. This regards not only provisions, but carts, horses, quar-
" ters; and, in short, all the wants of troops. With the aid of per-
" sons of this description our own Commissaries can do; but without
" them we can do nothing. The foundation of all this, must be an
" order to the authorities throughout the Provinces, to give every
" aid to the British, as to the Spanish troops. It is a matter of indif-
" ference who pays these Officers;—it would be more consistent
" with the dignity of Spain that they paid them; though we should
" reward them *according to their deserts.*

" With respect to magazines at Madrid, it is very likely to be a
" proper place for Spain to collect a considerable depôt of various
" kinds. It is their Capital, and they know best; but it does not
" strike me a place where the British could be called upon to make
" any collection. We shall establish small magazines for consump-
" tion in the neighbourhood where we are acting. These great
" reserves, which a country makes for general supply, should be made
" by Spain; when we approach it, we may draw from it, and pay for
" what we get. But Spain should make it, and be at the expence
" and trouble of its conservation: as I believe we are giving money
" to Spain, part of it may be applied by them in this manner; but
" it is they that should do it—not we.

" I have no objection to you, or Mr. Frere, representing the neces-
" sity of as many more British troops as you think proper. It is
" certain, that the agents, which our Government have hitherto
" employed, have deceived them. For affairs here are by no means
" in the flourishing state they are represented and believed to be
" in England; and the sooner the truth is known in England, the
" better. But you must observe, my Lord, that whatever is critical
" must now be decided by the troops which are here; the French,
" I suspect, are ready, and will not wait. I differ only with you

" in one point ;—when you say, the chief and great obstacle and
" resistance to the French will be afforded by the English Army.
" If that be so, Spain is lost. The English Army, I hope, will do
" all which can be expected from their numbers ; but the safety of
" Spain depends upon the union of its inhabitants, their enthusiasm
" in their cause, and in their firm and devoted determination to die,
" rather than submit to the French ; nothing short of this will
" enable them to resist the formidable attack about to be made upon
" them. If they will adhere, our aid can be of the greatest use to
" them; but, if not, we shall soon be out-numbered, were our force
" quadrupled.

" I am, therefore, much more anxious to see exertion and energy
" in the Government, and enthusiasm in their Armies, than to have
" my force augmented.—The moment is a critical one—my own
" situation is particularly so—I have never seen it otherwise ;—but
" I have pushed into Spain at all hazards ;—this was the order of my
" Government—and it was the will of the people of England. I
" shall endeavour to do my best, hoping that all the bad that may
" happen, will not happen; but that with a share of bad, we shall
" also have a portion of good fortune.

" This is a long letter for one who began by saying that he was
" jaded; but I have been gradually drawn on by the interest I take
" in the subject. You will communicate to Mr. Frere such parts as
" you think proper; and he will, I hope, act upon them. Be so good
" as to excuse me to him, for not particularly addressing himself.
" Lord Paget was at Corunna the 7th, with two regiments, the
" 7th and the 10th Hussars ; the other three were following fast

" I remain, &c.

" JOHN MOORE."

E

Two nights after writing the above, Sir John was awakened by an express from General Pignatelli, the Governor of the Province, to inform him that the French army had advanced and taken possession of the city of Valladolid, which is only twenty leagues from Salamanca.

It should not be forgotten that the General had been informed officially*, that his entry into Spain would be covered by sixty or seventy thousand men: and Burgos was the city intended for the point of union for the different divisions of the British army. But already, not only Burgos, but Valladolid, were in possession of the Enemy: and he found himself with an advanced corps in an open town, three marches from the French army, without even a Spanish piquet to cover his front.

He had at this time only three brigades of infantry without a gun at Salamanca. The remainder were moving up in succession, but the whole could not arrive in less than ten days.

This situation being extremely different from what he had been taught to expect, and that upon which the instructions of the Secretary of State were founded, called for very different measures. For if the French advanced in force, he had no option but to fall back on Ciudad Rodrigo; the country round which, being poor, could not subsist the troops long: and if he retreated to Portugal, he hardly improved his situation.

The General had long foreseen the possibility of the French advancing, to prevent the junction of the British troops; and was quite at a loss to comprehend the motives for the separation of the Spanish armies; one of which was posted in Biscay, and the other in Arragon, while the country in front was left open, as if to suffer the French to advance upon the British before they were united.

* Vide Appendix B.

It appeared also very singular, that the advance of the French so far into the country had produced no sensation among the people. The fact was established by a letter from General Pignatelli, the captain-general of the province; yet the news was brought by no other channel. The people were all tranquil, and employed in their ordinary occupations and amusements; and seemed to know or care very little about public matters.

The General assembled the Junta: he communicated to them the capture of the city of Valladolid, and explained the reasons " that " might render it necessary for him to retire at present to Ciudad " Rodrigo; that this temporary retreat ought not to discourage them; " but that they should employ every means in their power to rouse the " enthusiasm of the people, which seemed to be somewhat abated."

He represented, " that no nation had obtained independence with- " out making great sacrifices; and though the English would be " useful auxiliaries, that success could only be gained by the union " and effort of the Spaniards themselves."

He told them, " he must have the use of all the carts and mules " in the country to transport his magazines to Ciudad Rodrigo, " should it become requisite; and that the troops, with three days " provisions, should be kept in readiness. But," he added, " that " he had not yet stopt the advance of the rest of the army from " Portugal; he was desirous of assembling it there, and would " not retire without an absolute necessity."

All this was listened to with calm acquiescence. Indeed the pas- sive disposition of the Spaniards was most remarkable; for they heard of the generous intentions of the British, and of the destruc- tive ravages of the French, with almost equal indifference. The apathy of the people proved the inactivity of their rulers; for on such an occasion, there should not only have been numerous armies on foot, but every man in Spain should have been armed, and ready to act when required. Nor did this appear to be impracticable. For the supineness was not owing to disaffection among the people: the peasantry and lower orders were all well disposed; but in ascending to the higher ranks, the spirit of independence evaporated.

The General detached some intelligent officers, with strong patroles, to gain intelligence; by whom he soon learnt, that a thousand French cavalry, with two pieces of artillery, had entered Valladolid on the 13th, and retired to Palencia next morning. But he understood that no infantry had advanced beyond Burgos. He then sent orders to Generals Baird and Hope to concentrate their divisions, to advance with all speed to Salamanca, but to be upon their guard on their march.

It is necessary here to go back a very little, to mention that Mr. Frere arrived at Aranjuez at the beginning of November, as Minister Plenipotentiary of Great Britain. He of course superseded Lord William Bentinck and Mr. Stuart; who, from having resided some time in Spain, and from personal qualifications, had got acquainted with many of the leading men, and had acquired a clear insight into the state of affairs.

Their communications with each other, and with Colonel Graham who was at the head-quarters of the principal Spanish army; as well as their correspondence with Sir John Moore, were all conducted with harmony, and utility to the common cause.

This change in the administration of the civil department occurred at the period when events were hastening to a crisis.

Mr. Frere unfortunately had acquired his notions of Spanish politics in London; and his prepossessions were much too strong to be effaced by the observations of his predecessors, or even to be altered by the most opposing facts. His peculiar notions were totally unknown to Sir John Moore; who, to inform him of his situation, and to promote the public service, wrote as follows, from Almeida.

*From Sir John Moore to the Right Honourable J. Hookham*
*Frere.*

" SIR,                              *Almeida,* 10 *Nov.* 1808.

         " As Mr. Stuart mentioned in a late letter which I
" had the honour to receive from him, that he was in hourly expec-
" tation of your arrival at Madrid, I conclude that ere this you have
" reached that capital.

     " I shall not trouble you with any detail of my movements, as
" you will obtain every necessary information respecting them from
" Mr. Stuart and Lord William Bentinck, with both of whom I
" have been in correspondence ever since I was appointed to this
" command.

     " The Supreme Junta have fixed upon General Castanos, as the
" person with whom I am to correspond, and to combine whatever
" operations are to be undertaken by the troops under my command.
" This cannot but be considered as a step towards appointing him
" the Chief Commander of the Spanish army; and having gone so
" far, it is a pity they did not go a little farther, and at once give
" him the appointment. This decision of the Junta was only com-
" municated to me a few days ago, by Lord William, in a letter
" which I received on my road to this place. I have written to
" General Castanos, to give him every information with respect to
" the British force, the probable period of its junction; and I have
" requested to know from him, his plans, and his instructions, with
" respect to the co-operation he expects from us. It is needless to
" say what different measures I might have pursued, had I been
" sooner informed of the strength and condition of the different
" Spanish armies. As it is, the principal part of the infantry from

" Portugal is now passing the frontier; and by the middle of this
" month will be collected at Salamanca and Ciudad Rodrigo.
" General Hope, with the artillery, the cavalry, and 3000 infantry,
" will be in the neighbourhood of Madrid on the 22d; and the head
" of Sir David Baird's corps will reach Astorga on the 14th. If
" nothing adverse happens, we shall be united early in December,
" more or less advanced, according to the situation and movements
" of the armies now upon the Ebro. In the mean time I shall wait
" at Salamanca, with the troops assembling there, until Baird and
" Hope are more forward. Much is still to be done in the article
" of equipment and of commissariat arrangement. As I see more
" myself, of the resources of the country, I shall be able to decide the
" mode to be followed, for securing to us our supplies; for the
" present we must depend upon the Spanish Government, and their
" Chief Director, Don Vincenti.

" I understand from Sir David Baird that you were kind enough
" to spare him 40,000 l. from the monies you brought with you
" from England. I have to thank you for this supply; for when
" he applied to me, it was with great difficulty I was able to spare
" him 8000 l. We are now in the greatest distress for money, and
" if a quantity does not speedily arrive from England, we must
" depend upon the generosity of the Spaniards for our supplies. I
" doubt at present if there is wherewithal, after the 24th of this
" month, to pay the troops their subsistence. I fear that in Eng-
" land, until very lately, they were not aware of the impossibility
" of procuring money either in Portugal or Spain. I leave this to-
" morrow, and shall proceed by Ciudad Rodrigo to Salamanca;
" where I shall hope to have the honour to hear from you.

" I have the honour to be,

" JOHN MOORE.

" I trust you will have the goodness to excuse whatever is in-
" formal in this letter ; you may believe it proceeds from no dis-
" respect to you, but I have not been informed, and am quite ignorant
" of your appointment, whether Ambassador or Minister Plenipo-
" tentiary ; and thought it better to give you no titles, rather than
" the wrong one."

To this letter the following answer was sent.

*From the Honourable J. H. Frere to His Excellency Sir John
Moore, K. B.*

" SIR,                                        *Aranjuez, Nov.* 13, 1808.

" I HAVE this evening received the letter which you
" did me the honour to direct to me from Almeida, and which was
" delivered to me by Lord William Bentinck. His messenger, who
" sets off with the account, which I received only this morning, of
" the unlucky affair of the 10th near Burgos, enables me to thank
" you for the view which you have given me of your intended move-
" ments, and to mitigate the bad news, by the assurance which I
" think I can venture to give, that it has not created any visible
" degree of uneasiness or discouragement in the minds of the leading
" persons here. The people, though much irritated, as it is said,
" are still farther from being dejected than their leaders. 5000 men
" marched forward to-day from Madrid, and two regiments from
" Toledo. The fixed spirit of resistance which, without calculation
" of danger or of means, seems to have rooted itself in the minds
" of the people, appears superior to any reverses.
" You will have heard of overtures of negotiation: it seems doubtful
" whether Buonaparte meant to include Spain in the number of our
" allies with whom he proposes to treat ; and still more, whether he

32.

" would offer terms which it would be possible to accept. I should
" incline to think, therefore, that he had no other object than that of
" cajoling the Emperor of Russia, and facilitating the conscription.
" He will not disunite Spain and England; and I feel confident that
" he will not succeed in lowering the tone, or relaxing the spirit, of
" this country.

" You probably are already acquainted with the appointment of
" the Marquis Romana to the command of Castano's and Blake's
" army. His nomination is, I understand, a popular one at Madrid;
" and his long absence has given him an advantage which is pecu-
" liar to him, that of being wholly unmixed in the political intrigues
" of the day.

" I shall be obliged to Mr. Stuart for his assistance in the
" military as well as other parts of my correspondence; a circum-
" stance which I trust will not be unsatisfactory to you, as it will, I
" am persuaded, be conducive to the furthering of the public service.

" I have the honour to be,
Sir,
Your obedient humble servant,
" J. H. FRERE"

The preconceived notions of Mr. Frere were evinced, in this first
letter, by calling the defeat of the Estremadura army, the unlucky
affair of the 10th; and by the warm description of the spirit of resistance of a people, whom he had just come among.

The correspondence continues

*From Sir John Moore to the Right Honourable*
*J. Hookham Frere.*

" SIR,                                                  *Salamanca, Nov.* 16, 1808.

" I HAD last night the honour to receive your letter
" of the 13th, together with letters of the 14th from Mr. Stuart and
" Lord William Bentinck.

" It does not appear certain whether the French have advanced in
" any force to Valladolid; and there is no reason to think, from the
" information which reached me last night, that they have passed it.

" In the course of this day all this will be ascertained, from the
" reports of the officers and other persons I have sent out.

" General Pignatelli's conduct was certainly not such as became
" a person holding a situation of such trust. He seems to have
" run off upon the first alarm. It was right for him to retire,
" and put his person in safety, but no farther; there he should have
" stopped, and not have left the people without a head. It was his
" duty, I conceive, to have collected information, in order to com-
" municate it to me, and to those who, like me, were materially
" interested. I did not know, until I received Mr. Stuart's letter,
" that the defeat of the Estremadura army had been so complete.

" It was however nothing more than was to be expected, when
" so small a corps was committed so near to the strength of the
" Enemy.

" I have been unable hitherto to understand the movements and
" positions of the Spanish armies; but I have taken it for granted
" that they were formed from local circumstances, and a knowledge
" of the country, of which I was ignorant. I should otherwise have
" said they were upon a scale much too great for the strength of

F

" their armies. I begin to fear that this is the case, and that, if
" their system be not changed, we shall all of us very soon be beaten
" in detail. To cover and protect the British army, whilst upon its
" march from such distant points in order to unite, never seems to
" have been in the contemplation of the Spanish generals; and
" now, from the position the French have taken, the accomplish-
" ment of it is become exceedingly precarious. My position here is a
" bad one, in as much as my movements in it are confined, and
" leave nothing but a barren country to retire upon. I should un-
" doubtedly be. better at Valladolid; but it is impossible for me to
" go there, whilst the French in force are so near it, and the Spanish
" armies are at such a distance. Until my force is united, I must
" be covered and protected. As the corps come to me from such
" opposite directions, Corunna and Madrid, I cannot move towards
" one, without increasing my distance, and forsaking the other;
" and whilst they are each marching towards me, if I am forced
" to fall back, they will both risk to be destroyed. The difference
" hitherto between the position of the Spanish and French armies,
" as they have struck me, is this — the French, in order to con-
" centrate, or to strengthen either flank, move upon the chord, the
" Spaniards upon the circumference; the movements of the one are
" short, and can be easily concealed, those of the other extended,
" and exposed to be interrupted. I shall write to General Hope to
" consider it as his object to join me at this place with all expedi-
" tion; but to be guided by the information he receives of the move-
" ments of the Enemy, and to use his discretion. I shall direct
" General Baird to collect the whole of his corps at and about
" Astorga, whence his retreat to Corunna is safe; but not to come
" towards me, until I give him notice; and in this I shall be guided
" by what I perceive of the Enemy on this side of the Ebro, and
" from the information I expect to receive from the Marquis de

" la Romana, of his designs, and the direction he means to give to the
" Spanish armies. I know not where to address the Marquis; I
" have therefore written this military letter to you, and request
" you will communicate its contents to him.

" The contents of the two letters I addressed lately to General
" Castanos, and which were sent under cover to Lord William Ben-
" tinck, will of course be given to him;—the tone of conciliation
" which I have adopted in my letters to General Castanos, and which
" I shall continue to the Marquis Romana, I trust you will approve.
" I wish to impress upon whoever commands the Spanish armies,
" that I consider myself as having but one interest with him, and
" that he will find me as ready as any of his own Generals to follow
" and support his plans. The power and controul over the direction
" of my own army, which, as commanding an auxiliary force, I have;
" I shall keep out of sight, and hope never to be obliged to exert.
" You already know how much we are distressed for money. Mr.
" Stuart and Lord William both say that it is to be got by loan, or
" for bills, at Madrid. This differs from the information given to
" me by Mr. Kennedy; but I shall be happy to find that they are
" right, and that Mr. Kennedy has been misinformed. If Mr.
" Erskine were here, I should send him to Madrid for that purpose;
" for if money is to be found, (such are our necessities) that we must
" get it upon any terms; but, as Mr. Erskine has not joined me, and
" as, in his absence, I cannot spare Mr. Kennedy, I shall take it as
" a very particular favour if you will be kind enough to give me your
" assistance in this matter:—I have desired Mr. Kennedy to write
" to you upon it.

" With respect to our supplies, I do not apprehend want. If they
" exist in the country, and we have money, our Commissariat will
" procure them. What we want is, some persons conversant in the
" mode, and furnished with authority to call forth the aid of the

" country, and of the Magistrates and civil authorities; if Don
" Vincenti be the person entrusted by the Spanish Government
" for the supply of their army, some person from him, to whom
" he has delegated his information and his correspondence with his
" agents in the Provinces, is the person whom the Spanish Govern-
" ment should appoint to attend the British army, and aid with his
" knowledge and with his authority our Commissariat; — I should
" rather this person, were a man of character, not looking solely to
" making a property of us, but that could be trusted, and likely to
" be satisfied with having discharged an important duty, and with
" such pecuniary reward as would necessarily attend it.   *   *

" *   *   *   *   *   *   *   *   *   *
" *   *   *   *   *   *   *   *   *   *
" *   *   *   *   *   *   *   *   *   *
" *   *   *   *   *   *   *   *   *   *
" *   *   *   *   *   *   *   *   *   *
" *   *   *   *   *   *   *   *   *   *

" I have but one more subject to touch upon : — were the Officers
" employed with the different armies to correspond, they might
" have been useful before either you or I were sent to Spain, and
" when it was necessary for Government at Home to know what was
" passing ; but I own that I disapprove of any person being autho-
" rized to correspond officially with Government but you and me.

" *   *   *   *   *   *   *   *   *   *
" *   *   *   *   *   *   *   *   *   *

" If I want an English Officer at any time to assist my communi-
" cation with any of the Spanish Generals with whom I am acting,
" I can send one ; but, in general, I shall prefer a direct correspond-
" ence with the General himself, who will, of course, communicate
" many particulars to me, which it is unnecessary and highly impro-
" per for him to communicate to such Officers as are in general sent

" to them. My wish is, to overset the whole system ; to send them
" with their Spanish rank to England ; and to send, as they may
" occasionally be wanted either by yourself or me, Officers, or others,
" who will look to no rank or emolument but from their own country,
" in whose duty alone they should consider themselves employed, and
" who, when no longer wanted, return to their former occupations.

" I have the honour to remain,

" JOHN MOORE."

Some of the predictions contained in the above letter were but too
soon verified ; for next day a letter was received from Mr. Stuart at
Madrid, of which the following is an extract :

" *Madrid, 17th November,* 1808.

" THE defeat experienced by Blake on the 11th of
" this month, the occupation of Valladolid by the French, and the
" distance between the different divisions of your army, give room
" for the most melancholy reflections. The Orders which have
" been transmitted by the Junta, in consequence of this state of
" things, will, I fear, be very inadequate to meet the evil.

" The advance of a few regiments in Andalusia, the concentration
" of the runaways from Burgos, &c. at Segovia, and the attempt
" to render the passes of the Somasiera and the Guardarama defensible,
" will not save Madrid or Spain. And unless Blake effects his
" union with you, and Castanos brings together the whole of Arragon,
" Catalonia, Reding's division, &c. so as to form a force superior to
" opponents, who are increasing daily, I cannot flatter myself with
" any serious hope of a good result."

Other accounts were received of the defeat of General Blake's
army, which softened the misfortune. But letters were received

from Colonel Graham, who was stationed with the Central Army, and who gave a sad detail of cabals and divisions between the Generals, with the injudicious interferences of the Junta.

But neither reason, nor the experience of all ages, nor their own misfortunes, could prevail upon the Junta to appoint a Commander in Chief. Sir John Moore's ideas are best explained by himself.

### Sir John Moore to Mr. Frere.

" SIR, *Salamanca, 19th November,* 1808.

" A COURIER from Madrid brought me this morning
" letters from Mr. Stuart and Lord William Bentinck of the 17th:
" the former inclosed an order from the Supreme Junta of Ciudad
" Rodrigo, to place 20,000 dollars at my disposition, to be repaid
" hereafter. The Junta of this town are endeavouring to get money
" for us. Nothing can exceed the attention of the Marquis Cinalbo,
" the President; the Clergy, with Dr. Curtis at their head, exert
" themselves; and even a Convent of Nuns have promised five thou-
" sand pounds;—all this shews great good-will. The funds, how-
" ever, which it can raise, are small, and very inadequate to our
" wants. I trust that you will be able to supply us more amply
" from Madrid, until those from England arrive. A King's messen-
" ger brought me, on the night of the 17th, a Letter from Lord
" Castlereagh of the 2nd, in which he informs me, that two millions
" of dollars are upon their passage to Corunna; but his Lordship
" adds, that the difficulty of procuring silver is such, in England,
" that I must not look for a further supply for some months, and
" he impresses the necessity of taking every means of obtaining
" money upon the spot. The expected arrival of the above sum from
" England, must not, therefore, lessen your endeavours to get what
" you can for us at Madrid.

" The French, who entered Valladolid upon the afternoon of the
" 15th, left it the following morning; they were a thousand cavalry
" and two pieces of cannon; they returned to Placentia, and have
" not since advanced from it. I have written to Sir David Baird to
" advance a part of his corps to Benavente, and to close up the
" rest to Astorga; when this is done, he will forward that from
" Zamora, and follow with the rest; but as the propriety of these
" movements depends upon those of the Enemy, the execution of
" them is left entirely to Sir David's discretion, who must be guided
" by the information he receives;—his rear will not reach Astorga
" before the 4th of December.

" I heard of General Blake's defeat and retreat to Reynosa; but
" I knew no particulars, until I received this morning Mr. Stuart's
" letter. General Leith, who is employed with that army to cor-
" respond, has never written a line to me since I was in command.
" I want General Officers;—I have, therefore, written to him to
" leave any of the Officers with him, to carry on the correspondence,
" and to join Sir David Baird at Astorga.

" The scenes which Colonel Graham describes, in his letters,·
" as passing at the Head Quarters of the Central Army, are deplor-
" able. The imbecility of the Spanish Government exceeds belief.
" The good-will of the inhabitants, whatever it may be, is of little
" use whilst there exists no ability to bring it into action.

" I am in communication with no one Spanish army; nor am I
" acquainted with the intentions of the Spanish Government, or of
" any of its Generals. Castanos, with whom I was put in correspon-·
" dence, is deprived of his command at the moment I might have
" expected to hear from him; and La Romana, with whom I suppose
" I am now to correspond (for it has not been officially communi-
" cated to me) is absent—God knows where. In the mean time
" the French are within four marches of me, whilst my army is only

" assembling : in what numbers they are, I cannot learn. No
" channels of intelligence have been opened to me ; and I have not
" been long enough in the country to procure them myself. I state
" these particulars to you. I wish it were in my power to go myself
" to Aranjuez, or Madrid, to represent them ; for really if things are
" to continue in this state, the ruin of the Spanish cause, and the
" defeat of their armies, is inevitable ; and it will become my duty
" to consider alone the safety of the British army, and to take steps
" to withdraw it from a situation, where, without the possibility of
" doing good, it is exposed to certain defeat.

" I shall detain the King's messenger until I hear from you ; lest
" you should wish to send by him any dispatches to England. I
" shall beg of Lord William Bentinck to join the army, where, I
" think, his services will now be most useful.

" I have the honour to be,

" JOHN MOORE."

In this letter Sir John Moore complains of not having heard from
General Leith ; which was owing probably to the dilatoriness of the
messenger, who at last reached Salamanca with the following
tidings.

*From General Leith to Sir John Moore.*

*Renedo Valley of Caqueringa, Province*

" SIR,          *of Las Montanos de Santander,* 15th Nov. 1808.

" I REGRET to inform you that the army of General
" Blake, in which was lately incorporated the infantry of the Marquis
" de la Romana's division, has been defeated in several attacks since
" the 5th instant, and is entirely dispersed ; I have not time to enter
" into detail of this unfortunate reverse, carrying with it such

" serious consequences, for fear of delaying the intimation of that
" which is so essential to make known in general terms to the Com-
" mander of the British army advancing from Portugal to Galicia.
" The Estremaduran army has also experienced a reverse at Burgos.
" In short, the British army has nothing to depend upon in Las
" Montanos de Santander. In Asturias there are but a few battalions,
" totally undisciplined; and, by the last accounts, the French occupy
" from Reynosa to Burgos. Except what remains of the Estremaduran
" army, (the position of which I am ignorant) and the British army,
" there is nothing to prevent the Enemy from advancing towards
" Leon and Valladolid that I know of. I very much suspect that he
" will avail himself of this movement, to attack in detail the army
" of Palafox and Castanos, united *nominally*; and all of which are
" placed under the command of the Marquis de la Romana. The
" army has suffered principally from famine; and I do not think
" that it is possible to re-unite those who are flying in all directions,
" nearer than Astorga and Oviedo. It does not appear that there
" has been any want of spirit in the men; and in many instances,
" especially of the divisions of the North, distinguished conduct.
" Some of the new Officers have not behaved so well. Captain
" Pasly, Royal Engineers, who was sent to Head Quarters to obtain
" information, and to communicate with the British army, I hope may
" have given early intelligence of the state of things. Captain
" Lefebren, R. E. is the bearer of this letter, and will be able to give
" such information as may be required. I regret to state that Captain
" Rich, R. E. was wounded, but I hope he is doing well: I
" caused him to be embarked on board the Cossack frigate at Sant-
" ander, from whence I saw seventeen sail of transports, with war-
" like stores and provisions, when there appeared no chance of this
" Province remaining covered from the Enemy, who, no doubt, will
" occupy a point so useful to the Spaniards, and eventually to the

G

" British. Santander was in the power of the Enemy, after possessing
" the roads of Escudo and Reynosa. The accounts of their having
" entered that town are not yet received, however. The different
" attacks have been at Zorosa (between Durango and Bilboa)
" Valmaseda, Arantia; and the total deroute, after a defeat at Espi-
" nosa de las Montanax. About 7000 re-assembled at Reynosa on
" the 13th instant, but without any order; from thence they retreated
" after dark, and have arrived in this valley, as a half-starved and
" straggling mob, without officers, and all mixed in utter confusion.
" Never has there been so injudicious and ruinous a system begun and
" persisted in, as that which has led to the serious disasters of the
" present moment. The Marquis de la Romana, who is here, is
" quite of that opinion; and if the army on the other side, and near
" the Ebro, has not, or shall not have suffered before he can take
" this direction, I hope affairs may resume a more favourable
" aspect. I had prepared copies of reports on the different affairs,
" addressed by different Officers to Lord Castlereagh; but, unfortu-
" nately, all my papers are on board the Cossack man of war. Mr.
" Amiotte, the Deputy Commissary-General, has been in such bad
" health since his arrival, that it was difficult enough to get the stores,
" &c. embarked. I apprehend the convoy, chiefly consisting of
" warlike stores for the Marquis of Romana's division, and arms and
" provisions, under my orders, for the aid of the armies of Spain, has
" gone to Corunna; as they could not at this season keep the sea,
" and there is no good port nearer than the last-mentioned, from
" whence the roads towards Leon are not so good. I should hope
" soon to get near the British army. Under the present circumstances,
" I feel an awkwardness at leaving the Marquis de la Romana, with
" whom I have received particular instructions to communicate on
" any point still unsettled. I hope, however, he will soon be able to
" disengage himself from this part of the army (if such it can be

" called); and he may probably be obliged to go near the British
" army before he can communicate with the rest of his own troops.

" I have the honour to be,

" JANUS LEITH,<br>M. General.

" I inclose a rough idea of the situation of this valley, relatively
" to the great route from Reynosa to Santander."

Nothing certainly could be worse judged, than the orders sent
by the Junta to General Blake to fight the French army alone;
instead of directing him to fall back, and unite with General Baird
at Astorga; for this Spanish army was in no condition to contend
with regular troops. There were, it is true, between eight and
nine thousand regular soldiers, which had escaped from Denmark
with the Marquis of Romana, and who fought well; but they were
overpowered by superior numbers. The rest of this army consisted
of unfortunate peasants, who had suffered with constancy for four
months privations which would have annihilated a British army.

They had endured excessive fatigue, were without shoes, almost
without clothes, exposed to the cold on snowy mountains, obliged
frequently to depend for subsistence on such animals as they caught
by accident; on meat without salt, a food totally repugnant to the
habits of Spaniards. They passed many days without bread. Their
condition was so wretched, that it is not to be wondered at that they
were easily dispersed, and had no inclination to rally.

Some of the fugitives even passed Salamanca.

The Marquis Romana did not consider it prudent to remain at
Reynosa; he retired to Leon, to re-assemble as many as he could
collect.

It was now in the choice of Buonaparte either to turn his arms against Castanos, who was posted in Aragon, or to march against the British, prevent their junction, and compel them to retire to Portugal and to their ships.

Sir John Moore could do nothing to hinder this; for, being placed nearly in the centre between two divisions of his army which were approaching from different points, he was constrained to wait at Salamanca, in expectation that they should be permitted to join him. The following extract of a letter to one of his brothers marks his view of the state of affairs. It is dated Salamanca, November 26, 1808.

" Upon entering Spain I have found affairs in a very dif-
" ferent state from what I expected, or from what they are thought
" to be in England.

" I am in a scrape from which God knows how I am to extricate
" myself. But, instead of Salamanca, this army should have been
" assembled at Seville. The poor Spaniards deserve a better fate,
" for they seem a fine people; but have fallen into hands who have
" lost them by their apathy and * * * * * *.

" The Junta, jealous of their Generals, gave them no power; but
" kept them at the head of separate armies, each independent of the
" other. Thus they have prevented any union of action.

" They took no pains to recruit the armies, or to furnish them
" with arms and clothing. In short, during the interval that the
" French were weak, they did nothing either to overpower them
" before their reinforcements arrived, or to meet them with superior
" numbers when reinforced.

" When I marched into this country, in three divisions, from
" Corunna, Lisbon, and round by Madrid, instead of finding any
" army to cover the junction of the three corps, until our supplies
" and stores came up, which were necessary to enable us to act;

" I found that the Spanish armies were placed on each flank of the
" French; one in Biscay, and the other on the river Alagon; at
" such a distance as to be able to give no sort of support to each
" other, or to combine their movements; and leaving it also in the
" power of the French to attack either army with their whole force,
" as soon as they were ready.

" They accordingly attacked Blake, and have completely dispersed
" his army. Officers and men are flying in every direction. Many
" of them have passed this.

" They also got a corps, called the Estremadura army, beat at
" Burgos; where they sent it, without any motive, close to the
" strength of the French.

" I was desired to correspond with Castanos, and combine my
" movements with him; but as I began my correspondence, he was
" suspended, and the Marquis of Romana named to the chief com-
" mand; but who when I last heard was at Santandero.

" I am in no correspondence with any of their generals or armies.
" I know not their plans, or those of the Spanish government. No
" channels of information have been opened to me; and, as yet a
" stranger, I have been able to establish no certain ones for myself.

" The Enemy are at Valladolid, in what force I cannot make out;
" and I have my junction to make with Baird, whose whole force
" will not be at Astorga until the 5th of December, and with Hope,
" who will be at Arevola about the same time.

" Castanos and Palafox have about 40,000 men, mostly undisci-
" plined peasants, upon the Ebro and Alagon. And this is all the
" Spaniards have to oppose 100,000 French troops. The provinces
" are not armed, and as to enthusiasm I have seen no marks of it.

" That the Spaniards must be driven from Madrid is inevitable;
" they have no force to resist. When they will bring up, or if they
" will bring up at all, I cannot guess. In this province, and

" throughout Old Castile, there is no mark of any intention to
" make any effort. The French cavalry are overrunning the plains,
" raising contributions, to which the people submit without re-
" sistance.

" There may be more character in other parts. Enthusiasm, and
" an obstinate determination not to submit to the French yoke, may
" do much. But even in this case the Government has been impro-
" vident: arms, ammunition, and other means, are wanting.

" The probability therefore is that the French will succeed; and
" if they do, it will be from no talent having sprung up, after the
" first effort, to take advantage of the impulse, and of the enthusiasm
" which then existed.

" I understand all is fear and confusion at Madrid.

" Tell James it is difficult to judge at a distance. The Spaniards
" have not shewn themselves a wise or a provident people. Their
" wisdom is not a wisdom of action; but still they are a fine
" people; a character of their own, quite distinct from other nations;
" and much might have been done with them. Perhaps they may
" rouse again. Pray for me that I may make right decisions: if I
" make bad ones, it will not be for want of consideration.

" I sleep little, it is now only five in the morning; and I have
" concluded, since I got up, this long letter.

" Your affectionate brother,

" JOHN MOORE."

One of the qualities of the mind with which Sir John Moore was
gifted in a most extraordinary degree, was that of prescience. The
letters he wrote during the campaign to two military friends, as
well as those to his own family, prove that he foresaw very early
every event which afterwards took place. No movement was made

by Buonaparte, however artfully concealed, that was unexpected by him. Therefore, though the intelligence he received was always defective, and generally false, he was often able to supply the deficiency by a most extraordinary sagacity.

A circumstance occurred at this time, to the honour of the Spaniards, which is thus related in his Journal:

" Lord Proby was at Tordesillas reconnoitring, when a patrole of " French cavalry came into the town. They stayed some time. " Every man in the town knew that Proby was there, for he had " been two days among them; yet not a man betrayed him. And " when the cavalry left the place, and his Lordship came into the " street, they all testified their satisfaction, and declared that, though " they had no arms, they would have died rather than have allowed " him to be taken."

Sir David Baird in his march from Corunna had to struggle with difficulties of a kind totally new to him.

This General had distinguished himself in many campaigns in India, where the British army are always accompanied with so numerous a train of slaves, servants, and sutlers, horses, bullocks, and elephants, that the troops are not only abundantly supplied with necessaries, but even furnished with many luxuries.

But here Sir David had to encounter a thousand deficiencies; he met with a variety of obstacles to his progress, and received little aid from the Spaniards to overcome them. In order to procure sufficient supplies for the troops, and to be able to carry forward the baggage, he was obliged to divide his small corps into smaller detachments; each following the other at considerable distances. He arrived at Astorga November 19 with a part of his infantry; but the following extract of a letter which he wrote from that place, will explain his situation.

## Sir David Baird to Sir John Moore.

" MY DEAR SIR JOHN,                                          *November* 23d.

" THE more I consider our situation, the more I am
" convinced of the danger that would attend my making, at the
" present moment, any movement in advance, or attempt to join
" you, until my force is more collected. We have no kind of sup-
" port to expect from the Spaniards, who are completely dispersed
" and driven from the field. And if I were to move forward the
" infantry I have at present here, I should necessarily expose my-
" self to be beaten in detail, without a chance of being able to op-
" pose any effectual resistance.

" The Enemy are certainly at Majorga, and their parties have
" pushed forward almost close to Benavente. From my present want
" of cavalry I have not been able to ascertain how forward their infantry
" may be. But as they have had the army which defeated Blake
" unoccupied since the 13th, and that which routed the Estrema-
" durans since the 10th, I cannot believe that they are very remote.

" On my left they have pushed forward as far as St. Vincento de
" la Burena and Colombas, both of which places were attacked on
" the 19th instant. Of their being carried there can be little doubt ;
" as there does not appear to be any force in the Asturias sufficient
" to resist them. And should they have been successful, my com-
" munication with my rear may be endangered, by their advance
" on the road through Monderedo or Lugo.

" Under these circumstances I have felt it my duty to consult
" with the General Officers here, as to the measures it would be
" proper to adopt ; and their sentiments are perfectly in unison with
" my own ; that unless you should judge it absolutely requisite, it
" would not be advisable to attempt to advance, without I should

" be able to assemble my whole force at this place, previous to be-
" ginning to move. Should however the Enemy advance in force
" before that time, which will not be previous to December 4, from
" the general tenor of your letters to me, and particularly from the
" intention you express in that of the 15th of falling back on Ciu-
" dad Rodrigo, if the Enemy approach nearer than Valladolid, I
" shall instantly commence my retreat, taking care if possible to
" move by the time they are within three days' march of me, to
" prevent the confusion and loss necessarily attendant on a close
" pursuit.

" I had written thus far when I had the satisfaction to receive
" your two letters of the 19th instant; and it is particularly grati-
" fying to me to have your sanction to the measures I proposed to
" adopt. It is very extraordinary that I have been unable to ob-
" tain any sort of information respecting the position of the Enemy's
" infantry, although I have used every endeavour to get intel-
" ligence.

" I inclose a copy of some intelligence communicated by a person
" who was sent from Leon to obtain information respecting the
" movements of the French, and of a letter written by Colonel
" Graham from the head-quarters of Castanos' army.

" From the latter it is clearly apparent how very much exaggerated
" the accounts generally circulated of the strength of the Spanish
" armies have been. In all probability Castanos and Palafox may
" by this time have met with the same reverse as Blake; in which
" case the Spaniards could have no force deserving the denomina-
" tion of an army in the field.

" As it could never be intended by the British Government that
" our army should engage in the defence of this Country unaided
" and unsupported by any Spanish force, I confess, my dear Sir
" John, I begin to be at a loss to discover an object at this mo-
" ment in Spain: it being very evident that the Spaniards are

H

" not at this moment in a situation to be capable of assembling a
" force competent to offer any serious resistance to the progress of
" the French arms.

" It is very remarkable that I have not procured the least intel-
" ligence, or received any sort of communication, from any of the
" official Authorities at Madrid, or either of the Spanish Generals.
" Neither Mr. Frere nor Lord William Bentinck have written to
" me for a considerable time.

" I remain, my dear Sir John, &c.

" D. BAIRD."

This excellent letter shews how very just a notion Sir David Baird
entertained of the Spanish affairs; and it appears that both himself,
and the Generals in his army, saw the prospect of events in even
a more desponding light than Sir John Moore, who indeed states at
this period in his Journal—

" I see my situation as clearly as any one, that nothing can be
" worse; for I have no Spanish army to give me the least assistance,
" only the Marquis Romana is endeavouring to assemble the fu-
" gitives from Blake's army at Leon.

" Yet I am determined to form the junction of this army, and to
" try our fortune. We have no business here as things are; but,
" being here, it would never do to abandon the Spaniards without a
" struggle."

The difficulty of obtaining intelligence was one of the great embarrassments which the English had to contend with; and, what
was quite unexpected, the Spanish generals complained as much of
this as the English.

It was excessively difficult to learn the truth by private means,
and the public official reports were uniformly false. Many other
examples will occur in the progress of this narrative. On the

23d of November General Blake wrote from Leon, that the French had advanced from Sahagune, and were collecting a force at Ampudia and Rio Seco. And the Marquis Romana transmitted additional information, which was repeated through other channels, " that " the Enemy had, on the 24th instant, collected a corps of 14,000 " infantry at Rio Seco, and that they had in addition 4000 cavalry " in that neighbourhood." Sir David Baird naturally believed this information; and concluded that this corps was intended to fall upon him before his troops were collected in a body. He therefore prepared to retreat, and applied to Sir John Moore for directions, whether the cavalry should retire through Portugal, or be embarked, and go by sea.

Sir John however discovered, that Blake and Romana had been deceived by reports spread in consequence of a strong corps of French cavalry scouring the country. They had diffused a wide alarm; but the General learnt that the principal part of the French army was marching against Castanos. He therefore sent orders to Sir David Baird to advance and join him. The effect of these false accounts was, however, to retard the junction.

The situation of affairs in Spain was becoming more and more critical; and every account sent to Sir John Moore by men of sound judgment was filled with convincing proofs that the Spanish Government had most unwisely concealed their very desperate state from their ally.

Lieut.-General Hope, who always fulfilled the wishes of his Commander, had persevered in a toilsome march; and, by indefatigable exertions, and good arrangements, had provided for the subsistence of the corps placed under his command, and brought them forward to the neighbourhood of Madrid.

The accounts he wrote from that City, November 20, were just and discouraging. He there found Lord William Bentinck, who had transmitted so much useful and accurate information.

They both had a conference with the artful, subtle, and unprincipled Morla—a political hypocrite acting the part of a patriot, a Spanish nobleman despising honour.

This base man, foreseeing the probable superiority of Buonaparte, secretly combined with him; and was now cunningly retarding every useful measure, and suggesting every mischievous one which he durst, without exciting suspicion of his designs. As Sir John Moore * perceived there was no Spanish force in the North capable of opposing the French armies, he was considering of the expediency of carrying the English army to the South, and there making a stand, where there might be a probability of giving effectual aid.

In the above conference, Morla, aware of this judicious plan, did his utmost to prevent its being adopted, and endeavoured to entrap a part at least of the British army.

The words of General Hope's letter are,

" MY DEAR MOORE,                    *Madrid, 20th November,* 1808.

" IN consequence of a pressing letter from Lord " William Bentinck, I yesterday came to Madrid.

" This morning Lord William and I have had a long conversa- " tion with Don T. Morla, authorised by the Junta to converse with " us upon the state of affairs.

" Much desultory reasoning passed at this conference; and it is " perfectly evident that they are altogether without a plan, as to " their future military operations, either in the case of success or " misfortune.

" Every branch is affected by the disjointed and inefficient con- " struction of their Government.

* L. O.

" The only result of this conference that can be worth communi-
" cating to you is, that it is the decided opinion of Morla, and stated
" by him as what the Government also wish, that in case of the
" British force being now prevented from forming a junction, for the
" purpose of advancing to undertake active offensive operations, a
" junction of whatever part of that force it may be practicable to
" bring together should take place in the centre of Spain."

Men of strict honour and integrity, like. Lord William Bentinck
and General Hope, are never prone to suspicion.. It is from subsequent facts that it becomes clear, that this advice was insidiously.
given. Had it been followed, the British army, which was too
small to cope with the French even when combined, must have
been separated; and that portion which should approach the centre.
of Spain would have become an easy prey to Buonaparte; while the.
remainder would have been too weak to have been efficacious.

On the 27th of November this letter arrived.:

### Mr. Frere to. Sir John Moore.

" SIR,                                             Aranjuez, 25 Nov. 1808..

        " I SEND inclosed the copy of a Note which I addressed
" to M. Garay, secretary of. the Junta, and which contains the re-
" capitulation of a conference which I had with him (on the subject
" of your letters addressed to me and to Lord William Bentinck) in
" the presence of Mr. Stuart. I have likewise inclosed his answer,
" which I have just. received. It is difficult to account entirely for
" the want of information of which we have to complain. It is
" owing certainly in part to the mistaken notions of secrecy and
" mystery which are attached to the concerns of Government, which
" is incidental to people who are unexpectedly called to the manage-

" ment of public affairs. Something, I am afraid, is likewise to be
" imputed to a jealousy of Great Britain; as if we presumed upon
" the obligations under which this Country is placed. But most of
" all, the confusion of their own system of intelligence; or, more
" properly speaking, the want of system is the cause of the uncer-
" tainty in which we are left upon points of the greatest con-
" sequence.

" The accounts, however, which have been received to-day have
" been personally too alarming for concealment. A courier has
" arrived who left the advanced posts of the French at Medina celi;
" and an express has since come in from Torriga with an account
" of firing having been heard at Siguença, As the French are
" superior in cavalry, and there is nothing to stop them between
" that place and this, the Junta are in immediate expectation of
" their approach, and had determined this evening on retiring upon
" Cordova. I am in hopes that they have been prevailed upon to
" relinquish this plan, and to content themselves at present with
" retreating to Toledo. The following is the statement of the
" numbers of their troops in New Castile:

At Buitrago - - 5000
Segovia - - 4700
Somosierra - 6400
Madrid - - 5300

" The force of the Enemy is reckoned at about eleven thousand,
" men, of which six thousand cavalry under General Belliard.

" I inclose a report which has just been sent me relative to Blake's,
" army. I find upon enquiry, that the date of the attack is the 19th.
" at night. Columbres is not above two or three leagues from the first,
" village of Asturias. I learn at the same time, that one of the Asturian,
" Deputies to whom I had directed my enquiries has already left the,

" Sitio. The Marquis Romana on the 17th was attempting to make a
" stand at Torra de la Vega. General Leith had given orders, which
" had been properly executed, for evacuating the post of St. Ander.
" No courier has been received from Castanos; and it is clear, from
" the situation of the French, that the direct communication is cut
" off. Great discontent and perplexity are known to be prevalent at
" head-quarters.

" Mr. Stuart will be able to give you better accounts of the military
" condition of Madrid. There are about 8 or 10,000 musquets, and
" ammunition has been distributed.

" The Junta appear at present more anxious for your union with
" Blake than for covering Madrid. What they most deprecate, and
" I think with most reason, is a retreat upon Portugal. It would
" sink the hearts of the whole country, and would give the impres-
" sion of our having, after an ineffectual effort, relapsed into the old
" limited system of protecting Portugal.

" I must apologise for the apparent formality of this letter, which
" does not proceed from any inclination to commence a less confi-
" dential mode of communication between us; but is owing to the
" hurry which the circumstances I have mentioned will account for.

" Believe me, &c.

" J. H. FRERE."

There are two singular passages in this letter. The first is, it is
stated that the force of the Enemy is about eleven thousand men.
Where this force was, is not mentioned; but the Junta ought to have
known that at this period Buonaparte was advancing rapidly with
nearly 80,000; which information ought to have been communicated to Sir John Moore. The second is, that Mr. Frere strongly
deprecates a retreat on Portugal. This probably was not an ori-

ginal error of Mr. Frere's, but instilled into his mind by Morla; for otherwise a person totally ignorant of military affairs would hardly have ventured to express so decidedly his opinion of a military movement to an experienced General.

Morla was now become the chief ruler of the Junta; and was considered a man of the first abilities in Spain. He had been appointed President of the Board charged with military affairs, and was with great success effecting the destruction of the Spanish armies. Previous to his interference, the Generals Castanos and Blake had most judiciously acted upon the defensive: that system was now reprobated; and the Generals were impelled forward, contrary to their judgment. Morla was, however, not content with the destruction of the Spanish armies in succession: but, in order to complete the subjugation of Spain, he got himself appointed by the Junta * to treat with the English Generals; and empowered to proceed to the execution of such measures as were urgent and peremptory.

Being invested with this authority, he did not fail to exert it; and had his advice or requisitions been literally obeyed, not a man of the British army would have escaped.

The following is the requisition made by Mr. Frere to the Supreme Junta, in consequence of Sir John Moore's letter to him.

*Du Mr. Frere à son Excellence Mr. de Garay.*

" MONSIEUR,        " *Aranjuez*, 23 *Novembre*, 1808.

  " J'AI crû devoir adresser à votre Excellence, comme " Membre et Secrétaire de la Suprême Junta Centrale, une répré- " sentation qui m' a parû trop importante pour ne pas être communi-

* Vide Mr. De Garay to Mr. Frere, which soon follows.

" quée à cette assemblée par un de ses individus distingué par sa
" confiance et chargé de ses plus importantes fonctions.

" Des lettres qui me sont parvenues de la part de Sir J. Moore
" m'ont donné occasion de vous récapituler les plaintes qu'il m'adres-
" soit, et qu'il regrettoit (me disoit il) ne pas pouvoir adresser en
" personne à Aranjuez.

" Il se plaint d'abord de l'état d'incertitude dans lequel il se trouve,
" rélativement au nombre et aux positions de l'Ennemi, et même
" aux projets et événemens de la campagne, au point (me dit-il)
" que, lors de l'évacuation peu militaire de Valladolid par le Général
" Pignatelli, cet Officier n'a pas crû devoir lui en envoyer l'avis.
" Les détails de la route et de l'état effectif de l'Armée d'Estremadure
" lui ont été également long tems inconnûs; la retraite du Général
" Blake, et sa retraite sur Reynosa, lui ont été également inconnues
" jusqu'à ce qu'il en reçut enfin la nouvelle par la voye de Madrid.

" Il poursuit en ces termes : ' Je ne suis en communication avec
' aucune des Armées, ni au fait des intentions du Gouvernement
' Espagnol, ni d'aucun de ses Généraux.

' Castanos, avec qui on m'avoit mis en corréspondance, est démis
' de son commandement au moment où j'aurois pû attendre de ses
' nouvelles; et Romana, avec qui je dois maintenant, je suppose, entrer
' en corréspondance, est absent. En attendant, les François ne sont
' qu'à quatre jours de marche de mon armée qui ne fait que s'assem-
' bler; mais je ne peux encore apprendre l'état de leur force. Aucun
' canal d'information ne m'a été ouvert, et je ne suis pas assez long
' tems dans le pays pour me les procurer moi-même. Je vous fais
' part de ces particularités. Je voudrois pouvoir aller moi-même à
' Aranjuez, ou Madrid, en faire la réprésentation; car, vraiment, si
' les choses doivent rester dans cet état, la ruine de la cause d'Es-
' pagne, et la défaite de ses Armées, ne peut pas manquer; et il
' deviendra de mon devoir de ne regarder que la sécurité de l'Armée

I

' Britannique, et de prendre des mesures pour la tirer d'une situation
' où, sans la possibilité d' être utile, elle est exposée à une défaite
' certaine.'

" En réponse à ces observations rélatives au Général Castanos
" et au Marquis de la Romana, V. E. m' apprit, à ma très grande
" surprise, qu' il y avoit dix jours à peu près que des Ordres avoient
" été expediés au Marquis de la Romana pour venir prendre le com-
" mandement de l'Armée du Centre, en laissant celle du Nord et des
" Asturies aux ordres de M. Blake.

" Le secrét commun à une assemblée de 32 personnes auroit pû,
" ce me semble, être confié au Ministre de S. M. B. sans augmenter
" beaucoup le risque de sa divulgation, quand même il n' auroit pas
" été question d' un fait intéressant, et dont la connoissance étoit
" nécessaire pour la corréspondance dont pouvoit dépendre la sureté
" de l'Armée Angloise. Il m' a parû que V. E. ne se montreroit pas
" insensible à la justice de cette réflection ; à laquelle j' aurois pû
" ajouter que la nouvelle de l' entrée des François à Valladolid m' a été
" cachée ; qui, lors même que je demandois si le bruit public qui l'
" annoncoit avoit quelque fondement, on m' a répondu, qu' il n' étoit
" arrivé ce jour là aucune nouvelle officielle excepté sur le transport
" de quelques piéces d' artillerie, je crois, à Segovie. Il m' etoit donc
" impossible de croire, d' après une pareille réponse, que des nouvelles
" authentiques avoient apporté la certitude de l'événement sur lequel
" je demandois une explication, et qu'on avoit crû pouvoir la dissi-
" muler par une équivoque fondée sur la non-arrivée du rapport
" officiel du Commandant. La nouvelle de la défaite du Général
" Blake, nouvelle qui auroit pû causer la perte totale des deux
" divisions qui commençoient à se former sous les Généraux Moore
" et Baird, m' a été effectivement communiquée, mais le soir du
" lendemain de l' arrivée du Courier.

" Je suis bien loin d' éprouver le moindre sentiment d' aigreur
" personelle contre des personnes infiniment respectables, qui n' ont
" fait que suivie un systême qui leur aura été préscrit, tant pour
" les réponses que pour le silence; mais il est de mon devoir de
" réclamer hautement contre la continuation d' un systême, qui sans
" assurer le secret vis-à-vis des Ennemis, établit la défiance et le
" mystère à la place de cette confiance qui devoit servir de base äux
" combinaisons desquelles doit dépendre le sort de la guerre actuellé.

" J' ai appris avec beaucoup de plaisir la nouvelle du rappel de la
" Commission désorganatrice envoyée à l'Armée du Centre, ainsi que
" celle de la nomination de M. de Morla avec de pleins pouvoirs
" pour conférer et conclure avec nos Officiers sur tous les objets
" rélatifs à un systême de co-opération efficace; j'éspère que ces
" pouvoirs seront encore augmentés, tant pour la partie exécutive,
" que pour la délibérative.

" L' expedition d' un Courier pour le Marquis de la Romana lui
" aura, sans doute, apporté, selon les instructions de V. E. un ordre
" de s' aboucher avec le Général Sir J. Moore.

" Je ne puis finir sans remercier V. E. de l' attention avec laquelle
" elle a écouté, dans une prémiere conférence, les details d'une répré-
" sentation nécessairement facheuse.

" Je la prie, &c.

" J. H. FRERE."

This letter is certainly not written in very respectful terms; especially as the persons so harshly complained of were exercising
sovereign powers. The following mild answer was however returned:

TRANSLATION.

## " *To the Right Hon. J. Hookham Frere.*

" MOST EXCELLENT SIR,          *Aranjuez, Nov.* 24, 1808.

" I HAVE laid before the Supreme ruling Junta of the
" Kingdom the note your Excellency was pleased to address to me
" yesterday, relative to the complaint made to you by Sir John Moore,
" with regard to the state of ignorance in which he was kept with re-
" spect to the number and positions of the Enemy, and to the events
" and operations of our Armies.

" Of the evacuation of Valladolid, which was not a military move-
" ment, the Supreme Junta knows nothing ; neither of the particu-
" lars of an action in which one of the divisions of the Army of Es-
" tremadura was concerned.   The same is the case with regard to the
" details of the operations of General Blake ; who states that he has
" had two engagements—the one of which was in favour of our arms,
" and the other, though of no great advantage to the Enemy, obliged
" him to retreat to Reynosa.

" Each of the Generals had received positive orders from the Junta,
" which are now reiterated to them by extraordinary couriers, to com-
" municate with the English General, and to act in concert with
" him.   His Majesty would receive the highest satisfaction if Sir
" John Moore could appear personally at Aranjuez or at Madrid,
" to make such observations, and to adjust those points which he
" thinks might conduce to the removal of those circumstances which
" appear contrary to the good understanding, and which might pro-
" duce all the effect that may be expected from our union with the
" great power which with such generosity affords us assistance,
" and which the Junta could not see disappointed or weakened with-
" out the greatest regret.   This, however, could not happen, if, acting

" in concert, and with a perfect harmony, we avail ourselves of a
" speedy union of the forces, to complete the destruction of the Enemy,
" and of his plans; if, the English troops forming a junction with
" the left of our army, we compose a formidable body of 70,000 infan-
" try and 6000 cavalry, a force with which we should be certain of
" the blow, and which we never could be by any different conduct.

" Then the generous efforts of our ally, England, would complete
" the work; under whose happy and auspicious commencement the
" eternal friendship and alliance by which the two nations are for
" ever to be united began; so that neither interest nor policy will
" ever be sufficient to break the bonds by which they are united.

" When I spoke to your Excellency with regard to General Casta-
" nos, I had the honour to explain to you the strong and political
" motives that existed for acting as we had done. Your Excellency
" was convinced, and it was then determined, that he should not quit
" the command until the arrival of the Marquis de la Romana. In
" this there has been no secret, nor should there be any, however im-
" portant it may be, with regard to the Minister of a friendly nation,
" towards whom the Junta feels the greatest personal esteem and con-
" sideration, independent of his official character.

" The Junta knew of the Enemy's entry into Valladolid, and, after-
" wards, of the evacuation of that city by the French troops, who
" made but a very short stay there. General Morla is appointed to
" treat with the English Generals, to agree upon the necessary plans
" and operations, and to give information of them to the Supreme
" Junta; proceeding immediately to the execution of those measures
" which are urgent and peremptory.

" I have now only to assure your Excellency of the particular satis-
" faction and pleasure I derived from hearing your remarks on these
" matters, which led to this our first conference. I shall be ready to
" repeat it, with pleasure, as often as your Excellency may think

" proper; either at your house, or wherever else you may choose to
" appoint. In the mean time,

" I am, &c.

" MARTIN DE GARAY."

Sir John Moore did not think it expedient to accept of the invitation given in this letter to go to Aranjuez or Madrid, and leave the troops at Salamanca, in the present threatening posture of affairs.

His occupations were too important to admit of such an interruption; and the quantity of business he transacted may be conceived from the manner in which his time was daily employed.

He always rose between three and four in the morning, lighted his fire and candle by a lamp which was placed in his room, and employed himself in writing till eight o'clock, when the officers of the family were assembled for breakfast.

After breakfast he received the General Officers, and all persons with whom he had business; and the necessary orders were issued. His pen was frequently in his hand in the forenoon also; for he wrote all his letters himself. He always rode before dinner for an hour or two, either to view the troops, or to reconnoitre the country.

His table was plentiful; and the company varied from fourteen to twenty officers. He was a very plain and moderate eater, and seldom drank more than three or four glasses of wine, conversing with his officers with great frankness and cheerfulness. His portfolio was usually opened again before he went to bed; but, unless kept up by business, he never sat up later than ten o'clock.

By this regularity and assiduity all his affairs were transacted with order, and without procrastination.

The information conveyed by Mr. Garay's letter was by no means satisfactory. It contained no foundation upon which a decision could be built.

Therefore, as the troops were not yet assembled, Sir John wrote to learn the opinion of Mr. Frere.

*Sir John Moore to his Excellency J. H. Frere.*

" SIR, *Salamanca, 27 Nov.* 1808.

" I HAD the honour to receive last night a letter from
" Mr. Stuart, of the 24th inst. in answer to that which I addressed
" to you on the 19th.

" The conversation which Mr. Stuart states you to have had with
" the Secretary of the Supreme Junta, and the remonstrances with
" which you have followed it, are, perhaps, as much as can be done
" by you in your situation. The effect produced upon the Secretary,
" and the measures he said were determined, are very good, if we
" were looking to events six months hence; but the situation in
" which we are, calls for something more efficient and energetic.

" Madrid is threatened—the French have destroyed one army, have
" passed the Ebro, and are advancing in superior numbers against
" another : which, from its composition and strength, promises no re-
" sistance, but must either retire, or be overwhelmed. No other
" armed force exists in this country. I perceive no enthusiasm, or any
" determined spirit amongst the people.

" The French Cavalry, even in parties so weak as eleven or twelve
" men, enter the villages in Leon, and the neighbouring provinces,
" and raise contributions without opposition.

" This is a state of things quite different from that conceived by
" the British Government, when they determined to send troops to
" the assistance of Spain. It was not expected that these were to
" cope alone with the whole force of France; but as auxiliaries, to aid
" a people who were believed to be enthusiastic, determined, and
" prepared for resistance.

" It becomes, therefore, a question, whether the British Army
" should remain to be attacked in its turn, or retire from a country
" where the contest, from whatever circumstances, has become un-
" equal.

" I wish to throw no responsibility off myself, which properly be-
" longs to me.

" The question is not purely a military one. It belongs at least
" as much to you, as to me, to decide upon it. Your communications
" with the Spanish Government, and the opportunities you have had
" of judging of the general state of the Country, enable you to form
" as just an estimate of the resistance that is likely to be offered.

" You are, perhaps, better acquainted with the views of the British
" Cabinet; and the question is, What would that Cabinet direct, were
" they upon the spot to determine? It is of much importance that
" this should be thoroughly considered; it is comparatively of very
" little, on whom shall rest the greatest share of responsibility. I am
" willing to take the whole, or a part; but I am very anxious to
" know your opinion.

" The movements of the French give us little time for discussion.
" As soon as the British Army has formed a junction, I must, upon
" the supposition that Castanos is either beaten or retreated, march
" upon Madrid, and throw myself into the heart of Spain, and thus
" run all risks, and share the fortunes of the Spanish Nation; or I
" must fall back upon Portugal.

" In the latter case, I fall back upon my resources, upon Lisbon :
" cover a country where there is a British interest; act as a diversion
" in favour of Spain, if the French detach a force against me ; and
" am ready to return to the assistance of the Spaniards, should cir-
" cumstances again render it eligible.

" By marching into Spain, I detach myself from my resources,
" and should, probably, be able to take with me but a small portion

" of the military stores I have brought forward. In which case I
" should not be able, for a time, for much contest. But every thing
" could be sent from Lisbon to Cadiz, and thence join me.

" The movement into Spain is one of greater hazard, as my retreat
" to Cadiz or Gibraltar must be very uncertain. I shall be entirely
" in the power of the Spaniards; but perhaps this is worthy of risk;
" if the Government and People of Spain are thought to have still
" sufficient energy and the means to recover from their defeats; and,
" by collecting in the South, be able, with the aid of the British
" Army, to resist, and finally repel, the formidable attack which is
" prepared against them.

" It is impossible not to wish, and then it is more difficult not to
" hope, that the Spaniards may be at last successful in a struggle
" which does them so much honour. They are a fine people, and had
" they fallen into more able hands would have proved themselves
" fully equal to the contest. But I much fear the opportunity is now
" past; and that no efforts they are likely to make will be sufficient,
" or in time, to stand the armies they must engage. Upon this sub-
" ject, however, I cannot be very decided, and shall be most happy
" to find myself mistaken.

" I am, &c. &c.

" JOHN MOORE."

On the same day Sir John Moore wrote the following private letter
to Mr. Stuart, to whom he confided his thoughts most openly.

*Sir John Moore to Charles Stuart, Esq.*

" MY DEAR SIR,      *Salamanca,* 27 *Nov.* 1808.

  " I THANK you for your letter. You will see what
" I have written to Mr. Frere, and will, I hope, think with me on
" the necessity of deciding a question, which, surely alone, he being

K

" in the country, I could not with propriety decide for myself.
" Whatever be the decision, I shall be guided by events in the exe-
" cution of it.

" I have every inclination to think well of the Spanish cause: that
" I wish it well is most certain; and that I shall be most proud to
" give it every aid in my power. But, really, so little ability has
" been displayed by the Government, or by those employed to direct
" their armies; there appears so much apathy in the people, and so
" little means prepared for resistance, that I do not see how they can
" stand against the Enemy. The French will have troublesome sub-
" jects; but, in the first instance, they will have little more than a
" march to subdue the country.

" I have not a shilling. The Spaniards, I find, promise much
" more than they perform; and here we have not been able to get
" five thousand pounds. The house you mention in a former letter
" have money, but will not give it.

" Sir D. Baird, upon some false intelligence that the French had
" collected a large force at Rio Seco and Ampudia, has taken mea-
" sures to retreat, but I shall be able to stop him; and I hope by the
" 7th or 8th of December, we shall be able to make our junction.

" I hope to meet Romana on his passage to the army,—the intelli-
" gence was sent to Baird by General Blake. The French have
" many friends in this country; it is from them that a thousand
" reports are daily spread to the disadvantage of the *good cause.*
" I remain, &c.
" JOHN MOORE.

" P. S. There was a Colonel Charmilly here from England. He
" is gone on to Madrid, to offer to raise a regiment of cavalry. He
" is married in England: but I cannot help always having some dis-
" like to people of this description."

That no time might be lost, Sir John Moore wrote a letter the following day to Sir David Baird, to give him information of the movements of the French army, and to direct him to advance.

It is now requisite to state the catastrophe of the Spanish Armies of the Centre and Right.

On the 21st of November General Castanos' Head Quarters were at Cintruenigo, when the advanced guard of the French army appeared in sight. Castanos retreated in the night towards Tudela, and the French columns advanced by Soria and Lerona.

Behind Tudela there is a small ridge of hills; this was thought by the Representative of the Junta, and the Captain General of Arragon, a good position. Castanos did not approve of it, and wished to retire; but unfortunately he was overruled. He then drew up his main body near the centre of the ridge, concealing it from the Enemy; and advanced his two flanks on the small hills near Tudela.

The French attacked these points, and Castanos supported them from his centre. The Enemy were driven back on the left; but a strong corps of French pushed forward from Tudela, and made a fresh attack upon the left, and threw the Spaniards into confusion. They were a species of troops who could never rally; so all was disorder in a moment. Part dispersed themselves in the direction of Saragossa, and the rest towards Calatayud.

The only corps which preserved any kind of order was that of General La Pena, stationed at Coscante.

The news of this fresh disaster arrived at Madrid on the 27th of November. Mr. Stuart lost no time in transmitting the relation he had received to Sir John Moore, which he accompanied with a short and dismal note; in which are these words: — " I, therefore, lose " not a moment in dispatching this to you, that you may be enabled " to take such measures as, in this state of affairs, become absolutely " necessary for the security of our Army."

This dispatch reached Salamanca Nov. 28, which totally darkened the aspect of affairs.

While Castanos's army remained, there appeared to Sir John Moore a hope of resisting in the North of Spain; but now he thought there was none. It was also evident, that if Buonaparte chose, as might be expected, to push forward his advanced corps upon him, his junction with General Hope would be very doubtful, and that with Sir David Baird impossible *.

For these reasons he at once took the resolution of withdrawing the army from Galicia and Leon, and assembling it upon the banks of the Tagus.

The advantages of this measure were, that the whole British force would be collected and united with upwards of 10,000 men more, who were left in Portugal.

In the mean time, all the scattered corps of the Spanish army might fall back, to join such new levies as were raised in the Southern Provinces; which, when assembled, might still form an army capable of making a stand: and the British could then move to their aid in a formidable body. It appears from the previous correspondence, that it had always been the favourite plan of Sir John Moore to carry on the military operations from the South; and now that the three Spanish armies were beaten, the reasons for adopting it had acquired great additional weight.

If the Spaniards had constancy to hold out, and fortitude to continue the contest, an opportunity would still be afforded them. In the South all their energies might be put forth, and effectual assistance would be given them by the British army. And should they also be repelled in this effort; Cadiz and Gibraltar afforded them secure retreats.

* Vide Appendix F.

From these fortresses the war might be renewed, if circumstances favoured it; or if the contest was given up, the armies would still be in safety.

The following letters to Sir David Baird and General Hope were sent off the same evening.

### Sir John Moore to Sir David Baird.

"MY DEAR SIR DAVID,                    *Salamanca, 28th Nov.* 1808.

"I HAVE received this evening dispatches from Mr. "Stuart at Madrid, announcing the defeat and dispersion of Cas-"tanos's army. The French in Spain are estimated at 80,000 men, "and 30,000 are expected in the course of a week. It certainly was "much my wish to have run great risks in aid of the people of Spain; "but, after this second proof of how little they are able to do for "themselves, the only two armies they had having made so little "stand, I see no right to expect from them much greater exertions; "at any rate we should be overwhelmed before they could be pre-"pared. I see no chance of our being able to form a junction; as "certainly at Burgos the French have a corps which will now move "forward.

"I have, therefore, determined to retreat upon Portugal with the "corps I have here; and, if possible, with Hope's corps, if by forced "marches he can join me. I wish you to fall back on Corunna; "send back immediately your stores, under such part of your force "as you judge proper. You may then stay with the rest a little "longer; if you can depend upon knowing the movements of the "Enemy. I propose this, as were you at once to retire, it would "encourage the Enemy to push at once on Hope and me, and pre-"vent our junction; which is the more necessary, as I must stop "upon the frontier of Portugal, and cover Lisbon as long as pos-

" sible. On your arrival at Corunna, you will of course embark,
" and sail for the Tagus, where orders shall be waiting for you.
" Write immediately to England, and give notice of what we are
" doing; and beg that transports may be sent to Lisbon; they will
" be wanted: for when the French have Spain, Portugal cannot be
" defended.

" I remain sincerely,

" JOHN MOORE."

" This letter, though of the same date, is written on the evening
" of the day on which I wrote by Baron Tuyle.

" You will use your discretion as to sending the cavalry by sea
" or through Portugal. I shall not want them here, if I can get the
" two Regiments with Hope.      J. M.

" You will go to Lisbon with the whole of your force; the two
" regiments of cavalry included, not yet disembarked; unless you
" should receive orders from England to the contrary.    J. M."

Sir John Moore to Lieut.-General·Hope.

" MY DEAR HOPE,          Salamanca, 28th Nov. 1808.

     " I have received, by Mr. Vaughan, the letters from
" Madrid, which you had very properly opened.

" After due consideration, I have determined to give the thing up,
" and to retire. It was my wish to have run great risks to fulfil
" what I conceive to be the wishes of the people of England, and to
" give every aid to the Spanish cause; but they have shewn them-
" selves equal to do so little for themselves—their two principal armies
" having allowed themselves to be thus beaten and dispersed with-
" out almost an effort—it would only be sacrificing the Army without

" doing any good to Spain, to oppose it to such numbers as must now
" be brought against us : besides, I take for granted, a junction with
" Baird is out of the question ; and, perhaps, with you, problematical ;
" as there must be troops at Burgos, which must now push on to
" intercept us. I shall write this night to Baird to fall back on
" Corunna. I wish you, if possible, by forced marches, and in larger
" bodies, to push by Penaranda or Alba de Tormes ; whence, according
" to circumstances, you may join me here, or march at once on Ciudad
" Rodrigo ; should you, however, from any thing which comes to
" your own knowledge, deem it unsafe to push on to me, you are at
" liberty to use your discretion, and fall back on Guardarama and
" Madrid. It must, however, be my wish, that, if possible, you
" should join me ; for, as I must stop on the frontier of Portugal,
" I shall be in much want of your aid, and that of your corps ; but
" I leave you a discretion that you may use, should you see, which
" I do not at present see, a great probability of your being inter-
" cepted. This is a cruel determination for me to make ; — I mean
" to retreat ; but I hope you will think the circumstances such as
" demand it. I shall take measures for falling back ; but I shall stay
" at this place as long as I can. Provisions we shall want in Portu-
" gal ; and if you could get carts and send the provisions collected
" at Penaranda to Ciudad Rodrigo, it would be an object. It is
" unnecessary that it should be known, the determination we are come
" to ; other reasons may be given for your changing your march."

" Sincerely, &c.

" JOHN MOORE.

" *P. S.* Napier arrived as I had finished my letter to you, which
" is enclosed. You seem to have foreseen my wishes ; I have,
" therefore, nothing to add at present. I shall write to you by Na-
" pier in the morning ; and shall think of a movement towards

" you, should it appear necessary. The French have only a corps of
" cavalry at Valladolid."

It thus appears that Sir John Moore took the resolution of retreating, without waiting for Mr. Frere's answer to his letter of the 27th.
The defeat of Castanos totally altered the question; and the situation of the Army admitted of no delay. For, if Buonaparte should
detach his most advanced corps against the British, General Hope
might possibly be intercepted, and Sir David Baird might be hotly
pursued, and suffer loss in the embarkation.

He then assembled the General Officers, and shewed them the
intelligence he had received, and the plan he had adopted. He told
the Generals, " that he had not called them together to request their
" counsel, or to induce them to commit themselves by giving any
" opinion upon the subject. He took the responsibility entirely upon
" himself; and he only required that they would immediately prepare
" for carrying it into effect."

It ought to be mentioned, that the idea of retreating was very
generally disapproved of at Salamanca by the Army. The murmurs
against it from Officers of rank were heard in every quarter. Even
the Staff Officers of Sir John Moore's family lamented it; and, for
the first time, doubted the wisdom of his decision. He, however,
afterwards learnt, that General Hope agreed with him completely on
this, as on all other points.

The following letter signified his intentions to Mr. Frere and
Mr. Stuart.

*Sir John Moore to Mr. Stuart.*

" MY DEAR SIR, *Salamanca, 29th Nov.* 1808.

" I HAD determined to unite this Army, if possible, and
" to try what could be done for the Spaniards; though, I own, I saw
" but little chance of being able to do much good.  I had ordered
" Baird, though all his corps could not be at Astorga until the 4th,
" to march with such part as already are there to Benavente, on the
" 1st of December; and, on that day, I was to march myself with a corps
" from this to Toro, and to send others to Zamora.  Hope was to have
" marched to Tordesillas, and we should have taken up a line upon the
" Duero, to cover the arrival of our stores, and then to have acted ac-
" cording to circumstances: but the destruction of Castanos's army,
" announced by your letter which Mr. Vaughan brought to me yester-
" day afternoon, changes the case.  My junction with Baird is no
" longer practicable; but, if it was, the little resistance made by the
" Spanish armies gives no hope of our doing any good.  We should
" now have the greatest force of the Enemy to encounter single-
" handed, and this we are not equal to.  I have, therefore, come to
" the determination to retire.  I have ordered Baird to fall back upon
" Corunna.  I shall endeavour to unite with Hope, and retire upon
" the frontier of Portugal.  I shall be at hand to return, if affairs
" take a more favourable turn; or the Army may be transported by
" me to some other point, where they may still be useful; if this
" Government be overset, and another rises up, directed by men of
" more ability.

" Mr. Vaughan sets off to-day for Corunna.

" If you can possibly send me any money to Almeida, do it.

L

" I send this by Colonel Lopez, who, as yet, knows not the mis-
" fortune which has befallen Castanos, nor of my resolution.
                " Believe me always, &c.
                                        " JOHN MOORE.

" I address this to you; you will, of course, make a communication
" to Mr. Frere."


Two days afterwards, when Sir John Moore was waiting for the
arrival of General Hope's Corps, at Salamanca, he wrote to Mr. Stuart
a more full explanation of his motives.

*Sir John Moore to Charles Stuart, Esq.*

" MY DEAR SIR,                    " *Salamanca, 1st December,* 1808.
        " GENERAL HOPE forwarded to me your letter of the 29th,
" and I received it last night.
        " My letter to you of the 29th, after I had seen Mr. Vaughan,
" would inform you of the resolution I had come to.  It was with
" reluctance, you may believe, that I formed such a determination;
" but I had no alternative; and reflection since has confirmed me in
" the opinion, that I have done right.  There is nothing so easy,
" as for the Junta, with their pens, to form armies; and they have,
" I see, in this manner, collected one of eighty thousand men in Leon.
" But Romana, whom they have put down at twenty thousand, has
" only five thousand fugitives from Blake, without arms, clothing,
" stores, or ammunition; without organization, or officers to make
" any; the soldiers neither disciplined, nor (Romana complains)
" susceptible of taking any; when checked, they go off.  The Junta
" neglected the opportunity to form armies, and to prepare the Pro-
" vinces, before the arrival of the French reinforcements;—it is
" now too late under the beards of a victorious Enemy; and Spain

" has no chance now but from a force, if collected in the South, and
" at a distance. I consider this letter, and that which I wrote to you
" on the 29th, as if written to Mr. Frere, and, as such, I beg you
" will have the goodness to communicate them to him. I continue
" in the same determination I was in then, with respect to my own
" movement, which will take place the moment that General Hope
" is out of danger; but he has found it necessary to go round by
" Avilla, whence I hope he will be able to join me. I have not heard
" from Sir David Baird since my letter to him by Mr. Vaughan;
" but, as he was prepared, I take for granted he has commenced
" his movements on Corunna. The communication with Madrid is
" become less secure from the incursions of the Enemy's cavalry; I
" cannot, therefore, enter into more particulars; but if the Spaniards
" make head, I conceive the British force can still, in one way or
" another, be taken to their assistance. I am sorry when Hope
" sent Mr. Smith to Madrid, * * * * * * * * * *
" that he did not give him special instructions : Mr. Kennedy writes
" to him by this opportunity. But such is our want of money, that
" if it can be got at a hundred *per cent.* we must have it; do there-
" fore, if possible, send me some at any rate; but it must make a
" circuit by Avilla, at least; and, if Smith is still at Madrid, I wish
" you would tell him from me, that he cannot render such service as
" by bringing money at any discount.

" The Enemy do not, at present, seem to have any thing but
" cavalry on this side of Valladolid; they certainly have a division at
" Burgos, and the thirty thousand from France will be there shortly;
" and they will detach from the army which has defeated Castanos;
" and may have done so already, unless they first choose to enter
" Madrid. It is from the Centre and South, that an effort should be
" looked for : in this quarter the business is up, and the people
" without enthusiasm think they have nothing left for it, but to
" submit.

"The armies you see are also without enthusiasm, or even com-
"mon obstinacy—they do not stand—and the individuals we see
"passing as fugitives are not ashamed, nor are they thought ill of
"by the people, nor indignation excited. In this province, and it
"is probably the same in others, there is no head to direct—the
"Captain-general Pignatelli is a weak old man. A man of a firm
"and active mind could, by taking the means which exist, have done
"much. At Zamora there are three or four thousand stand of arms,
"in other places there may be more. If they remain collected in
"towns they will be taken by the Enemy, for the towns will make
"no defence; but if put into the hands of the peasants, with ammu-
"nition, they would protect their property, kill small parties and
"stragglers, and harass the Enemy; and, when assembled at any
"time in bodies, they would form the best materials for an army.

"This and a thousand measures could be adopted, if the Junta had
"selected men to employ; but they have acted with all the imbecility
"of an old established weak government of the old *regime*. Lord
"William is this moment arrived, having narrowly escaped being
"taken at Arevalo.

"I shall be glad to hear from you and Mr. Frere; but your mes-
"senger must be cautious, and advance on information of the
"Enemy.

"I have the honour, &c.

"JOHN MOORE."

On the 2d of December Sir John Moore received ample dispatches; all softening the losses of the Spaniards, and giving more
favourable accounts of their remaining resources. Mr. Stuart was
in regular communication with Morla, as is mentioned formerly.
The principal part of the intelligence contained in the following

letter was from him. Mr. Stuart narrates all he has heard, but with great good sense does not venture to give an opinion upon the military movements.

*Charles Stuart Esq. to Sir John Moore.*

"MY DEAR GENERAL,                              *Madrid*, 30 *Nov*. 1808.

      "I HAVE this moment received your's, dated the 29th,
"announcing a determination to retire on the frontier of Portugal,
"in consequence of the intelligence conveyed through Mr. Vaughan
"respecting the army of Castanos. I have to inform you that two
"other Officers have arrived from Arragon, by whom the Govern-
"ment have received accounts somewhat more favourable. Having
"however received nothing from Graham, Whittingham, and Doyle,
"and being equally deprived of letters from the Sitio since they came,
"I cannot say to what extent matters are retrieved. I know, how-
"ever, that the Enemy have made three attacks on San Juan near
"Sepulveda, and have been as often repulsed. And, from the large
"force, particularly of cavalry, which were engaged in the late
"affair at Borja and Tudela, it is impossible they can have any
"thing so considerable as General Hope represents in the neigh-
"bourhood of Valladolid and Olmedo. They have 10,000 cavalry
"in Spain: 1500 are at Sepulveda. If, therefore, 4500 were in
"Valladolid, there would remain but few on the other points they
"have so lately attacked. Every report brought in here states,
"that several small parties are scattered in Castile, for the purpose
"of obtaining provisions, gaining intelligence, and inspiring terror
"throughout the province. And this accords so well with all the
"positive intelligence which has reached us, that I really believe it
"to be true.

" You must, however, certainly know best the chances of effecting
" a junction between your different divisions; and it does not become
" me to hazard an opinion on the subject. With respect, however,
" to the consequences of their distinct retrograde movements, I can
" tell you, that they are very likely to produce an effect here, not
" less serious than the most decisive victory on the part of the Enemy;
" and I shall, I own, be surprised if a change of government is not
" the immediate consequence, when the reasons for your retreat
" are known."

A part is here omitted, which chiefly consists of observations on
the Paymaster's department. He then goes on—

" I had written thus far, when I saw Morla, who informs me,
" that Castanos is bringing the greater part of his force, though he
" did not say what, from Calatayud to Siguenza, for the purpose of
" effecting a junction with San Juan. Reports from the latter add,
" that the French have reinforced their corps at Sepulveda, and
" that he expected to be attacked yesterday or to-day.

" He has received an addition of four new regiments; and on
" the result of the affair about to take place, it is thought his
" union with Castanos will depend. He likewise tells me again,
" that he believes the Enemy have merely small parties throughout
" Castile, not sufficient to impede the union of your divisions. He
" declares that his report from Olmedo merely mentioned the arri-
" val of thirty dragoons in that village, which were detached from
" Valladolid; where he insists that their present force is not suffi-
" ciently considerable to impede your movements. He added, that
" according to the declarations of prisoners Buonaparte is at Burgos.

" You will take all this as it is given. He declares he speaks on
" official reports, and your own accounts will enable you to ascertain
" how far it is worthy of credit. This much is certain, that the

" accounts of the Enemy are magnified, both by their own details
" and by the fear inspired in the country. If it be true that
" Buonaparte is at Burgos, it certainly looks like a great effort
" either on the side of Somosierra or Valladolid. Though Segovia
" would appear to be his object, if his cavalry are pushed beyond
" the latter town.

" Truly yours,

" CHARLES STUART."

After perusing these alleviating details, on the authority of Morla,
the following dispatch was opened.

*Mr. Frere to Sir John Moore.*

" SIR,           *Aranjuez, Nov.* 30, 1808.

  " I HAD just written my other letter of this date when
" I received a messenger from Mr. Stuart with the communication
" of a note addressed to him, but intended equally for myself. I do
" not know that I can in any way express with less offence the en-
" tire difference of our opinions on the subject of it, than by forward-
" ing what I had already written in the ignorance of the determi-
" nation which you had already taken.

" I have the honour, &c.

" J. H. FRERE."

As Sir John Moore's letter to Mr. Frere previous to his knowing
the defeat of Castanos, solicited his political opinion; and as all his
letters were written in most respectful terms, it was impossible for
him to expect such an answer. Mr. Frere appears not to be at
all aware of how much importance it is for a Minister to restrain the
ebullitions of temper. The reasons contained in that which follows
would certainly be as likely to produce conviction in the mind of his
Correspondent, had the above letter been omitted.

*Mr. Frere to Sir John Moore.*

" SIR, *Aranjuez, Nov. 30, 1808.*

" You will find inclosed a letter, of which I think it
" right to say, that if there appears any thing in the form or mode
" of transmitting it which may appear deficient in respect, it is, I
" am persuaded, wholly unintentional\*; and, trusting to your candour
" for seeing it in that light, I have not thought it worth while to
" make any remark to Mr. Garay on the apparent dryness of his
" communication.

" Respecting Mr. Escalante, it may be proper that you should
" know, that he is understood to have behaved very unfairly towards
" General Castanos. I mention this only as it may lead you to
" admit his opinion on subjects connected with that General's con-
" duct with some degree of caution.

" In what I said respecting a retreat upon Portugal, I wished to
" confine myself to a simple political opinion ; which, supposing
" other considerations not to be decidedly adverse, might, I thought,
" determine for a retreat upon Galicia, or the strong country about
" Astorga, in preference to Portugal, supposing of course a retreat
" to have been determined upon as absolutely necessary.

" If, however, you do me the honour to consult me respecting
" the general state of the country, and the means of resistance to
" be expected from it, I should say that the provinces which you
" have hitherto seen are of all Spain the least distinguished for a

\* This apology is curious, and shews that Mr. Frere thought the most delicate
expressions ought alone to be employed to the Commander of the Forces. Though
Mr. Garay's letter which follows does not appear to require any apology.

" military, patriotic, or provincial spirit. No man ever calls himself
" a Leonese. The Junta of that province (at the time when Galicia
" and Asturia were sending deputies, and seemed to be almost put-
" ting themselves on the footing of independent states) quietly gave
" their full powers to the Asturians, and acquiesced in what they
" determined and obtained for them. With the exception of La
" Mancha and the city of Madrid, the same description will apply to
" nearly the whole of Old and New Castile.

" In the course of the late events they have been wholly passive,
" and have seen their country successively occupied by the stronger
" party. And indeed it is difficult to blame them: living in open
" villages, in vast plains, without arms, and without horses, they
" have neither the means of defence or escape.

" Yet even here we have seen that the towns are abandoned at the
" approach of the French; that no magistrate has been brought over
" to take an oath of allegiance to the Pretender; nor have the French
" been able to enlist a single soldier.

" The whole of this country has in all times belonged to the party
" which was superior in cavalry; while, in the extremities of the
" kingdom, powers in every respect inferior have been able to pro-
" tract their independence for ages.

" From every thing that I can learn of the disposition of the other
" provinces, they seem to be possessed by the most ardent and deter-
" mined spirit; which, even in the event of the defeat of the levies
" which they are raising for the general defence of the kingdom,
" would lead them individually to continue a desperate resistance,
" under the direction of their separate Juntas, with such assistance
" as England could afford them, by flotillas, disembarkations, &c.
" But it must, I apprehend, be the wish of Government, on every
" account, to prevent things from being brought to this extremity.
" There seem to be two modes of acting with this view: one which

M

" you justly state to be of greater hazard, inasmuch as we effectively
" place ourselves in the power of the Spaniards; but, as you observe
" at the same time, with great truth, this may be worthy of risk, if
" the people of Spain and their Government have sufficient energy
" to recover from their late defeats. Of the people I have no doubt:
" the Government are new, and have been hitherto too numerous
" to be very active; but I trust that this inconvenience will soon be
" remedied. They are resolute, and, I believe, every man of them
" determined to perish with the country. They will not at least set
" the example (which the ruling powers and higher orders of other
" countries have exhibited) of weakness and timidity.

" The military system is certainly defective in its two main points,
" reward and punishment; but the circumstances of the times must
" prove the necessity of varying from the old system in this re-
" spect; and I am persuaded that your representation on this, as
" on all other points, would be listened to with the greatest de-
" ference.

" If you should determine upon marching into Spain, exclusive
" of the importance of covering the capital, there are, I think, great
" advantages which would result from hastening the measure. We
" have now in New Castile an army of 20,000 men, upon which
" Castanos (as you will see) is falling back. Reinforcements are
" passing through here every day from the provinces, and the
" addition of the British would give a force very much, I should
" apprehend, superior to any thing which the French would be able
" to assemble by that time; especially having a strong country in
" arms against them to their left the whole way from the Pyrennees:

" There is besides at present a great delay in the arrival of the
" reinforcements which were promised them; and which, if they
" had been sent, would by this time have composed an enormous
" force.

" There are reports that the resistance to the conscription has
" been much more obstinate than usual; and the pastoral letter of
" the Bishop of Carcapone seems to imply that such reports cannot
" be wholly groundless.

" Every great effort on the part of France has been preceded by
" a similar interval of weakness and internal disturbance; an ad-
" vantage, therefore, which should be obtained at the present moment
" would be doubly valuable, inasmuch as it would render a conscrip-
" tion for a third attempt infinitely difficult, if not impracticable.
" But if, on the other hand, the French are allowed with their pre-
" sent forces to retain their present advantages, and to wait the
" completion of their conscription, they would pour into Spain with
" a number of troops which would give them immediate possession of
" the capital and the central provinces.

" The war would then be reduced to an absolute competition
" between the two countries which would stand out longest against
" the waste of population, enormous as it must be on both sides.

" I cannot but think, therefore, that considerations both of policy
" and generosity call upon us for an immediate effort.

" If, however, this view of the subject should not appear to you
" sufficiently clear or conclusive to induce you to take a step which
" would, I am well convinced (since you do me the honour to refer
" to me on that subject) meet with the approbation of His Majesty's
" Government, I would venture to recommend retaining the posi-
" tion of Astorga. A retreat from that place to Corunna would (as
" far as an unmilitary man may be allowed to judge of a country
" which he has travelled over) be less difficult than through Portugal
" to Lisbon; and we ought in that position to wait for the rein-
" forcements of cavalry from England; which would enable the
" army to act in the flat country, which opens immediately from
" that point, and extends through the whole of Leon and Old Cas-

" tile.  My political reasons on this head I have already troubled you
" with.

" I mention this, however, merely as, in my humble opinion, the
" least objectionable of the two modes of retreat.  Our first object,
" as it appears to me, ought to be, to collect a force capable of re-
" pulsing the French before they receive their reinforcements.

" The covering and protecting Madrid is surely a point of great
" moment, for effect in Spain, and still more in France, and in the
" West of Europe.  It would be a point of the utmost importance
" for Buonaparte to be able to publish a decree, or to date a letter,
" from Madrid.  The people of the town are full of resolution, and
" determined to defend it, in spite of its situation, which is judged
" to be an unfavourable one.  This determination ought surely to
" be encouraged by some shew of support.  The siege of Madrid
" by a Pretender to the throne would be a circumstance decisive
" against the claim, even if in other respects it were a legitimate one.

" I enclose a copy of two official reports from Castanos.

" Believe me, &c.

" J. H. FRERE."

The official reports from Castanos were such descriptions of the
actions at Tudela as it was thought good policy to present to the
public, and were printed in the Spanish newspapers.

A translation of the letter from * Mr. Garay announcing the
arrival of two Spanish Generals, and communicating their powers,
is here subjoined.

* Vide Appendix, T.

They corroborated the statement made by Mr. Frere of the strength of the Spanish armies; asserted that they were undismayed and augmenting every hour; and that General San Juan, with 20,000 brave Spaniards, was in possession of the pass of Somosierra; which he had fortified so strongly as to render the approach to Madrid impracticable.

After listening to this flattering statement, Sir John Moore exceedingly surprised these Spanish Generals by introducing to them Colonel Graham, who had just brought certain accounts that San Juan's corps had been charged by a body of French cavalry, and were completely routed; and that there was no doubt that the French army was in full march for Madrid.

As Colonel Graham had supped the night before with San Juan, in his way from Madrid, his intelligence could not be questioned.

Sir John by his interrogations seems to have completely sounded the depths of these Generals' capacities; and, finding them very ignorant of facts, was little affected by their requisition to move to Madrid. Nor was he altered by Mr. Frere's letters; one of which was written previous to his knowledge of Castanos' defeat; and the short one, which was written after that event, contained no fresh information. He was not even shaken by Mr. Stuart's intelligence, but persisted in his resolution to retire, and waited only for the arrival of General Hope *.

But Don Morla, no doubt instigated by Buonaparte, tried other means, besides his influence with Mr. Frere, to stop the retreat of the British army, and to bring them to the neighbourhood of Madrid.

With this view, on the 2d of December, when Morla was inducing the inhabitants to submit to the Conqueror, who was at the gates of Madrid †; the following dispatch was sent off, by a Government Messenger.

* Vide Appendix, P. R.      † Vide Appendix, U.

This letter was brought to Salamanca by a messenger of the Junta, December 5, 1808. The Prince of Castelfranco and Don Thomas Morla were Deputies of the Supreme Junta entrusted with the government of Madrid; and the latter was the person appointed to concert all Military movements with the English General, as has been mentioned. While Sir John was taking this paper into consideration, Colonel Charmilly arrived with the following dispatches from Mr. Frere.

### Mr. Frere to Sir John Moore.

" SIR,                                             Dec. 3, Talavera.

" THOUGH I have little to add of the general represen-
" tation respecting the means of resistance at present existing in
" Spain, which I had the honour of stating in my letter of the 30th
" of last month; yet the report which is just brought me by Colonel
" Charmilly of the state in which he left Madrid, is so strong a con-
" firmation, or more properly speaking, so much exceeds every thing
" which I had ventured to say of the spirit and resolution of the peo-
" ple, that I cannot forbear representing to you in the strongest
" manner the propriety, not to say the necessity, of supporting the
" determination of the Spanish people, by all the means which have
" been entrusted to you for that purpose.

" I have no hesitation in taking upon myself any degree of re-
" sponsibility which may attach itself to this advice. As I consider
" the fate of Spain as depending absolutely for the present upon the
" decision which you may adopt. I say *for the present*, for such is
" the spirit and character of the country, that, even if abandoned by
" the British, I should by no means despair of their ultimate success.

" You will see by the date of this that the Junta are removed
" from a situation in which they were exposed to be made prisoners.
" They have determined to retire to Badajoz; where I shall hope to
" be honoured by your answer.

" I have, &c. &c.                          "J. H. FRERE."

This letter was sent in to the General, and Colonel Charmilly the bearer pressed vehemently to see him; asserting that he had important communications to make. Sir John at length came out from an inner apartment, and questioned him upon the intelligence he brought. The Colonel described in lofty terms the patriotic zeal with which all ranks of persons at Madrid were animated. The whole inhabitants of the city, he said, were in arms, and had united with the troops. The streets were barricaded; batteries were erecting all round; the peasants were flocking to the capital; and, in fine, the enthusiasm was unexampled.

He added, that there were most favourable accounts of the rising ardour of the South of Spain.

Sir John Moore listened to all this without uttering a word which could indicate his thoughts. But, when alone, he reflected seriously upon the extraordinary demands which were transmitted to him, not only by the Spanish Government, but also by the British Minister: and he called to mind, that he had been commanded to receive * the requisitions and representations of both with the utmost deference and attention.

But, independent of these positive requisitions, the intelligence brought was of the most favourable kind; and from so authentic a source that it could not be doubted. The letters were official, and from the highest authorities: and Mr. Charmilly, who was deputed by the British Minister, had been an eye-witness of the effervescence of Madrid.

The General was thus persuaded that a great and unexpected improvement in the public affairs had taken place; and he judged, that he ought not to pursue the plan which he had devised previous to these events. Was it becoming him to fly when the common

* Vide Appendix K.

N

Enemy was threatening the ruin of Madrid, and when the inhabitants of that city had bravely determined to perish, rather than yield? This was impossible; and, having the strongest reasons to believe that the causes for retreating had altered, he abandoned his intention, and resolved to support the Capital to the utmost of his power. In short he embraced upon this, as upon all occasions, the determination which he thought would be most useful to his Country, and which was most congenial to a noble mind.

It is now, however, completely ascertained, that, notwithstanding the apparent correctness of the intelligence, all was false. For the Prince of Castelfranco and Don Thomas Morla wrote their perfidious statement on the very day they had begun to capitulate: and they pressed Sir John Moore to hasten to their assistance, though they knew that Madrid must belong to Buonaparte, before the letter could reach its destination *.

But it could never enter into the conception of Sir John Moore, that the two Chiefs of the Junta had conspired to betray the capital of their own country, and to entice the army of their ally into the power of the Enemy. Nor could he suspect, when the confidential agent of Mr. Frere was representing Madrid as in little danger, that, in fact, it had already submitted at the very sight of the French army; that the Spanish Chiefs were crouching at the feet of Buonaparte; and that the people were overwhelmed with terror and despair. Nor was it imaginable, that the British Minister should be so grossly deceived, as to send, for his instruction, intelligence the reverse of truth; and to require of him, in so positive a manner, to succour a city which had actually surrendered.

As no human penetration could discover the real state of affairs under such representations, the General would have been highly

* Vide Appendix U.

reprehensible, had he persisted in his design of retiring to the South. So, to stop Sir David Baird as soon as possible, he wrote to him that night, as follows;

*Sir John Moore to Sir David Baird.*

" MY DEAR SIR DAVID,               *Salamanca, 5 December, 1808.*

          " THE City of Madrid have taken up arms, have
" refused to capitulate to the French, are barricading their streets,
" and say they are determined to suffer every thing rather than sub-
" mit.   This arrests the French ; and people who are sanguine enter-
" tain great hopes from it. — I own, myself, I fear this spirit has
" arisen too late ; and the French are now too strong to be resisted in
" this manner.   There is, however, no saying ; and I feel myself the
" more obliged to give it a trial that Mr. Frere has made a formal
" representation, which I received this evening.   I must beg, there-
" fore, you will suspend your march until you hear from me again,
" and make arrangements for your return to Astorga, should it be
" necessary. — All this appears very strange and unsteady ; but, if the
" spirit of enthusiasm does arise in Spain, and the people will be
" martyrs, there is no saying in that case, what our force may do.
" I hope in the mean time the regiment of cavalry is coming to me,
" which I asked you for.
          " Believe me, &c.
                                        " JOHN MOORE."

    After more full deliberation he wrote again next morning.

*Sir John Moore to Sir David Baird.*

" MY DEAR SIR DAVID, *Salamanca,* 6 *December,* 1808.

" I WROTE to you last night to suspend your retro-
" grade movements. I now write to you to beg that you will put to
" the right about, and return bag and baggage to Astorga.

" The people of Madrid, it is said, are enthusiastic and desperate;
" and certainly at this moment do resist the French—the good which
" may result from this it is impossible to say; I can neither trust to
" it, nor can I altogether despise it. If the flame catches elsewhere,
" and becomes at all general, the best results may be expected; if
" confined to Madrid, that town will be sacrificed, and all will be as
" bad, or worse than ever. In short, what is passing at Madrid
" may be decisive of the fate of Spain; and we must be at hand to aid
" and to take advantage of whatever happens. The wishes of our
" Country, and our duty, demand this of us, with whatever risk it
" may be attended. I mean to proceed bridle in hand; for if the
" bubble bursts, and Madrid falls, we shall have a run for it. Let all
" your preparations, as far as provisions, &c. go, continue to be
" made for a retreat, in case that should again become necessary.
" Establish one magazine at Villa Franca, and one or two further
" back; to which let salt meat, biscuit, rum or wines, forage, &c.
" be brought up from Corunna. Send to me to Zamora two regiments
" of Cavalry, and one brigade of Horse Artillery; keeping one regi-
" ment of Cavalry and one brigade of Horse Artillery with yourself;
" and send on your troops by brigades to Benavente. The Enemy
" have nothing at present in that direction; we must take advantage
" of it, and by working double tides make up for lost time. By

" means of the Cavalry patroles, you will discover any movements
" immediately near you; and I take for granted you have got other
" channels of information; and both you and me, although we may
" look big, and determine to get every thing forward, yet we must
" never lose sight of this, that at any moment affairs may take that
" turn, that will render it necessary to retreat.

" I shall write by this opportunity to the Marquis of Romana; and
" it would be satisfactory if you kept an officer constantly, or sent
" one occasionally to him, to judge his force, and its state of prepa-
" ration for service, to let us know how far we can depend upon its
" action. I wish you would forward the money to me.

" I remain, my dear Sir David, &c.

" JOHN MOORE."

It luckily happened that Sir David Baird had proceeded no farther
than Villa Franca, so that little time was lost; and General Hope by
rapid marches had brought his division close to Salamanca. The
position of the British Army had therefore become much more secure.
Sir John had now a complete though small corps, with Cavalry and
Artillery; and, by a movement to the left, his junction with Sir
David Baird was certain.

Being desirous of obtaining the co-operation of the only Spanish
Corps within reach, he wrote immediately to the Marquis of Romana,
who was at Leon.

*Sir John Moore to the Marquis de la Romana.*

" SIR,                                     *Salamanca, 6 Dec.* 1808.

" I HAD the honour to receive your Excellency's letter
" of the 30th November. I shall in general write to you in French,
" as you desire it; but I hope you will excuse me, if I address this
" to you in English, as I am at this moment a good deal hurried..

" Since my arrival in Spain, I have been put in no communication
" with any of the Spanish Armies, and have been kept perfectly in
" the dark with respect to their movements, the plans of their Gene-
" rals, or their Government — and during the time my army was on
" its march to assemble and unite itself, I have been left exposed
" without the least support.

" My wish has always been to co-operate with the Spanish Armies
" for the good of the common cause : but at last, finding that I was
" left to myself, it became necessary for me to think of myself alone ;
" and to consider, after the two armies of Generals Blake and Casta-
" nos were beaten, what steps I could take for the British Army,
" which was then collecting at Astorga, and this place ; thus the
" more helpless from its separation, but even, if united, not sufficiently
" strong to encounter the whole force of the Enemy, which I saw
" would immediately be turned against us. I therefore felt myself
" obliged, however reluctantly, to order the corps at Astorga to fall
" back on Corunna ; and I meant myself, with the corps I had here,
" to retire upon Portugal, from whence I should be ready to return
" to the assistance of Spain, whenever their affairs were better ma-
" naged, and an opportunity offered of doing them any good. Per-
" haps this opportunity has already occurred. The French have turned
" a great part of their force against Madrid. The people there have
" armed themselves, and say they are determined to resist. If this
" enthusiasm which actuates the people of Madrid last, and they
" continue resolute, and, above all, if the example of the capital is
" followed, and the enthusiasm becomes at all general throughout
" Spain, and induces large armies to come forward to the assistance
" of Madrid — Spain may still hope to recover from her misfortunes,
" repel the French, and re-establish her independence. As my re-
" treat was forced, and made with reluctance, so it is stopped the
" moment I see a chance of acting for the advantage of this country.

" I have ordered Sir David Baird to return with his corps to Astorga,
" and from thence to Benavente. My wish is to unite with you;
" and to undertake with you such operations as we may judge best
" for the support of Madrid, and the defeat of the Enemy. The
" French have driven General St. Juan from the Somosierra; and are
" in possession of that and the pass of the Guardarama. General
" Castanos is said to be at Siguenza. The Supreme Junta have re-
" tired to Badajos. The Duke of Castelfranco and Mr. Morla are at
" the head of the Junta, Civil and Military, at Madrid.

" I have written to you with that frankness which becomes a Mili-
" tary Man; I shall act with you in the same manner. I have the
" greatest respect for your character; and you will find me always
" ready to undertake whatever is practicable for the advantage of the
" Spanish Nation.

" I have the honour to be, Sir,

" Your Excellency's, &c.

" JOHN MOORE."

In the morning of December 6, Col. Charmilly again appeared at
Head Quarters, and presented the following letter, which he had
been desired not to deliver unless it was necessary.

*Mr. Frere to Sir John Moore.*

" SIR,                                           *Dec.* 3, 1808.

" IN the event which I did not wish to presuppose of
" your continuing the determination already announced to me of re-
" tiring with the army under your command, I have to request that
" Colonel Charmilly, who is the bearer of this, and whose intelligence

" has been already referred to, may be previously examined before a
" Council of War.

" I have, &c.

" J. H. FRERE."

Mr. Frere's mind must have been strongly wrought upon to view
the retreat of the British Army to the Tagus, as so injurious a measure. For, not content with sending intelligence of the brilliant state
of Spanish affairs, and employing arguments, requisitions, and depu-
tations : he here attempts to controul the Commander of the Forces ;
and seems to have expected to compel him by a Council of War to
obey, even against his will.

It may easily be conceived, that a high-spirited officer could not
read such a proposition without expressing great indignation at the
writer. And he was astonished to find, that Mr. Frere had had the
imprudence to entrust Colonel Charmilly with the secrets contained
in the important dispatches he brought.

The General however, not choosing to repose any confidence in
this Frenchman, did not utter a syllable which could give him the
slightest indication of his plan; and, not even approving of his presence with the army, directed the Adjutant-General to write an
order for him to retire.

The Colonel was thus dismissed, with the conviction that Sir John
Moore was still determined to retreat, and he returned to Mr. Frere
to communicate the bad success of his mission.

But, notwithstanding this conduct of Mr. Frere, Sir John wrote
to him an answer so calm and dignified, as to form a striking
contrast with the style of the other. For, as Mr. Frere was the
King's Minister, he was desirous, if possible, of preserving a correspondence which was necessary for the public service.

*Sir John Moore to Mr. Frere.*

" I HAD the honour to receive on the 2nd inst. your
" letter of the 30th, in answer to that which I addressed to you on
" the 27th November. Had this army been united and ready to act
" at the time of General Castanos' defeat, much as I think it would
" have been risking it, yet it was my intention to have marched on
" Madrid, and to have shared the fortunes of the Spanish nation. If
" I could not have sustained myself there, I thought, by placing my-
" self behind the Tagus, I might give the broken armies, and the
" people of Spain, if they had patriotism left, an opportunity to as-
" semble round me, and to march to the relief of the capital. That
" this was my intention is known to the Officers with me, who are in
" my confidence; it is known also to Lord Castlereagh, to whom I
" had imparted it in one of my late letters. I wished to have my
" opinion confirmed by yours; which was the reason of my address-
" ing you on the 27th. Had you seen the affairs of Spain in a different
" light, and had you been adverse to the army being committed in the
" heart of Spain, your opinion upon such a subject would, I may
" say, certainly have decided me to have altered my intention.

" With respect to the determination I made on the evening of the
" 28th, upon receiving from Mr. Stuart the account of Castanos' de-
" feat, I should, had you been with me, have communicated it to you;
" but should never have thought of asking your advice or opinion,
" as that determination was founded on circumstances with which you
" could not be acquainted: and was, besides, a question merely Mi-
" litary, of which I thought myself the best judge. At that time

" the army was divided into three different corps, and could not possi-
" bly be united before the 13th or 14th of this month ; before which
" period there was every reason to believe that it would be attacked
" by all the force of the Enemy : as, after General Castanos' defeat,
" I know of no Spanish army from which it could receive the small-
" est assistance.   The army I commanded was weak from separation ;
" and when united amounts to only 26,000 men fit for duty.   I had
" been left without any communication with any of the Spanish ar-
" mies ;  I expected no assistance from any,  and it behoved me to con-
" sider the safety of the British troops.   I therefore directed Sir David
" Baird, whose corps would not have been collected at Astorga until
" the 4th of this month, to fall back on Corunna.   I directed General
" Hope by forced marches to join me here, where I intended, if I
" was permitted, to wait his arrival ; and I took measures for retir-
" ing, with him, into Portugal ; with a view either to defend that
" frontier, and, ultimately, to return to Lisbon, or to return to Spain
" should any change of affairs there render it eligible.

   " The resistance made by the people of Madrid has occupied the
" French, and has prevented any corps from being detached against
" me.   This example of enthusiastic patriotism in the capital, if it
" holds, may be followed by the most happy effects, if the flame com-
" municates, and the example is followed by the Provinces.   There
" has been no example of any such resistance in any other part of
" Spain ;  and, though I hope this will produce it, I have neither seen
" nor heard of much enthusiasm elsewhere.   Their armies are devoid
" of both ; and, though I trust it will prove otherwise, I cannot but
" consider it as doubtful, whether the people of Madrid will continue
" firm when they come to be pressed.   If they yield, the whole is
" gone.   I received yesterday a letter from the Junta of Madrid.   I
" have ordered Sir David Baird to march back to Astorga ; and have
" stopped my preparations for a retreat on Portugal.   I have put my-

" self in communication with the Marquis Romana, at Leon; and
" without being able exactly to say in what manner, every thing shall
" be done for the assistance of Madrid, and the Spanish cause, that
" can be expected from an army such as I command. I cannot make a
" direct movement on Madrid, because the passage of the Guardarama
" and Somasierra are in the hands of the French. Besides, until joined
" by Sir David Baird I am much too weak. I have thought it my
" duty thus calmly to explain to you the reasons which have and do
" actuate my conduct; and I wish anxiously, as the King's Minister,
" to continue upon the most confidential footing with you : and I hope,
" as we have but one interest, the public welfare, though we may
" occasionally see it in different aspects, that this will not disturb the
" harmony that should subsist between us.

" Fully impressed as I am with these sentiments, I shall abstain
" from any remark upon the two letters from you, delivered to
" me last night and this morning by Col. Charmilly, or on the mes-
" sage which accompanied them. I certainly at first did feel and ex-
" pressed much indignation at a person like him being made the
" channel of a communication of that sort from you to me. Those
" feelings are at an end; and I dare say they never will be excited
" towards you again.

" If Mr. Charmilly is your friend, it was, perhaps, natural for you
" to employ him : but I have prejudices against all that class ; and
" it is impossible for me to put any trust in him. I shall, therefore,
" thank you not to employ him any more in any communication with
" me. It is impossible not to remark, that, whatever enthusiasm
" exists in the country, a small portion of it belongs to the Junta ;
" who would otherwise, I think, have found some place more central
" and less remote than Badajos for their residence.

" I have the honour to be, &c.

" JOHN MOORE."

*Sir John Moore to Mr. Frere.*

" SIR,                                        *Salamanca, 6th Dec.* 1808.

" I NEGLECTED to mention to you in my letter of
" this date, that the General Officers Escalante and Bueno had been
" with me; who are mentioned in that extraordinary paper which
" you sent me with your letters of the 30th Nov. signed by Martin
" de Garay, Secretary of the Junta. The two Generals seemed to
" me to be two weak old men, or rather women, with whom it was
" impossible for me to concert any military operations, had I been so
" inclined.

" The persons with whom such operations can be concerted at
" present are the Generals who command the armies, not men like
" these two, who have no information upon which such plans can
" be formed, except the official papers, always incorrect, which have
" been given to them from public offices. Their conference with
" me consisted in questions and in assertions with respect to the
" strength of different Spanish corps, all of which I knew to be
" erroneous; and they neither knew that Segovia nor Somosierra
" were in possession of the Enemy. I shall be obliged to you to
" save me from such visits, which are very painful.

" I mentioned to you in my letter of this day that I had had a
" letter from the Junta at Madrid. My instructions direct me, that
" all my communications with the Spanish Government should go
" through you; and I should be very happy, on every account, to
" comply with them : but I do not see how this can be, if you con-
" tinue at Badajos. I shall, however, send you copies of them, if
" you wish it.

" I have the honour to be, &c.

" JOHN MOORE."

The following short passage in the General's Journal shews the ideas at this time revolving in his mind, while waiting for the junction of Sir David Baird.

" After Castanos' defeat the French marched to Madrid. The " inhabitants flew to arms, barricadoed their streets, and swore to " die, rather than submit.

" This has arrested the progress of the French, and Madrid still " holds out. This is the first instance of enthusiasm shewn. There " is a chance that the example may be followed, and the people be " saved. I have stopped Baird's retreat, and am taking measures to " form our junction, whilst the French are wholly occupied with " Madrid.

" We are bound not to abandon the cause as long as there is hope. " But the courage of the populace of Madrid may fail; or at any " rate they may not be able to resist. In short, in a moment things " may be as bad as ever, unless the whole country is animated, and " flocks to the aid of the capital.

" In this part the people are passive. I have sent Colonel Gra- " ham to Madrid, to let me know exactly what is passing; for we " find the greatest difficulty to get people to bring us information."

The following is the letter entrusted to Colonel Graham.

*Sir John Moore to the Duke of Castelfranco and M. de Morla.*

" *Salamanca,* 6 *Dec.* 1808.

" I HAD the honour to receive, last night, a letter " signed by the Duke of Castelfranco and M. de Morla, in the " name of the Junta Military and Civil established at Madrid. " Hitherto I have been left without communication or support from " any of the Spanish armies; and as the army I command was sepa- " rated at Astorga and Salamanca, at which place it had been

" ordered to collect, at the time when the army under General
" Castanos was defeated, it became necessary for me to consider
" what steps were necessary for the security of the British army,
" which was helpless from its separation, and when united not
" sufficiently strong to encounter the whole French force, which
" was about to be turned against it. I had therefore ordered the
" corps at Astorga to fall back on Corunna, and was about to
" retire with the corps from this to some place of greater secu-
" rity, from whence I might return to the assistance of Spain, when
" a more favourable opportunity offered. Those measures I have
" now stopped. The corps under Sir David Baird shall return to
" Astorga. I have put myself in communication with the Marquis
" de la Romana, at Leon; and I shall, in concert with him, under-
" take such operations as are deemed best for the interests of Spain,
" and for the relief and assistance of Madrid. I should hope that.
" the example of patriotism given by the capital will be followed by
" the provinces, and that the people will flock up to its assistance;
" when, headed by the armies, the best results may be expected.
" The Junta may rest assured that every thing shall be done by me
" that can be expected by such a corps as I command. This will be
" delivered by Colonel Graham, whom I send to the Junta that he
" may explain the particulars of my situation, and communicate to
" me the wishes of the Junta, and the relative positions and strength
" of the people of Madrid, and the French opposed to them.

" I have the honour to be,<br>
" Your Excellency's, &c.<br>
" JOHN MOORE."

This letter was written in consequence of the intelligence sent
by Mr. Frere, who imagined that both Castelfranco and Morla had

resolved to fight to the last extremity, and, rather than suffer their country to be enslaved, to perish in its ruins.

But it is now fully ascertained that Madrid was basely betrayed. The Chiefs who signed the capitulation abandoned every principle which they had sworn to maintain, and stipulated for advantageous conditions for themselves: while the inhabitants at first resisted with noisy vociferation, and then quietly surrendered their arms.

Castelfranco and Morla when they wrote to Sir John Moore knew that Castanos' troops were cut off from Madrid by Marshal Bessieres, and were flying towards Cuenca.

They themselves had ordered the gates of Madrid to be shut against the corps of San Juan; who, from mistaken fury, murdered their General, one of the ablest of the Spanish officers; and after this horrid deed fled in confusion to Almares.

Such was the conduct of the misguided troops; and the two high-born Spanish Chiefs sheathed their swords at the sight of the Enemy of their country, and by his order employed their perfidious pens to betray the British army. In the letter to Sir John Moore the signature il Principe de Castelfranco is written with a steady hand; but Thomas Morla's appears to have trembled in signing his infamy.

Buonaparte, with affected grandeur, pretended to extend his clemency to these degraded Spaniards. To conceal their concert with him, and to gratify his spleen, he cunningly taunted Morla for his former perfidy in breaking the Capitulation with Du Pont. But so shallow a device is easily comprehended.

Morla made good terms for himself and his base associates. His fortune and military rank were preserved to him, and he stoops to exist under the protection of the Usurper of his country.

" *Vendidit hic auro patriam, dominumque potentem*
" *Inposuit, fixit leges pretio atque refixit.*"

But these dismal truths were all unknown to Sir John Moore. He never saw the men, and had no means of judging of the sincerity of their professions. He perceived very clearly the folly which predominated in the Spanish councils, but conjectured nothing worse.

On the 7th of December he had the pleasure of receiving the following patriotic address from the City of Toledo *.

*The Junta of Toledo to his Excellency Sir John Moore, &c. &c.*

" EXCELLENT SIR,          *Toledo, 5th December,* 1808.

      " THE Junta of Toledo, most anxiously wishing to
" save their country, have signified to General Eredia, the Comman-
" dant of this Capital, that it is their intention to reunite here the
" dispersed armies; and to take the proper measures to enable him
" to defend this City to the last extremity.

" The Junta is besides in communication with Aranjuez, and other
" points of union; and have the satisfaction to assure your Excellency
" that they are resolved to die in defence of their country. They
" transmit this information for the guidance of your Excellency,
" wishing you many years."

(Signed by the MEMBERS OF JUNTA.)

Sir John Moore rejoiced at this new proof of rising spirit in Spain, and immediately returned the following answer.

* Vide Appendix X.

*Sir John Moore to their Excellencies the Junta of Toledo.*

" GENTLEMEN,                                *Salamanca,* 7 *Dec.* 1808.

" I HAVE received this morning the letter which you
" have done me the honour to address to me.

" The sentiments it contains, and the determination you express
" to die for your country, do you and the City of Toledo the greatest
" honour. If similar sentiments animate the rest of Spain, and the
" Spaniards will adhere faithfully to each other, there can be no
" doubt of your ultimate success, whatever temporary advantages the
" French may perhaps gain. The example given by Madrid is
" worthy of a great nation: it will, I hope, excite the enthusiasm
" of all good Spaniards; make them collect, and march to the
" assistance of a town which ought not to be sacrificed.

" The British army, like the British nation, is desirous of render-
" ing every assistance to the Spanish cause, and you may depend
" upon its best exertions. I am uniting the different corps of the
" army, and preparing to act.

" The Marquis of Romana is at Leon, collecting the army that
" was with General Blake in Biscay; and, in concert with him,
" whatever is possible on this side shall be done.

" I shall hope to continue in correspondence with you, and that
" you will inform me with the progress you make; and with what-
" ever movements are made, either by the Enemy or by the armed
" force assembling at Toledo. You shall be equally informed by me
" of every thing on this side. In order to facilitate this correspondence,
" I shall send a British officer to reside at Toledo, which I trust will
" meet your approbation.

" I have the honour to be, &c.

" JOHN MOORE."

An officer was accordingly sent to concert measures for the defence of Toledo; but the Junta at the approach of a French corps suddenly changed their resolution, and, instead of dying, or even fighting for their country, very prudently retired: and the Duke of Bellune took possession of this peaceful City. This was one of the usual disappointments Sir John Moore met with from his ally; who was constantly proclaiming the most daring intentions; and when expectation was wound up to its height, and the most strenuous deeds were looked for, in a moment exertion relaxed, and every resolution yielded.

Indeed few Generals have been entangled with so many embarrassments as Sir John Moore; who not only had to contend with the distrust of the Spanish Government, always exaggerating their resources, and concealing or glossing over their disasters; but also to guard against the secret plots of unsuspected traitors, hid in the bosom of the Junta. While the British Minister, instead of assisting him with correct information, perplexed him with false intelligence, harassed him with vexatious missions, and thwarted him with pertinacious requisitions. And, lastly, he had to encounter the power and genius of Buonaparte.

Madrid had now fallen, and the indefatigable Emperor was resolved to give the discomfited Spaniards no time to rally; but to disperse their dispirited troops, and penetrate with celerity to the South.

Marshal Bessieres was chasing the Central Army on the road to Valencia; the Duke of Bellune had entered Toledo; and the Duke of Dantzic, with a strong division, was marching to Badajoz, with the design of either seizing upon Lisbon or Cadiz; the Duke of Treville was proceeding against Saragossa; the Duke of Dalmatia was preparing to enter Leon; and Buonaparte, from Madrid, was ready to support all these movements; and complete the subjugation of Spain.

There are no certain documents to ascertain what were the actual numbers of the French army who invaded Spain.

Buonaparte announced that his intention was to carry there 200,000 men; and the French Officers who were taken prisoners believed that their army consisted of fully that number.

The following statement shews that in this there was probably little or no exaggeration.

| | |
|---|---:|
| Various accounts agree in calculating the French force in Spain, in autumn 1808, which was stationed behind the Ebro, at - - - - - - - - - - - - | 45,000 |
| There were at the same time, in the Town of Barcelona, and in the Province of Catalonia, - - - - - | 15,000 |
| According to the intercepted letter from the Governor of Bayonne to Marshal Jourdan, there would enter Spain by Bayonne, between 16th October and 16th November*, | 72,000 |
| An army, chiefly from Italy, entered Catalonia about the same period - - - - - - - - - - - - - - | 15,000 |
| Junot's division entered, in the beginning of December | 30,000 |
| | 177,000 |

From reports there is reason to believe that there were other French corps besides the above; which would make the numbers nearly accord with Buonaparte's declaration.

It is not however to be imagined, that there ever was at one period so great an effective French force as the above; for deaths and casualties always occasion a great reduction of the numbers of an army.

Considerable pains have been taken to ascertain what was the real British force which entered Spain; for a very false estimate may be

* Vide Appendix, E.

made by examining only the total numbers of official reports. After an accurate * examination it is found, that the whole effective force of the corps which marched from Corunna under Sir David Baird consisted of 9550 men; and of those which proceeded from Portugal was 18,416; making altogether an army of 25,631 infantry and 2450 cavalry. The artillery was numerous, but of too small a calibre; including a brigade of useless three-pounders, it amounted to fifty guns.

Sir John Moore was now joined by General Hope's division, and was desirous of uniting himself with Sir David Baird's; having resolved to prosecute the war in the North of Spain. But neither the arts of Morla, the news of Charmilly, nor the arguments and requisitions of the Junta and Mr. Frere could induce the General to advance to Madrid. He knew that the passes of Somosierra and Guardarama were possessed by the French, and that an attempt to force them would be destructive; yet, if he continued where he was, or only guarded the frontiers of Galicia, every thing valuable in Spain would be quickly subdued. The first of these plans was rejected as rash, and the others as futile; but he formed and executed a plan for stopping the progress of the French, and relieving Spain, which has been highly admired by masters in the art of war. This will be gradually developed. But, as he found that the Spanish Generals who had been deputed to him were quite incapable of discussing a plan, or giving him any advice, he thought it would be imprudent to confide his intentions to them. He considered it most advisable to trust no one with his designs, except the Government, and the Generals commanding armies who were to co-operate with him.

This appears to have given great offence to one of the Deputed Generals, who wrote the following letter.

* Vide Appendix Y.

*Don Ventura Escalante to His Excellency the Commander of the Forces of His Britannic Majesty \*.*

" MOST EXCELLENT SIR,　　　　*La Calzada de Banos, Dec.* 7, 1808.

　　" I IN vain exhausted every means, military as well as
" political, to induce your Excellency to give up the project of retir-
" ing with your troops to Ciudad Rodrigo and Portugal, and of
" withdrawing that part of the British army which is at Astorga to
" Galicia. And your Excellency having observed, that the Marquis
" of Romana was only able to collect five thousand men, I left Sala-
" manca yesterday morning to meet the Supreme Junta, considering
" my mission at an end. But to-day I have received a courier with
" a letter from the Marquis of Romana ; of which I transmit a
" copy to your Excellency, in hopes that it will have more influence
" than my observations, and induce you to change your plan. For
" if, instead of uniting the two divisions of your army with the army
" of the Marquis of Romana at Zamora, or some other point that
" may impose upon the Enemy, you persist in putting your design
" in execution, you will immediately occasion the destruction of
" Spain, and perhaps your Excellency will be under the necessity
" of embarking for England. But if your Excellency will accede
" to the said junction, it is very probable that the Enemy will aban-
" don his intention of attacking Madrid, and will retire. This would
" give time to the army of the Centre to concentrate, and take other
" positions.

　　" I request your Excellency to give an answer to the bearer, that he
" may send it to me. And it would be important if your Excellency
" would be so good as to write to the Marquis of Romana your final
" determination.

" VENTURA ESCALANTE."

* Vide the original Spanish, C. C.

The answer that was sent to this letter was one of pure civility, Sir John choosing only to write confidentially to the acting Generals.

*De Sir John Moore à son Excellence le Marquis de la Romana.*

" MONSIEUR LE MARQUIS,         *Salamanca, ce 8 Decembre.*

" Un Officier que j' expédie au Général Sir David
" Baird, m' offre l' occasion de vous écrire. Je n' ai pas encore reçu
" des informations sûres, à l' égard de Madrid; j' ai lieu de croire que
" le peuple tient encore. Une lettre du Junta de Toledo m' a com-
" muniqué l' intention de rassembler un corps d' armée là; et que le
" peuple est déterminé de mourir, les armes à la main.

" Le Général Castanos a reçu ordre de se rétirer à Carolina, de
" l' autre côté du Sierra Morena.

" Dans cette partie de l' Espagne les habitans sont trop tranquilles :
" ils disent qu' ils n' ont point d' armes; ils ont besoin d' une tête pour
" les remuer et pour les réunir, et pour les commander. Je propose,
" le 10 courant, de faire un mouvement sur Zamore et Toro, pour
" me rapprocher du Corps du Général Baird et du votre. Quand je
" sais quel progrès vous avez fait dans l'organisation de votre armée,
" nous pourrons combiner quelque chose; et j' attends avec impa-
" tience de recevoir une réponse à la lettre que j' eus l' honneur de vous
" écrire le six. Deux Officiers Généraux etoient ici, il y a quelques
" jours, envoyés de la part du Junta Suprême. Ils ne m' ont pas paru
" d' avoir ni les pouvoirs ni les informations nécessaries pour combiner
" une opération. J' ai cru pouvoir m' appliquer plus clairement avec
" vous, Monsieur le Général, et j' ai refusé d' entrer avec eux en
" matiere : ils etoient le Général Escalante et le B. Général Bueno.

" J' ai l' honneur

" d'être, &c.

" JOHN MOORE.

The following instructions were then dispatched to Sir David Baird.

*Sir John Moore to Sir David Baird.*

" MY DEAR GENERAL,        *Salamanca*, 8th Dec. 1808.

" MADRID still holds out, and I have some reason to
" believe that some efforts are making to collect a force at Toledo,
" and a still larger one on the other side of the Sierra Morena. As
" long as there is a chance, we must not abandon this country. The
" conduct of Madrid has given us a little time, and we must en-
" deavour to profit by it. My first object must be to unite with
" you, and thus connect myself with the Marquis Romana. I shall
" move a corps from this on the 10th, to Zamora and Toro. To
" which last place I shall move Head Quarters.

" I should wish you to push on your people by brigades to Be-
" navente. I have desired General Clinton to send you, for your
" *private* information, the manner I propose dividing the army.
" I think you will prefer commanding a division to being second in
" command without any. I send you this *private*, that you may
" consider it, and let me know if you would wish it altered in any
" particular. But I should not wish it to be shewn to any of the
" Generals, which might draw upon me applications which I could
" not grant. You will have the goodness to point out to me any
" alterations, respecting the corps with you, which might improve
" the arrangement.

" You never noticed the letter I enclosed to you, long since, for
" General Leith, ordering him to join you. I am, therefore, ig-
" norant whether he is with you. He is placed, like all the cor-
" responding officers, under my command; but he has never written

" me a line. I shall thank you to tell me where he is, as also
" the Officers who were employed in the mission under him.

" In the mean time I am anxious to know the real strength and
" condition of the troops Romana and Blake are assembling; and
" I shall thank you to send an intelligent officer to Leon to see
" them; and who is capable of judging without allowing him-
" self to be humbugged. You will of course order whatever
" troops arrive at Corunna to be immediately landed and moved
" forward.

" I have sent Colonel Graham (90 Reg.) to Madrid, and expect
" to hear from him this evening.

" I remain, &c.

" JOHN MOORE."

Colonel Graham, who had been deputed with the answer to
Castelfranco and Morla, instead of travelling directly to Madrid,
thought it most prudent to go first to Talavera, to obtain intelligence. He arrived there late at night on the 7th of December.
The following letter explains his proceedings; but, as the Spanish
messenger was slow, and the Colonel was indefatigably active, he
returned to Salamanca on the 9th, before the letter arrived.

*Colonel Graham to Sir John Moore.*

" MY DEAR GENERAL,     *Talaveira de la Reina,*
*Wednesday Night late,* 7-8 *Dec.* 1808.

" OWING to the extreme difficulty in getting horses, I did
" not get here till past eleven to-night: and hearing there was a part
" of the Junta Central still in this place, I immediately waited on
" them to obtain information: the amount of which I send by an

" extraordinary courier, as the most likely means of its reaching you
" soon; as he will get on much faster than I could, requiring fewer
" horses.

" It seems on the 3d, Castelfranco and Morla made some sort of
" agreement with the French, who on the day before got posses-
" sion of the Retiro and Prado of Madrid. They are suspected of
" treason in this proceeding; having refused to admit the troops
" under St. Juan and Hereida who were at the gates on this side;
" and whose presence, it is asserted, would have enabled the citizens
" to have defended the town. Castellar, the Captain-General, and
" all the Military Officers of rank, refused to ratify the agreement,
" left the town, and brought away 16 guns; and the inhabitants re-
" fuse to deliver up their arms. In this state of things the Enemy
" remain in the Retiro, without having taken possession of the dif-
" ferent posts within: and they (the two Deputies here) do not think
" there is any chance of any part of the French force (between 20
" and 30,000 men) being detached from Madrid.

" Castanos' army, meanwhile, commanded by General La Péna,
" second in command, is at Guadalaxara; and they say amounts to
" about 30,000 men. There are about 12,000 of the remains of St.
" Juan and Hereida's army here, going to occupy the bridge of Al-
" maraz; where great exertions are making by the Junta to assemble
" a large force. Meanwhile St. Juan has been sacrificed to the popu-
" lar fury for retreating from Madrid; and was this morning mur-
" dered here. One of the members now here is to proceed imme-
" diately to Leon, to concert measures with the M. de la Romana;
" whose force they state, by the accounts received this day, to ex-
" ceed 30,000 men; and every where, where the country is not occu-
" pied by the Enemy, they say the most active measures are taking
" to increase the military force of the country. They state the whole
" of the French force in Spain not to exceed from 70 to 80,000 men;

Q

" a part of which is before Saragossa. They deny any reinforcements
" more being on their way to join the Enemy. They are most anx-
" ious that you should join Romana. I shortly explained to them,
" the divided state of your army, and the necessity you was under to
" begin a retreat, instead of completing the junction, on hearing of
" Castanos' defeat. I assured them, that, whatever might be your
" determination from circumstances, you have nothing more at heart
" than to serve effectually the cause of Spain; but that the British
" auxiliary army could do little in that by itself, and that every thing
" depended on their being able to bring forward a powerful Spanish
" army, that could unite with it. I mean to return by the Placentia
" road. I am afraid I shall not be able to get the Courier to send this
" till to-morrow morning.

" I remain ever most truly yours,

" THOMAS GRAHAM.

" P. S. I think they mean that La Péna should retire on Anda-
" lusia: though they do not seem to have quite given up hopes of the
" people of Madrid resisting, should they be able to introduce a few
" thousand men. The Junta is at Truxillo. You see that all that I
" can do is to repeat what I have heard; for I have no means at this
" moment of judging for myself."

*(Paper inclosed.)*

" *In the Morning of the 8th.*

" I HAVE just heard, from good authority, that the Enemy
" have gone towards Saragossa with a large force; and that that and
" Madrid are their objects.

" P. S. Official accounts are just come that they attacked Sara-
" gossa on the first, and were repulsed with great loss."

This letter exemplifies the manner in which the Spanish Junta cloaked their calamities from the sight of their ally. Not being able absolutely to deny the capitulation, they softened it into a kind of agreement; adding, that the indignant inhabitants had refused to deliver up their arms, and that the French had not ventured to enter the city. They also sunk down the numbers of Buonaparte's army, and exaggerated their own in the same proportion: completely disguising from the British General the relative strength of both.

He was thus misled by the persons who ought to have instructed him; and taught to believe that Madrid, instead of surrendering, had only formed a species of armistice with the Enemy. That Spanish corps were preparing to advance to its relief; and that the chief portion of Buonaparte's force must be occupied in controuling it.

It appears from Sir John Moore's letters, that he neither credulously trusted, nor totally disbelieved this authenticated account; though it was likewise confirmed by many private reports: particularly by the testimony of a Friar, who had come from Madrid. Notwithstanding his doubts, he considered himself compelled to make every effort in his power for the relief of the capital, and accordingly advanced from Salamanca.

The movement was made from the left flank, by brigades, towards the Duero.

The reserve and General Beresford's brigade were marched to Toro; there to unite with the cavalry under Lord Paget, who had reached that place from Astorga. He moved with the remaining divisions towards Alaejos and Tordesillas. At this last place the whole were intended to unite, whence he proposed to proceed to Valladolid. Sir David Baird's corps were not yet all collected; but he was directed to push on his brigades to Benavente, to support or join him.

The intention of this movement was to threaten the communication between Madrid and France : but the design is expressed in the following letters.

Sir John Moore to Sir David Baird.

" MY DEAR SIR DAVID,  *Salamanca, 12th December, 1808.*

 " I HAVE received both your letters of the 8th, in answer
" to mine of the 5th and 6th.

 " Lord Paget is at Toro, to which place I have sent the reserve,
" and General Beresford's brigade; the rest of the troops from this
" are moving to the Duero. My quarters to-morrow will be at
" Alaejos; Hope's at Tordesillas; Fraser will be with me with his
" division on the 14th; on which day Lord Paget, with the Cavalry
" and Infantry from Toro, will move along to Duero, towards us,
" so as to enable the whole to reach Tordesillas and its neighbour-
" hood the 15th, and Valladolid on the 16th. I have no answer
" from the Marquis de la Romana, to whom I wrote upon the 6th,
" and with whom it is my wish to form a junction, and to co-operate.
" But, although I am disappointed in not hearing from him, and must
" forego any assistance from him; and although your corps will not
" be up in time, yet I think it an object with the troops I have
" to march to Valladolid; from whence, according to the information
" I receive, I may move on to Palencia and Burgos; and thus threa-
" ten the Enemy's communications, and cause a diversion in favour of
" Madrid or Saragossa, or any movement which may be in contempla-
" tion from the South of the Tagus. I shall, at all events, cover you
" whilst assembling at Astorga and Benavente, and may bring you
" on to me, or fall back upon you, as occasion requires; and, in the
" mean time, I shall be just as safe as at Salamanca or Zamora. I
" think I shall call on to me Colonel Crawford with his corps, either

" by Toro or Medina de Rio Seco, of which I shall give you notice
" from Alaejos. I have attached one brigade of artillery to each
" division of the army; whatever is over, is considered as reserve.
" To each division also there is attached ten rounds of musket car-
" tridges *per* man carried in carts, and four mules with pack-saddles,
" for the purpose of bringing the cartridges, when wanted, from the
" carts to the troops; besides which, I am forwarding musket-ammu-
" nition, and ammunition for guns, to Zamora. I think if you bring
" on with the troops two brigades of artillery, besides the two of
" horse artillery, one of which is with Lord Paget, this will suffice;
" leave the other two at Astorga, ready to come forward when called
" for. I wish you would make the same arrangement for carrying
" with your brigades, or divisions, ten rounds a man, besides the sixty
" in pouches. I shall enclose a letter from Colonel Harding, com-
" manding the artillery, explanatory of every thing else. I consider
" Benavente as a place to have certain stores advanced to; the rest
" you should divide between Astorga and Villafranca.

" All the money at Corunna should be brought up to Villafranca;
" we shall want it. I am much obliged to you for your opinion upon
" the Galicias and Vigo; and it is that which now, probably, I
" shall follow, should such a measure become necessary. I am,
" therefore, most anxious that magazines should be formed on that
" communication. I have written home, to direct that all transports,
" &c. should call at Corunna, and Vigo, unless otherwise directed.
" Corunna must be the place for all supplies from England;—the
" communication through Portugal is difficult and tardy.

" Forward the inclosed to the Marquis de la Romana as soon
" as possible; and send me any letters which may come from him
" without delay. An Officer will remain at Salamanca to forward
" letters to me. Should you not prefer the direct road by Toro to
" Tordesillas, or Valladolid, you will not think it necessary to have

" more cavalry with you whilst I am in your front. I shall enclose
" a letter for Lord Castlereagh *, which I shall thank you to for-
" ward to Corunna.

" Believe me sincerely,

" JOHN MOORE."

*Sir John Moore to Mr. Frere.*

" SIR,            *Salamanca, December 12th,* 1808.

     " I LEAVE this to-morrow, and I expect to be in Valla-
" dolid on the 16th, with that part of the army which came from
" Portugal, joined by 1500 Cavalry which came with Sir David
" Baird; the rest of Sir David's corps he is assembling at Astorga
" and Benavente; but I have thought it advisable to make this
" movement without him, rather than wait longer. He will be in
" my rear, and can join me when he is ready. I have heard nothing
" from the Marquis de la Romana, in answer to the letters I wrote
" to him on the 6th and 8th instant. I am thus disappointed of
" his co-operation, or of knowing what plans he proposes.

     " I am in ignorance of the state of Madrid. It was attacked the
" 2d, and capitulated the 3d. The French then had the Retiro;
" and the people kept their arms. Whether this continues their
" relative situation, I cannot learn. The difficulty of obtaining
" information surpasses what I ever met with.

     " The object of my movement is to threaten the French communi-
" cations, and attract their attention from Madrid and Saragossa, and
" favour any movement which may be projected by the armies form-
" ing to the South of the Tagus.

     " If no advantage is taken of it, if no efforts are made, and
" if every one continues quiet, as they did when Madrid was attacked,
" the French will have their option to turn against me what portion

* Vide Appendix B B.

" of their force they please ; it will, of course, not be one inferior in
" number, and I need not state to you what is likely to be the conse-
" quence.

" The French in the North of Spain have from 80 to 90,000
" men :—it is said that more are advancing, and I believe it ; as
" many of the letters, found in the intercepted mail, mention a seventh
" and eighth division, preparing to enter Spain. I have seen
" nothing in the conduct of the Spaniards that gives me the least
" hope that they will resist such formidable numbers. They have
" shewn nothing like resolution hitherto. Madrid, after so much
" boasting, held out but one day. This army is now in motion, and I
" shall make with it what diversion I can, to favour any resistance,
" or any attacks made elsewhere. If the forces, collected to the
" Southward of the Tagus, will move forward in great numbers,
" and like men determined to rescue their country, Madrid may still
" be saved ; if the inhabitants keep their arms, and if the French,
" notwithstanding the capitulation, have not dared to enter the city ;
" but nothing short of some very decided measure will save either
" Madrid or Spain at this moment. I shall continue to keep you
" informed of my movements ; and your Courier coming by Ciudad
" Rodrigo, will be informed where to find me.

" I have, &c.

" JOHN MOORE."

It appears by this letter, that Sir John Moore was still ignorant
of the submission of Madrid ; and he was led to entertain hopes
that his movements might be useful to save that city.

On the same day, December 12th, Lord Paget, with the principal
part of the cavalry, marched from Toro to Tordesillas ; while Brigadier-General Stuart, commanding the 18th and King's German
Dragoons, was moving from Arevolo. The Brigadier got informa-

tion that a party of French cavalry and infantry were posted in a village called Rueda.

Captain Dashwood secretly reconnoitred the place at night, and marked the position of the guards. The Brigadier then rode up to the village with a party of the 18th Dragoons, surprised the Enemy, and killed or took prisoners almost the whole detachment.

This was the first encounter of the French and British in Spain. The march of the British had been so well concealed, that the French were astonished to find that there were any English troops there. The prisoners declared that it was universally believed they had re-treated.

The Head Quarters were, on the 14th December, at Alaejos, where Sir John received a letter from the Marquis of Romana, who, he thought, had been rather too long of writing. The Marquis here distinctly expresses a perfect approbation of the reasons for the retreat which Sir John Moore had before projected; and, from caution, he adds not a word respecting the forward movement, lest his letter should fall into the hands of the Enemy.

There is often in the Marquis's letter one or two English words, and the French is a little incorrect.

*A. S. E. Mr. le Général Sir John Moore, Commandant Général de l'Armée Angloise en Espagne.*

" SIR,                              *Head Quarters, Leon,* 11*th December,* 1808.

" JE vois par les deux lettres de V. E. du six et huit
" courant, la cause des mouvemens retrogrades qu' elle avoit prescrit
" aux corps d' Armée sous ses ordres; et je la trouve très fondée et
" très juste. Craignant d'aventurer une réponse aux articles des
" deux lettres, je me reserve de le faire par le moyen d'un Officier
" que j'expédierai demain pour aller à votre rencontre à Zamora,

" tandis que je me prépare pour faire avec V. E. la jonction si désirée.

" J'ai l' honneur de renouveller à V. E. l' hommage de ma haute
" estime, et de la parfaite considération avec laquelle

" Je suis votre très humble,

" et très devoué serviteur,

" LE MARQUIS DE LA ROMANA."

On the same day on which the above was received, a packet of letters from the Head Quarters of the French Army were brought to Sir John Moore. The Officer who had them in charge was intercepted, and murdered by some Spanish peasants.

The following dispatch from Marshal Berthier to the Duke of Dalmatia was very important.

*A Monsieur le Maréchal Duc de Dalmatie, commandant le 2 Corps d'Armée, à Saldana. Le V. Connétable, Major Général.*

" *Chamartin, le* 10 *Decembre,* 1808.

" A MONSIEUR LE MARECHAL DUC DE DALMATIE,

" J' AI lu à l'Empereur, Monsieur le Maréchal, votre
" lettre du 4 Decembre, apportée par l' un de vos officiers ; sa Ma-
" jesté, Monsieur le Duc, approuve tout ce que vous avez fait. Le
" 8me Regiment de Dragons, le 22me de Chasseurs, le Regiment du
" Colonel Tascher, le Regiment Hannoverin, font quatre Regiments,
" formant deux Brigades commandées par les Généraux de Brigade de
" Belle et Franceschi : ces deux Brigades de Cavalerie sont sous vos
" ordres ; et vous pouvez les faire manœvrer comme il vous convien-
" dra. L'Empereur pense qu' avec la Division Merle, avec la Divi-
" sion Mouton, les 4 Regiments de troupes à cheval, vous n' avez
" rien qui puisse vous résister.

" Qu' avez vous à faire ? Vous rendre maitre de Leon, rejetter
" l' ennemi en Galice, vous emparer de Benavente et de Zamora ;

R

" vous ne devez pas avoir d'Anglais devant vous, car quelques Regi-
" ments sont venus à l'Escurial, à Salamanque, et tout porte à pen-
" ser qu'ils sont en pleine marche rétrograde : notre avant-garde est
" aujourd'hui à Talavera de la Reyna, sur la route de Badajoz : elle
" sera bientôt sur cette ville. Vous sentez assez que ce mouve-
" ment (s' il ne l' a pas déjà fait) va forcer les Anglais à accourir sur
" Lisbonne. Au moment, Monsieur le Maréchal, que vous serez
" certain, comme tout porte à le présumer, qu'il n'y a pas d'Anglais
" devant vous, vous pouvez marcher droit et à tête baissée ; il n'y a
" rien en Espagnols qui puisse tenir contre vos deux divisions. Faites
" faire des souliers et des capottes à Leon, à St. Ander, à Palencia.
" Sa Majesté approuve toutes les demandes que vous ferez ayant pour
" but d'ameliorer votre materiel : vous pouvez également requérir des
" mulets pour remonter votre artillerie, et des chevaux pour remonter
" votre cavalerie, en mettant dans tout cela les formes et tout ce qui
" tient à la bonne administration. Il est possible qu' aussitot que la
" division de Dragons du Gén. Miller arrivera en Espagne, l'Empe-
" reur vous l'envoye ; mais cette division ne sera pas en Espagne au
" moins de 15 jours. A la distance ou vous vous trouvez de nous,
" Monsieur le Duc, vous ne pouvez vous conduire que par vous-même,
" et regarder tout ce que je vous écris à un si grand éloignement
" comme une direction générale.

" Sa Majesté pense que vous prendrez toutes les mesures pour sou-
" mettre le pays entre le Duero et la Galice et les Asturies, en gar-
" dant toutesfois, et précieusement, St. Ander. Le 5me corps, que
" commande le Maréchal Duc de Trevise, a reçu l'ordre de se diriger sur
" Sarragosse. Le 8me corps aux ordres du Duc d'Abrantès, dont la
" 1r Div°⁰ arrive à Vitoria vers le 12, va vraisemblablement recevoir
" des ordres pour se réunir à Burgos. Des gabarres et des batiments
" de toute espèce, armés au guerre, ont l'ordre de se rendre à St.
" Ander ; faites les charger de marchandise Anglaise saisie, de coton,

" de laine, d'artillerie, et qu'on les expedie sur France. Enfin tenez
" Valladolid et Zamora dans la soumission : Valladolid est une bonne
" ville, et qui s' est bien conduit ; on dit qu' il seroit très intéressant
" d'occúper Zamora. Enfin, Monsieur le Duc, l'Empereur pense que
" vous pouvez tout faire du moment que les Anglais seront retirés sur
" Lisbonne.

" Cinq divisions de Castanos, composées des meilleurs troupes, ont
" été culbutées plus facilement encore que vous n' avez culbuté vous-
" même l'armée d'Andalousie à Burgos. Les débris de l'Armée de
" Castanos sont poursuivis par le Maréchal Bessieres, qui leur a coupé
" la route d'Estramadure, et qui les poursuit sur celle de Valence à
" plusieurs journées au delà du Tage. L'Empereur a son quartier
" général à Chamartin, petite campagne à une lieue et demi de Ma-
" drid ; sa Majesté jouit de la meilleure santé. La ville de Madrid
" est très tranquille ; les boutiques sont ouvertes, les spectacles ont
" repris, et il ne parait pas que les premiers pourparlers ayent été
" appuyés de quatre mille coups de canon.

" LE PRINCE DE NEUCHATEL,<br>" Major Général.

" Je vous enverrai demain la proclamation et les arrêtès pris par
" l'Empereur ; vous y reconnoitrez celui fait pour commander à tout."

This letter gave Sir John Moore not only a correct account of the
disposition of most of the French divisions, together with the intentions of the Emperor ; but also included an exact summary of the
Spanish operations, and of the state of Madrid.

The most important service that Mr. Frere could perform to Spain
and to his Country, was certainly to send intelligence of all important
events to the Commander of the Forces. This duty was of course in-
culcated in his instructions from the Secretary of State, in which is
the following clause : " You will on your part keep him (Sir J.

" Moore) regularly informed of any political event of importance
" which may arise, and which can in any degree affect the safety, or
" influence the movements, of the army." It cannot be questioned
that the surrender and total submission of Madrid was a political event
of some importance ; and likely to affect the safety, and influence the
movements, of the British army. Yet Mr. Frere never transmitted to
Sir John Moore this intelligence ! It was the more requisite to do
so, as, by his letters from Aranjuez when close to Madrid, and by
those from Talavera when near it, and by the mission of his friend
Charmilly, he had sent the strongest assurances of the determination
of the inhabitants of the capital to hold out to the last extremity.
Yet Mr. Frere never intimated to Sir John Moore that this expectation had proved fallacious ! To conceal such intelligence, would have
been highly criminal : it must, therefore, be concluded that Mr.
Frere was totally misinformed and deceived. Yet one is quite at a loss
to conceive how the Junta and Mr. Frere could find any difficulty in
obtaining intelligence from Madrid. For this city never was surrounded by the French ; the communication with the country was left
open by their consent, for the admission of provisions. And though
the Governor and a few others were traitors, yet the city was full of
loyal citizens, undoubtedly disposed to send true accounts.

No satisfactory explanation appears for the want of true intelligence, and the transmission of false ; or for mingling both together,
as was the present case. For the Junta had actually communicated to
the British Commander that Madrid had capitulated ; but they had added
that the city had remained in some sense hostile, and that the French
troops had not ventured to enter within the gates. This impression
of course continued upon his mind ; and it was from Marshal Berthier that he was indebted for the knowledge of the truth. But it
was now too late to resume the former plan of carrying his arms to
the South ; and he still had some reliance on the favourable advices
which had been sent him on the other points.

Along with the unfavourable intelligence communicated in Berthier's letter, it was some consolation for Sir John Moore to find that Buonaparte believed he was retreating. But as he perceived that Soult's corps was stronger than had been represented, he considered it no longer advisable to march to Valladolid, least Sir David Baird should be attacked in forming his junction. He thought it preferable to move to Toro, to approach nearer to Sir David, and accordingly wrote to him this intention.

### Sir John Moore to Sir David Baird.

" MY DEAR SIR, *Head Quarters, Alaejos, Dec.* 14, 1808.

" I RECEIVED last night your letters of the 10th and 11th
" inst. It was my intention to have moved to-morrow on Valladolid ;
" but by a letter from Buonaparte to Marshal Soult at Saldanha,
" which we have intercepted, the officer who carried it having been
" murdered by the peasantry, I am induced to change my direction,
" and shall be to-morrow with all the troops I have at Toro, and its
" immediate neighbourhood. It appears that Marshal Soult, Duc de
" Dalmatia, has with him two divisions at Saldanha, besides one
" under the Duc d'Abrantes which is collecting at Burgos, and ano-
" ther under the Duc de Trevile which has received orders to march
" on Saragossa, but which of course may be recalled. Madrid has
" submitted, and is quiet ; and the French from thence are marching
" upon Badajos. Their advanced guard was at Talaveira la Reina on
" the 10th instant. My object is now to unite the army as soon as
" possible : you at Benavente, and I at Toro ; from whence, either
" by a forward or flank movement, the two corps can be joined. I
" shall direct all my stores from Zamora to be forwarded to Benavente.
" The arrangement with respect to yours which I communicated to
" you in my letter of the 12th inst. may go on ; by which we shall

" have a certain portion at Benavente, and the rest at Astorga and
" the rear. It appears from the intercepted letters, from deserters,
" and from prisoners we have taken, that the French are in complete
" ignorance of the present movements, and think we have retreated:
" As they will now know the truth, what change this may make in
" their march to Badajos. I know not: but Marshal Soult will cer-
" tainly be checked in his intended operations; which were projected
" upon the supposition that he had nothing but Spaniards to oppose
" him. Every arrangement which I before directed with a view to
" enable us to live in the Galicias, should be strictly attended to;
" for, though in the first instances we may not have opposed to us
" more than we can face, it will be in the power of the Enemy to in-
" crease their force far beyond our strength. I have received a letter
" from the Marquis of la Romana, and I expect an officer from him
" every hour. Whatever I determine with him shall be communi-
" cated to you; in the mean time I shall thank you to let him know
" that I have changed my intention of going to Valladolid, in conse-
" quence of information; and that I am collecting the army at Toro
" and Benavente.

" Believe me, &c.

" JOHN MOORE."

Though Sir John Moore had received no answer to the letters he
wrote to Mr. Frere on the 6th and 10th, he continued sending him
exact information of his movements

*Sir J. Moore to Mr. Frere.*

" SIR,

" Marshal Soult, Duke of Dalmatia, is with a corps at
" Saldana: Junot, Duke of Abrantes, is marching with another by
" Vittoria on Burgos; and there is a corps under another Marshal,
" Duke of Trevise, destined for Saragossa. Madrid is quiet; and
" the army, or rather a portion of it, is on its march to Badajos; the
" advanced guard was at Talavera de la Reina on the 10th. Buona-
" parte is at Chamartin — in the belief that the British have retired
" into Portugal. Marshal Bessieres is in pursuit of the army of Cas-
" tanos; has intercepted its march to Estremadura, and is following
" it to Valencia. This information, which I received yesterday, has
" determined me to unite the army with all possible speed; and in-
" stead of proceeding to Valladolid I have marched to this place, in
" order to make my junction with Sir David Baird, who is assembling
" his corps at Benavente. I met a King's messenger on my coming
" to this town who was in search of you: I have directed him to go
" to Ciudad Rodrigo; where, according to the information he re-
" ceives, he will proceed straight to Badajos, or enter Portugal.

" I have the honour to be, &c.

" JOHN MOORE."

The British Commander was now very desirous that the Duke of
Dalmatia should move forward, and meet him halfway; though he
could hardly flatter himself with this expectation. He resolved therefore to march towards him, form his junction with Sir David Baird
on the road, and, if possible, encounter Marshal Soult before he was
reinforced, and before any French corps should be pushed forward
on his right flank to endanger his retreat.

With this design he had marched to Toro, which he reached on the 16th. Here he received the following letter from Lieut.-Col. Symes, who had been deputed by Sir David Baird to ascertain the strength and condition of the Marquis of Romana's troops.

*Lieut.-Colonel Symes to Sir David Baird.*

" SIR, *Leon, 14th Dec.* 1808.

"I HAVE the honour to acquaint you that I arrived at " Leon yesterday evening; the difficulty of procuring post-horses " greatly retarded my journey. Between Membibre and Manzanal I " met a brigade of Spanish artillery, viz. two howitzers, and six field- " pieces; they were proceeding to Ponteferada, for what precise " object I could not learn;—possibly to defend the passes of the " mountains.

" At a league North of Astorga, I came on another brigade of " Spanish guns, drawn up on a rising ground. These guns had only " three or four men to guard them, and no regular centinels. I was " told that the gunners and cattle were in the neighbouring village. " I examined the state of the guns and the ammunition, as closely as " I could without giving offence. They appeared very defective; " the men said they came from Leon fifteen days ago, and knew not " whither or when they were to proceed. At Orbigo, four leagues " from Leon, I found the place occupied by a numerous body of troops; " I was told 4,000 under Major General Don Jenars Trigader. " There were five regiments; three of the line — El Rey, Majorca, " and Hibernia; and two of militia — the Maldonada and another. " The equipment and appearance of these troops were miserable. " I had an opportunity of inspecting the arms of the General's " Guard, which were extremely imperfect; the springs and locks " do not often correspond; either the main spring was too weak for

" the feather-spring, or the feather-spring too weak to produce
" certain fire from the hammer. I tried sixteen; of this number
" only six had bayonets, and these were short and bad. The ammu-
" nition pouches were not proof against rain: the clothing of the
" soldiers was motley, and some were half naked. They were in
" general stout young men, without order or discipline, but not
" at all turbulent or ferocious; and nothing of intoxication was ob-
" servable. Soon after I left Orbigo, I met the regiment of Vittoria
" on its march from Leon, destined, I was told, for Ponteferada:
" the men were wretchedly clad and armed.

" I got to Leon early in the evening, and waited on the Marquis
" de la Romana; he had not heard of the capitulation of Madrid;
" expressed himself vaguely on the subject of moving; stated his
" force at 22,000 infantry and 300 cavalry; complained much of
" the want of officers; had intended to form his army into five divi-
" sions, but could not for want of Officers to put at their head: he,
" therefore, meant to divide his army into wings; one under General
" Blake, the other under himself; that his force was daily increasing
" by the return of fugitives. He expressed hopes, that we had
" light troops to oppose those of the French, who were very expert;
" and added, that he was training 6,000 of his men to that species
" of warfare. There was to be a general review the next day, at
" which I expressed a desire of the honour of attending his Ex-
" cellency. In the morning I waited on the Marquis, and pressed
" him, as far as I could with propriety, on the subject of joining
" Sir John Moore; to which he evaded giving any more than general
" assurances. He does not think that the force of the Enemy in the
" North exceeds 10,000 men in all; and that there is no danger of
" their penetrating into Asturias. He recommends to Sir John
" Moore, to break down all the bridges between Toro and Aranda —
" five in number; that Zamora be fortified and made a depôt; and

" that magazines be formed at Astorga and Villafranca; regretted
" his want of cavalry; expressed a wish to procure 2,000 English
" muskets, and shoes for his army. When I asked him for 100 draft
" mules for General Baird's army, he replied, it was impossible; he
" had not one to spare. Whilst we were talking, a courier brought
" intelligence of the repulse of the French at Madrid. It may be
" true, but seems at present to stand in need of confirmation.

" I attended the review. The troops were drawn up in three
" columns; each might, perhaps, consist of 2,500 men. The Mar-
" quis, on horseback, addressed each column separately; when that
" was over, the troops formed into lines; the right wing was badly
" armed, and worse clothed; the left was better, being chiefly pro-
" vided with English firelocks; and a corps of 1,000 men in uniform,
" who, I was informed, were light troops, might be called respect-
" able. Their movements from column into line was very confusedly
" performed, and the Officers were comparatively inferior to the
" men; there was only one brigade of artillery in the field; and I
" doubt whether there is any more in Leon. The guns were drawn
" by mules. No ammunition-waggons were brought into the field
" for inspection. On the whole, from what I have been able to
" observe, since I came here, and from the tenor of my conversations
" with the Marquis, I am disposed to doubt his inclination of moving
" in a forward direction to join Sir John Moore. I suspect he rather
" looks to secure his retreat into Galicia, unless the aspect of affairs
" materially alters for the better; and if he were to join Sir John, I
" doubt whether his aid would be found essentially useful. My reasons
" for these conclusions are as follows:—If the Marquis meant to
" advance, why send his artillery and troops into the rear? and why,
" as he is assured of the time when Sir John Moore intends to be
" at Benavente, decline to fix any precise day to make a movement?
" I do not know what communication he may have made to you

" through Captain Doyle, or by letter to Sir John Moore, to whom
" he says he has written fully; but to me he has certainly given no
" cause whatever to suppose that he will move in concert with your
" army, or that of Sir John Moore : I hope I may be mistaken.

" My motive for doubting, whether the aid which he might bring
" would be of any importance, arises from a sense of the inefficient
" state of his army; and the want of discipline in the men.  It is
" morally impossible that they can stand before a line of French
" infantry.  A portion of, at least one third of, the Spanish muskets
" will not explode; and a French soldier will load and fire his piece
" with precision three times before a Spaniard can fire his twice.
" Men, however brave, cannot stand against such odds; as to charg-
" ing with the bayonet, if their arms were fit for the purpose, the men,
" though individually as gallant as possible, have no collective con-
" fidence to carry them on, nor Officers to lead them; they will
" therefore disperse, probably on the first fire, and can never be
" rallied, until they voluntarily return to their General's standard;
" as in the case of the Marquis de la Romana's present army, almost
" wholly composed of fugitives from the battles of the North.  A
" striking instance of this is given by the Marquis himself, who as-
" sured me that the Spaniards did not lose above 1000 men in
" their late actions with the French; a proof not of the weakness
" of the French, but of the incapacity of the Spaniards to resist
" them.  In fact, the French light troops decided the contest; — the
" Spaniards fled before a desultory fire; — they saved themselves,
" and now claim merit for having escaped.

" By a repetition of such flights and re-assembling, the Spaniards
" may, in the end, become soldiers, and greatly harass the Enemy;
" but, as we cannot pursue that mode of warfare, our allies are not
" much calculated to be of use to us on the day of battle, when we
" must either conquer or be destroyed.

" I do not mean to undervalue the spirit or patriotism of the
" Spaniards, which I highly respect, and which, in the end, may
" effect their deliverance ; but they are not now, nor can they for a
" long time be, sufficiently improved in the art of war, to be coad-
" jutors with us in a general action : we must, therefore, *stand or*
" *fall through our own means* ; for, if we place any reliance on
" Spanish aid for success in the field, we shall, I fear, find ourselves
" egregiously deceived.

" I think the Marquis de la Romana should immediately be called
" upon, to say upon what day he will march, and on what day and at
" what place he will join Sir John Moore.

" I have thought it my duty, Sir, thus to enter at length into the
" subject, with a view to prevent hereafter any disappointment on a
" matter of such high importance.

" I have the honour to be, &c.

" MICHAEL SYMES,<br>" Lieut.-Col."

This account of the Marquis of Romana's troops, was most discouraging. It was evident that little reliance could be put on a
force so imperfectly organized. The following letter from the Marquis gives no very flattering description of his army, though it was,
in many points, an exaggeration.

*The Marquis of Romana to Sir John Moore.*

" SIR, *Leon, le* 14 *Dec.* 1808.

" VOYANT les mouvements que l' Armée sous les ordres
" de V. E. execute en avant, je prens le parti de lui dépêcher mon
" aide-de-camp Mr. O'Niell avec cette lettre, qui l'instruira, et de
" la destination de mon Armée et de mes desseins. Je me trouve
" avec 20 mille hommes presents sous les armes, que j'ai commencé

" à habiller, et à les mettre en état d' agir ; mais il s' en faut encore
" beaucoup que j' aie completé l' ouvrage, et il-y-a encore les deux
" tiers au moins qui ont besoin d'être habillés de neuf et en entière.

" Presque toute l'Armée se trouve sans havre-sacs, sans gibernes,
" et sans souliers ; et malgré toute l' activité que j'ai mis pour cet
" effet, je n' ai pu y parvenir à cause du peu de ressources qu' offre le
" pays. J' attends d' un jour à l' autre tous ces objets ; mais
" l' éloignement où ils se trouvent de ce point-çi retardent l'exécution
" de mes ordres. Si les Provinces mettoient un peu plus de zéle, je
" ne doute pas que l'Armée se trouverait dejà en état d'agir de
" concert avec celle de V. E. Voici quant à la situation de mes
" troupes, je vais à présent exposer à V. E. mes desseins. Si je
" n' avois point d' Ennemis en face, je ne douterois pas un instant de
" réunir toutes mes forces avec celle de V. E. et de concerter un at-
" taque décisif sur les troupes qui cernent Madrid dans ce moment :
" mais il-y-a un corps d'environ huit à dix mille hommes d'après les
" meilleurs enseignemens qui s' étend depuis *Sahagun* jusqu' à
" *Almanza*, et dont l' objet à ce que je crois est de tenir en échec
" mon Armée, également que d'entretenir les communications avec
" les montagnes de Santander. La position est le long de la petite
" rivière de *Cea*, et il occupe les villages de *Sahagun*, où il appuye
" sa gauche ; *Saldana*, où se trouve son corps principal ; *Cea* et
" *Almanza*, où il a ses avants-postes. De ce dernier point il pousse
" ses reconnoissances jusqu' à *Pedrosa* à l'entrée de *Valdeburon*, et
" il prétend gêner ma gauche. Tant que ce corps sera dans cette
" position, je ne pourrois pas abandonner la mienne, tant parceque
" je ne puis pas laisser à découvert ni abandonner ce pays où je tire
" beaucoup de subsistances, comme aussi parceque je laisserais libre
" et degagée à l' Ennemi l' entrée des Asturies, et qu' il ne tarderoit
" pas à s' emparer aussitôt de ce pays-çi, et à menacer l'entrée en
" Galice. Je compte dès que je serois en état de manœuvrer de pousser

" le corps qui est devant moi ; et en même temps Sir David Baird
" pourroit montrer les têtes de Colonnes en avançant depuis Benavente
" sur la route de Palencia. Ce mouvement combiné obligeroit ce corps
" ennemi à se replier sur Reynosa, ou même à Burgos ; une fois degagé
" de cette partie, je ne trouve pas qu'il fut difficile à V. E. de venir se
" joindre à nos corps, tant à celui de Sir David Baird comme égale-
" ment au mien.

" Je voudrois bien avoir une entrevue avec V. E. : nous applanirons
" bien des difficultés ; si je puis l' exécuter sans faire faute ici, je me
" rendrois au plus tôt à Tordesillas, et je ne manquerai pas de vous
" en avertir d' avance.

" J'ai l' honneur d' être, Monsieur le Général,

" vôtre très humble et dévoué, Serviteur,

" LE MARQUIS DE LA ROMANA."

While Sir John Moore's whole attention was engrossed with the
attack on the French army, which he was meditating, a new mission
from the Supreme Junta and Mr. Frere overtook him this day at Toro.

A member of the Junta, accompanied by Mr. Stuart, presented the
following dispatch :

*Don Martin De Garay, Secretary of the Supreme Junta, to His
Excellency J. Hookham Frere, &c. &c. &c.* *

" SIR,

" THE Marquis de la Romana has informed the
" Supreme Junta, from his Head Quarters in Leon, under data
" the 2nd inst. that eight days ago he was treating with the English
" General Sir David Baird, who commands the troops of his nation
" at Astorga, to proceed with them and twelve or fourteen thousand
" picked men of the army under his command, to Zamora, to unite

* Vide Original in Appendix, W.

" with the General Sir John Moore, by the road he had pointed out;
" in order to make a movement against the Enemy, towards the
" point that might be thought most convenient.    But, when he
" flattered himself that General Baird would agree thereto, he re-
" plied, that he had positive orders to go by land or sea to unite
" with Sir John Moore in Portugal.    That he had repeated his
" request to both Generals; and that on the preceding day General
" Baird had definitively answered him, that he was withdrawing
" his artillery to embark it at Corunna, and that he intended to go
" with his troops to Portugal, along the coast of Galicia, or by the
" province of Tras los Montes upon Almeida.    That he wrote him,
" in conjunction with General Belande (who had arrived that night
" at Leon), acquainting him of the consternation that he would throw
" that country into by his retreat; the impossibility of the Marquis's
" marching alone, without any cavalry, towards Zamora; the evils to
" which that province remained exposed, and the risk with which it
" threatened the kingdom of Galicia *.

" The Supreme Junta has learnt with the greatest surprise and
" pain this resolution of the English General; which, if put in exe-
" cution, would afford great advantages to the French arms, and
" would bring on the most terrible consequences upon the Spanish
" arms.    The generous and ready succours that England afforded us,
" and the troops with which she assisted us, increased the enthusiasm
" of the whole country, and strengthened the just hopes that this
" union would secure the happiest results to the enterprize.    For
" the same reason, the dismay and consternation that will now arise
" from seeing the British army retreat without acting or uniting,
" will excite feelings contrary to the good cause, will weaken the

* Vide page 120, where the Marquis states an opinion exactly the reverse of
this; namely, that it appeared to him, that the cause for Sir John Moore's ordering
a retreat was well founded, and very just.

" enthusiasm and ardour which, hitherto, confidence in the uniformity
" of ideas, and in the operations of the British army united with our
" troops, has sustained.

" Besides the irreparable injury that we should feel, Portugal
" would remain exposed to see herself for the second time subjected
" to the French; who would then disconcert, most completely, all
" the plans and measures that would alone save these two kingdoms,
" allies of England, who by the ultimate result would only have
" afforded us succours and troops to make us rely on their effective
" assistance, and withdraw them in the most critical and interest-
" ing moment. In reality, the Enemy has never been nearer his utter
" ruin (if the English and Spanish armies act with judgment and
" energy) than in the moment when, weakened by what his late
" efforts have cost him, we might profit of the advantage of seeing
" his army divided in covering such an extended line.

" All these considerations, and the melancholy consequences the
" retreat of the British troops would produce, cannot be hidden from
" your Excellency's penetration, and that of his Britannic Majesty's
" Generals; but, if the British army were united to ours, it would con-
" tribute to give liberty to Spain and Portugal; finish the generous
" work for which the friend of Spain destined them; immortalise their
" name, and render service to all the Continent.

" Although our troops have experienced reverses, there are no
" grounds for dismay. The state of things rather promises that,
" by the number of English and Spanish troops, and by the enthu-
" siasm and confidence their union will produce, advantages will
" occur which must secure us victory.

" The Marquis de la Romana will see Sir John Moore, and join
" him with fourteen thousand chosen men from his army; and with
" the active and energetic measures the Supreme Junta has directed,
" in a month it will augment its numbers with thirty thousand con-

The following is the letter brought by Mr. Stuart.

*To Sir John Moore.*

" SIR, "                                    *Truxillo, Dec.* 8, 1808.

" APTER the representations which have been made
" to you from other quarters, I can hardly hope that a farther
" remonstrance on my part can produce any effect: when high
" military rank and authority, and the influence of persons whom I
" am told you honour with your private esteem, have been found
" unavailing. The advantages which Mr. Stuart possesses in this
" respect will, I hope, enable him to urge you with the warmth of
" regard, what I may be allowed to state with impartiality and
" candour, towards a person with whom I am no otherways ac-
" quainted than by the honour which he has done me by his cor-
" respondence: I mean the immense responsibility with which you
" charge yourself by adopting, upon a supposed military necessity,
" a measure which must be followed by immediate if not final ruin
" to our Ally, and by indelible disgrace to the Country with whose
" resources you are entrusted.

" I am unwilling to enlarge upon a subject in which my feelings
" must be stifled, or expressed at the risk of offence; which, with
" such an interest at stake, I should feel unwilling to excite. But
" this much I must say, that if the British army had been sent
" abroad for the express purpose of doing the utmost possible mis-
" chief to the Spanish cause, with the single exception of not firing
" a shot against their troops, they would, according to the measures
" now announced as about to be pursued, have completely fulfilled
" their purpose.

" That the defence of Galicia should be abandoned must appear
" incredible.

" I inclose a note which I have just received from Mr. Garay,
" Secretary to the Junta, and remain, with great truth and regard,

" Sir,

" Your obedient humble servant,

" J. H. FRERE."

This letter, and this second mission, shew the decided interference
of Mr. Frere in the military operations; and they prove how determined he was that Sir John Moore should be governed by him.

It must be very superfluous to add a word in justification of Sir John
Moore's original plan, since it appears, by Berthier's letter, that Buonaparte presumed that his movement would of course induce the
English to retire on Lisbon. We do not, however, suspect that
Mr. Frere thinks himself a superior general to Buonaparte; we only
perceive that his understanding was completely warped by traitors.
The stile of the letters, however, do not admit of the same apology;
and the whole transaction displays an extraordinary specimen of
diplomatic authority. Had it not been recorded, no one could have
suspected how Commanders of Armies might be treated by British
Plenipotentiaries.

The forbearance of Sir John Moore on receiving these letters is
very remarkable: he sent no answer till the 23d, which will appear
in its place. In his Journal there is the following passage.

" I halted at Toro on the 16th, when Mr. Stuart came to me
" from Mr. Frere, accompanied by a Member of the Junta, to re-
" quest I would connect myself with the Marquis of Romana. This
" I told them I was about to do, and that I had written to the
" Marquis from Salamanca.

" I explained to Mr. Stuart Mr. Frere's extraordinary conduct to
" me, and I shewed him his letters, which surprised him. He was

"not much pleased at having been sent upon a mission with only a
" half-confidence."

It is mortifying to observe, with how much more propriety and
judgment the political details are managed by the French, even when
conducting an atrocious usurpation, than by the English, when engaged in the justest cause.

Let Marshal Berthier's letter be compared with Mr. Frere's. The
instructions contained in the former are perspicuous, and the language is concise and polite. And though Marshal Soult only commanded a detached corps, he is left with ample discretionary powers,
and free from the fetters of diplomatic men.

But what above all things merits imitation, the best information
which had been received is sent him, and the state of affairs is
fairly described, neither exaggerating nor disguising the truth.

It thence appears that the correspondence between public officers
in France is of an opposite nature from the pompous Bulletins.
The latter are intended to deceive the vulgar, the former to instruct
their officers. And the French are too wise politicians to suppose
that successful measures can be founded on false information.

Sir John Moore * had now resolved to threaten the communications between France and Madrid; and, if a favourable opportunity
offered, to attack the Duke of Dalmatia's corps, or any of the covering divisions that should present themselves. He foresaw that this
would necessarily draw upon him a large French force, and of course
would prove an important diversion in favour of the Spaniards; who
would by this means have the opportunity of collecting in the South,
and restoring their affairs. The army was now near the French
position. The cavalry under Lord Paget were pushed so forward,
that their patroles reached as far as Valladolid, and had frequent

* Vide Appendix, DD.

successful skirmishes with the Enemy. Colonel Otway met a detachment of French cavalry, charged them, and made the whole prisoners.

On the 18th of December Sir John Moore's Head Quarters were at Castro Nuevo, and Sir David Baird's at Benavente, on the road to join him.

Sir John was very desirous of obtaining the co-operation of the Marquis of Romana, who unluckily was beginning to retire on Galicia. This proceeded from the Spanish and English Commanders being independent, instead of the one being subordinate to the other.

*Sir John Moore to the Marquis de la Romana.*

" SIR, *Castro Nuevo*, 18th Dec. 1808.

"I HAD the honour to receive, at Toro, on the 16th
" inst. your Excellency's letter of the 14th, delivered to me by your
" Aid-de-camp, Mr. O'Niell. I have deferred to answer it until
" I approached nearer to you, and until I knew what measures you
" might propose to pursue, in consequence of the information I had
" directed Sir David Baird to communicate to you. Upon a know-
" ledge that Marshal Soult had a corps so near as Saldana and
" Sahagun, which would soon be joined by another coming from
" France under General Junot, I judged it expedient to make my
" junction with Sir David Baird in this neighbourhood, as speediest
" done, rather than at Valladolid. I therefore marched from Ala-
" ejos, on Toro, and yesterday came here; where I occupy rather
" an extended cantonment. My intention was to march towards
" Saldana and Sahagun, as soon as Sir David Baird's corps was come
" forward; which I thought would either lead to an action with
" the corps under Marshal Soult, or induce him to retire. In either

" case I expected to disembarrass you from a troublesome neigh-
" bour. In this operation I of course expected the co-operation of
" such part of your corps, if not the whole, as was fit to move.

" I received, upon my arrival here yesterday afternoon, a letter .
" from Sir David Baird, inclosing one which he had just received
" from you, dated the 16th; in which you mention your intention
" immediately to retreat, by Astorga and Villafranca, into the
" Galicias. I beg to know whether this be still your Excellency's
" determination, as it is one which must materially affect my move-
" ments. I own that I expected that your Excellency would have
" left the road through the Galicias to Corunna open for the British
" army, as it is that by which we must receive our supplies; and by
" which, if obliged, we can alone retreat. I expected that your
" Excellency, with the Spanish troops, would have entered the
" Asturias, and have thus protected the left flank of the commu-
" nication on Corunna. I was the more induced to think that this
" would have been your mode of acting, as it is stated in a paper
" given, I believe, by your Excellency to the British Government;
" and by which they were induced to prefer the disembarkation of
" their troops at Corunna, and the assembly of the British army in
" Leon.

" As is was my wish, on coming here, to combine my movements
" with those of the Spanish army under your command, I hope you
" will have the goodness to communicate to me your intentions. You
" know the successes the French have met with, you know the forces
" they have in Spain, and you should be able to judge better than
" I can, what chance there is, after the recent defeats, of an army
" being assembled in the South of Spain able to resist, or occupy
" the attention of the French, sufficiently to oblige them to withhold
" any considerable portion of their army from being sent against us.

" I have no accounts from Saragossa; but it is reasonable to
" suppose that it cannot hold out long against a regular attack.

" I had forgot to mention to you, that a Member of the Supreme
" Junta waited upon me at Toro, to request in the name of the Junta
" that I should act in concert with your army. The Junta were at
" Truxillo; but have retired to St. Mary's, near to Cadiz.

" I shall wait anxiously for your Excellency's answer, and have the
" honour to be,

   " Sir,

     " Your most obedient, &c.

       " JOHN MOORE."

The General continued his march on Villapando and Valderos.
On the 20th December he reached Majorga; and here he was joined
by Sir David Baird, with the Guards and General Manningham's
brigade.

The British army were now united; and, independent of some
small detatchments left to keep up the communications, it amounted
to 23,000 infantry, and 2000 two or three hundred cavalry. The
Head Quarters were at Majorga, but the cavalry and horse-artillery
were advanced to Monastero Melgar Abaxo, within three leagues of
Sahagun; where it was understood that near 700 of the Enemy's
cavalry were posted.

The weather was extremely cold, and the ground covered with
deep snow; yet Lord Paget endeavoured to cut off this detachment.
His Lordship marched at two o'clock in the morning, and sent General Slade with the 10th hussars along the Cea to enter the Town;
while he proceeded towards it in another direction, with the 15th
dragoons and horse-artillery.

His Lordship approached the town at dawn, and surprised a piquet: but two or three men escaped, and gave the alarm.   He pushed

forward, and discovered the Enemy formed up, not far from the town. The two corps manœuvred for some time, each endeavouring to gain the flank of its opponent. At first the ground was unfavourable to Lord Paget; particularly from the situation of a hollow. But by superior skill his Lordship surmounted this difficulty; passed the hollow, completely out-manœuvred the Enemy, and charged them at a favourable moment; for the French having wheeled into line, very injudiciously halted to receive the shock. But this they were unequal to; they were overthrown in a moment, and dispersed in every direction. Many of the French were killed; and the prisoners amounted to 157, including two Lieutenant Colonels. The loss of the British was trifling. The 15th Regiment of Hussars, about 400 strong, encountered in this action near 700 French, and surpassed them both in skill and intrepidity.

Sir John reached Sahagun in the morning of the 21st of December, and established there his Head Quarters. As the soldiers had suffered a great deal from the forced marches (for the weather was severe, the roads were very bad, and covered with snow) he halted a day, to enable them to recover.

The following letter was received this morning from the Marquis of Romana.

### The Marquis of Romana to Sir John Moore.

" SIR,                                         *Leon, le 19 Decembre,* 1808.

  " Je m'empresse de répondre à la lettre de V. E. de hier, " datée de Castronuevo, en lui exposant que si j'avois pensé faire une " retraite, ce n'étoit qu'en raison des nouvelles que je recevois de Sir " David Baird; autrement ce n'etoit nullement mon intention. J' ai " placé mes avants-postes de façon à pouvoir me retirer en bon ordre ; " et tant que le Corps du Maréchal Soult ne recevroit pas de renforts

" plus considérables, je n' ai rien à risquer dans ma position, qui n' est
" que momentanée, et uniquement pour rétablir l'armée. Je voudrois
" co-opérer au mouvement que V. E. pense faire sur Sahagun ; et je
" n'attendrois pour cela que le moment de sçavoir quand votre Excel-
" lence pense le mettre en exécution, pour me mettre en marche.
" Je ferai longer les Montagnes de Leon jusqu' à *Guardo* par un
" corps de troupes légères ; tandis que le gros de mes troupes marchera
" sur *Almanza*, et de-là cotoyant la Rivière de Cea se portera sur Sal-
" dana, où doit se trouver le Corps du Maréchal Soult, à moins
" qu'il n' ait changé de position comme on le dit depuis deux jours.
" Les avis annonçent qu'ils n' ont laissé à *Saldana* que 1500 hom-
" mes, et qu'ils ont fait filer les autres vers *Guardo*, en se rapprochant
" des Montagnes. On prétend qu'ils ont à *Guardo* 3 mille hommes, et
" que ce Corps peut bien être augmenté par les détachements qui ont
" quitté *la Liebana*, ou les Montagnes de Santander, qui confine
" avec *Leon* et les *Asturies* ; au reste il n'y a pas un grand fond à
" faire sur les rapports des Paysans, car outré qu'ils ne voyent pas
" exactement, ils sont brouillés dans leur comptes par les marches
" continuelles et les contre-marches que les Ennemis font. J'ai
" l'honneur de prévenir V. E. qu'ils ont fait barricader le Pont et
" l'entrée de *Sahagun* avec des charriots.
" Si V. E. a d'autres projets en tête j'espère qu'elle voudra bien
" m'en donner connoissance, dans la persuasion que je ne désire autre
" chose que concerter en tout mes opérations avec celles de V. E. et
" l'appuyer de mon mieux dans toutes les entreprises. Je crois que
" pour le moment il ne doit pas être question de retraite, mais bien de
" tâter, l'Ennemi, et l' obliger à s'éloigner de la Capitale. Si V. E. le
" jugeoit à propos, nous pourrions avoir une entrevue à *Benavente*,
" et peut-être il seroit plus facile alors d'établir un plan d'opérations.
" J' ai eu ce soir des lettres de la Junta datée de *Merida* en Estre-
" madure le 13, dans lesquelles ils m'annonçent que le Peuple tient

u

" encore bon à Madrid, que les François ont été repoussés et battûs
" allant à Saragosse, et que les choses vont très bien en Catalogne.
" Je prie V. E. d'agréer l'hommage
" de mon sincère et respectueux attachement,
" LE MARQUI DE LA ROMANA."

The Marquis in this letter expresses his approbation of the present measures, and his willingness to co-operate in the attack proposed to be made on Saldana; but his intelligence is in every point erroneous. The last paragraph, mentioning the information sent by the Junta, is most extraordinary.

Could it be possible, that on the 13th of December the Junta did not know that Madrid had completely submitted ten days before; when they themselves had been chased by the French army from Talavera, which is sixty miles beyond Madrid?

It is true that Mr. Frere in his remonstrance of the 23rd of November * reproached the Junta for concealing information from him, and even for equivocating upon the subject. But it is quite incredible, that they should intentionally deceive their own General, and through him the British Commander. We must therefore suppose that the Junta transmitted the best intelligence they had; and must pity most sincerely a country so governed.

The following letter from the Duke of Infantada is dated the 13th of December, the same day with that from the Junta to the Marquis of Romana. Let them be compared.

* Vide page 58.

*Du Duc de l' Infantado à S. E. J. H. Frere.*

" MONSIEUR,                          *Cuença, ce* 13 *Decembre,* 1808.

" JE me fais un devoir de vous annonçer, comme à
" notre très bon et fidèle Allié, qu' ayant été envoyé à cette armée du
" Centre pour tâcher d'accélerer son arrivée auprès de la Capitale, à
" fin de sauver celle-ci, s' il étoit possible, n' ayant pu réussir dans
" mon projet, et me disposant en conséquence à me rendre auprès de
" la Junta Suprême, je me suis vû obligé par les Généraux, et forcé
" par les circonstances, à prendre le commandement de l' armée, en
" attendant la décision de la Junta. C' est malheureusement l' esprit
" d' insurrection et de mécontentement du soldat qui m' a placé au
" poste que j' occupe; et c'est assurément une situation bien désagré-
" able que celle d' avoir à corriger des maux invétérés, et de débuter
" par des mesures nécessaires pour rétablir l' ordre et la discipline
" totalement négligés.

" Je ne saurais vous dépeindre l' état où j' ai trouvé ce corps de
" troupes affamé, sans chaussures, une grande partie sans uniformes,
" manquant de munitions, ayant perdu la plupart de ses bagages;
" réduit à peu près à 9 mille hommes d' infanterie et deux de cava-
" lerie, et surtout ayant totalement perdu la confiance en ses Chefs.
" J' ai crû d'après cela, devoir suivre le plan adopté par mon prédé-
" cesseur, celui de venir dans ce pays montueux pour y passer le peu
" de jours nécessaires à rétablir un peu l' armée; pour me faire rejoindre
" par quelques traineurs, et quelques recrues, donner la chaussure et
" du repos au soldat et aux chevaux, et partir ensuite pour de nouvelles
" opérations. Mais il seroit bien important pour leur réussite qu' elles
" marchassent d' accord et de concert avec celles des autres armées,

" surtout avec celles de l' armée Angloise ; et il seroit, par consé-
" quent, indispensable que nous connussions mutuellement nos pro-
" jets.  Le Colonel Whittingham se trouve malade dans ce moment-
" ci, et je désirerois d' après celà qu' il me fut envoyé par S. E. le
" Général en Chef Moore un officier de confiance et connoissances
" militaires, qui pût me rendre compte du plan adopté par le
" Général pour cette campagne, et lui rendre de ce que nous accor-
" derions ensemble quant à la part que le corps d' armée pourroit
" prendre à son exécution.  Je serai bien charmé si le choix pouvoit
" tomber sur le Colonel Graham, qui j' ai eu l' honneur de connoître
" chez M. Stuart.

" Je ne sais, Monsieur, où cette lettre-ci vous parviendra, car
" j' ignore encore le lieu où la Junta s' est détenue ou fixée, et je
" pense que vous êtes auprès d 'elle.  Ma lettre n' en sera pas moins
" l' organe de ma très-sincère affection, ainsi que de l'assurance de
" ma plus haute considération, avec laquelle

" J' ai l' honneur d' être, &c.

" LE DUC DEL INFANTADO."

What folly, deceit, and distress, does this most natural letter
detect !  Here is a genuine description of the Spanish army, and a
true account of its numbers.  And it is lamentable to observe,
that while the British army, almost by the command of the Junta,
is hazarding its existence to make a diversion in favour of the
Spanish army, the General of the Spanish army knows nothing about
the matter.  What concert could there be between the various armies
employed for the defence of Spain, when the Junta, the centre of
intelligence, kept them all in absolute ignorance of the state of things?

Had Sir John Moore been so fortunate as to find so candid a correspondent as the Duke of Infantado, a person who would describe
things as they were, there is no doubt that the events and conclusion

of the campaign would have been very different. But this most important letter, dated Cuenca, Dec. 13, was sent to Seville, and was there enclosed in one to the General from Mr. Frere *, dated Dec. 22. It contained the only correct information he had hitherto sent. But instead of being carried according to its address, it was conveyed to London. The packet was unsealed by Sir John Moore's Executors.

On the 22d of December, while the troops were enjoying a short repose at Sahagun, and preparing for action, the following letter arrived.

*Mr. Frere to Sir John Moore.*

" SIR,         ·      *Merida*, 14 *Dec.* 1808. [*Received* 22 *Dec.* 1808.]

" I WAS last night honoured by your letter of the
" 10th, and was sincerely gratified at learning that, with hopes
" infinitely less sanguine than I confess myself to entertain of the
" final success of the Spanish cause, you had determined to make
" an effort in its favour. A resolution taken with such views must
" have been in a great measure founded upon feelings similar to
" those which you will have seen very strongly expressed in a letter
" of which, Mr. Stuart was the bearer; and of which I wish to say
" nothing more, than that I feel highly gratified in the idea of your
" having partaken them with me, and that, without communication
" between us, the same sentiments which at that very moment
" were influencing your conduct, were guiding my pen.

" Your letter happened to be delivered to me while I was with
" the Junta; and, after communicating such parts of its contents
" as were most important and gratifying to them, with the reserve
" which you pointed out, I mentioned Mr. Pignatelli's conduct,

---

* It was considered improper to print this letter of Mr. Frere's, as it was not received by the General.

" and was told that it had been already determined to remove him
" from his command, and that he should be sent before a Court Martial
" for his conduct at Valladolid; that the same resolution had been
" taken with respect to an Engineer Officer of high rank, whom his
" brother officers had denounced to the Marquis of Romana, for not
" having appeared in the moment of action. That, with respect to
" Avila, the Authorities of that town should be displaced, and
" General Romana directed to treat them in the manner which their
" conduct has deserved. You know, I presume, that he is invested
" with the authority of Captain General of Leon and Old Castile,
" Galicia and Asturias; and I can congratulate you on having to do
" with a man whom, upon all subjects of this sort, you will find of
" a perfectly right mind, and determined to keep every man to the
" performance of his duty.

" The placing the towns which you mention in a state of defence,
" suitable to the means of attack which the Enemy might at present
" be able to direct against them, would, I imagine, fall within the
" limits of his authority; but I shall state the subject to the Junta,
" and I have no doubt of their approbation of any measure which
" you suggest. The one of giving a temporary species of defence
" to the open towns has, I think, great advantages in a country like
" this, which is not over-run with luxury and timidity, and where a
" kind of provincial pride exists, not only in every province, but
" almost in every town. The people would be amused and animated
" not only against the Enemy, but in rivalry with each other;
" the Enemy would be obliged to overcome, at the price of his blood,
" obstacles which had been opposed to him by mere labour; and a
" thousand barriers would be interposed against that deluge of panic
" which sometimes overwhelms a whole nation, and of which, at
" one time, I was afraid I saw the beginning in this country.

" With respect to what you mention of directing the public mind
" by proclamations, and other means of popular impression, Marquis
" Romana is, with very few exceptions indeed, the man whom I have
" seen most capable of judging rightly. I send inclosed an ordon-
" nance which has been published in Aragon, and which has not
" yet appeared in the papers. I will thank you to forward it to
" Marquis Romana, if it is not printed. In the mean while, you
" will be glad to hear that it is much approved of by the Junta; and
" that they are well persuaded that it is only in this way that things
" can be done. They are almost all of them men of mild tempers and
" good humour, such as it is natural to expect in men who have been
" the object of a popular choice, and it will cost them some struggle
" to get the better of their natural dispositions, unless (which I think
" most likely) they put the thing out of their own hands, by erecting
" a special tribunal for Military offences.

" The extinction of the popular enthusiasm in this country, and the
" means which exist for reviving it, would lead to a very long discus-
" sion. I would only say, that if I am at all right in my judgment
" of the cause of the evil, it is already removed by the act of the
" Junta; and I trust that its effect will not long survive.

" I have been persuaded to write to the Commander in Chief in
" Portugal, to reinforce the army under your command with all the
" troops he can spare; and have already transmitted home a repre-
" sentation to that effect. The Portuguese who have been offered by
" the Regency, I apprehend, you would hardly wish for; I have
" therefore suggested their being sent to Badajos or Alcantara.

" No official report has yet been received of the capitulation of
" Madrid, nor is it by any means certain, that any formal stipulation
" existed. Nothing has been heard from Morla, Castellar, and
" Castelfranco; nor is it known where they are. An order has been
" drawn up and is to be published, prohibiting all persons concerned

" in the capitulation, or holding any command in the town at that
" time, from approaching the residence of the Junta.

" The army of Aragon had repulsed an attack on the 2nd. Pala-
" fox's official report of the unfortunate action of Tudela represents it
" as an exceedingly bloody one; and that the French confess to a loss
" of 4000 men. All the reports from Madrid represent the force of
" the French as much reduced. I have heard no estimate above
" 26,000 men. All these estimates are vague; but officers who were
" witnesses to the attack, are confirmed in the opinion of the weak-
" ness of the Enemy, by what they observed of his appearance and
" mode of approach. The Catalans appear to be entirely at their ease,
" following up the blockade of Barcelona. Whenever it falls, it will
" set loose a considerable reinforcement; Mr. Jovellanos made out to
" me a regular detail of 25,000, besides peasantry and irregulars,
" who are employed there.

" The Junta are on their way to Seville, a situation on many ac-
" counts preferable, in my opinion, to any other they could have
" chosen; unless circumstances could have allowed them to have
" stopt at Toledo. I shall follow them from hence to-morrow.

" This province is raising horses and men with great zeal, and send-
" ing them forward to defend the passes of the Tagus; particularly to
" Almanaz. The Junta have been received with general respect by
" the people, and with great deference by the inferior Juntas.

" I have the honour to be, with great truth and respect, Sir,
" Your most obedient humble servant,
" J. H. FRERE."

The exertions of the Supreme Junta and of Mr. Frere are singularly
displayed by this letter. After the armies of Spain are beaten, and
the capital is taken, Mr. Frere informs Sir John Moore, that he intends to state to the Junta a proposal for placing a few towns in a state
of defence.

As this plan was suggested by Sir John Moore in his letter of the 10th of December, it was not requisite to make any great effort to convince him of its utility. But Mr. Frere is fired by the idea; he displays the expected advantages in a fine flow of elocution; and at length rises in his diction to the sublime metaphor of interposing a thousand barriers against a deluge of panic.

These phrases were an inadequate substitute for dearth of intelligence; for Mr. Frere does not yet declare, whether Madrid has submitted or not: his expressions are still vague; he writes, there is no " official report of the capitulation."

Did Mr. Frere expect that Morla or Buonaparte would report to the Junta? And does he acquire no intelligence but by official reports? Mr. Frere was certainly not a person to be depended upon for information; for this letter, which only hints darkly at the capitulation of Madrid, reached the General on the 22nd of December; whereas an explicit account of the surrender of Madrid had been conveyed to Paris, and thence to London, and was printed in the English newspapers three days sooner *.

But it would be doing injustice to Mr. Frere to assert that his letter gives no intelligence; since he informs Sir John Moore that the force of the French is much reduced; and that no estimate he has heard of their numbers at Madrid exceeds 26,000 men: he consequently is desirous that the General should rely upon this intelligence; yet he owns, that the Junta are on their way to Seville—a measure which he very much approves of.

What! after all the boasted enthusiasm of the Spanish nation, does Mr. Frere approve of the Supreme Junta flying to the extremity of the Peninsula from the dread of 26,000 Frenchmen? If there had been no greater number the Junta need have taken no alarm, though

* Vide Appendix, U.

not a Spaniard had been in arms : for 25,000 British were now advancing into the heart of Spain.

Buonaparte's intelligence is somewhat different. He declares, in his 20th bulletin, that he reviewed his army on the 18th of December at Madrid, which consisted of 60,000 men, with 150 pieces of artillery : and this was independent of two large corps under the Dukes of Bellune and Dantzic, at Toledo and Talavera; and others in the neighbourhood. The account of the review, we believe, was no exaggeration. It was confirmed by the prisoners who were afterwards taken by the British ; and the terror inspired by such a force forms a sufficient excuse for the retreat of the Junta.

On the same day the General received another letter from Mr. Frere ; which was written only two days later, yet of a totally different tenor.

### Mr. Frere to Sir John Moore.

" SIR,  *Las Santos, Dec.* 16, 1808.

" THERE was a part of the letter with which you
" honoured me on the 10th, to which I hope I shall now be able to
" send a satisfactory answer. The subject of the ships in Cadiz had
" not escaped me ; but I thought it so very dangerous to suggest to
" the Junta any idea except that of living and dying on Spanish
" ground, that I avoided the mention of any subject that could seem
" to imply that I entertain any other prospects. The measure of
" confining the French prisoners on-board of them, seems to offer an
" opportunity for making arrangements which, without damping the
" spirit of the country, may provide a resource in case of the worst.
" This measure has been taken by the Junta of Seville, whose energy
" was so conspicuous in the course of the last summer. They have,
" as I judge from their proclamation, determined to assert themselves

" very vigorously; for they have reassumed their old title, and directed
" the Commander of Cadiz to correspond with them directly, as they
" do not know what is become of the Central Junta. I hope I shall
" succeed in keeping the peace between them.

       " I have the honour to be, &c.

                        " J. H. FRERE."

This letter should be read with particular attention, as the hints it
contains are very extraordinary.

Mr. Frere here acknowledges the reasons that he would not notice
sooner the subject of the Fleet of Cadiz to the Junta. He thought it
dangerous to suggest " any idea except that of living and dying on
Spanish ground;" and he avoided the mentioning any thing that would
seem to imply that he entertained other prospects. It thus appears,
that Mr. Frere did, in fact, think of the ships of Cadiz, and that he
did entertain prospects different from those he depicted to the Junta,
but that he disguised his thoughts from policy.

The wisdom of these concealments to an ally is a diplomatic question. But it was not from the Junta alone that Mr. Frere hid the
melancholy forebodings in his mind; he also kept them a profound
secret from the Commander of the British Forces; and, not contented
with a bare concealment, in every former letter he drew a flattering
picture of the Spanish affairs. Let the letter even of the 14th of
December be again examined: he there states — that the cause of
the extinction of enthusiasm is now removed — that no official account of the capitulation of Madrid has yet been received — that
the army of Aragon has repulsed the French — that the force of
the French is much reduced, only 26,000 being at Madrid — that
the Catalans are at their ease, and Barcelona about to fall. This is
an abstract of the agreeable description written on the 14th; and
on the 16th, no new event having occurred, Mr. Frere is making
arrangements for the worst!

With regard to the British Army, the discovery of Mr. Frere's real sentiments comes too late. It is now on the banks of the Carrion close to the position of the French.

The Commander wrote early in the morning to the Marquis.

*Sir John Moore to the Marquis de la Romana.*

" SIR, *Sahagun,* 22 *Dec.* 1808.

      " I HAD the honour to receive your Excellency's letter of
" the 19th yesterday morning early, as I was getting upon my horse
" to march with the troops to this place, where I arrived in the fore-
" noon. Six or seven hundred French cavalry were stationed at this
" place; a part of my cavalry marched the preceding night, attacked
" and defeated them at day-light yesterday morning, killed a good
" many, and took two Lieutenant-Colonels, eleven officers, and 144
" men prisoners.

     " The body of the French under Marshal Soult is still at Saldana.
" I shall march in that direction to-morrow, and shall attack them the
" moment I can. If your Excellency can make any movement in
" favour of this attack, or to take advantage of any success I may
" meet with, I take for granted you will do it. But time to me is the
" most precious of all things; and I cannot delay my movement.

     " With respect to the information sent to you by the Junta, you
" may depend upon it, it is erroneous. Madrid is quiet; Buonaparte's
" proclamations are dated from it; and nothing but the greatest exer-
" tion on the part of Spain, and all good Spaniards, will preserve
" them from conquest.

            " I have the honour to be, &c.

                        " JOHN MOORE."

The following letter arrived on the evening of the 22nd.

## The Marquis of Romana to Sir John Moore.

"SIR,  Leon, 21 *Decembre*, 1808.

"J'ai eu l'honneur de vous écrire le 19 en réponse à la
"lettre que V. E. m'avoit remis par mon aide-de-camp Mr. O'Niell,
"et n'ayant pas eu d'avis depuis, je dois lui exposer que pour faire
"l'attaque de Saldana comme il paroit que c'est l'intention de V. E.
"je desirerois de coopérer de mon côté, afin que la réussite soit com-
"plette. L'Ennemi en rassemblant toutes les forces qu'il a dissé-
"minées sur tous les points de ces environs, aura tout au plus, d'a-
"près les meilleurs renseignemens que j'ai pris, environ 8 à 9 mille
"hommes d'infanterie, et mille chevaux, avec 8 à 10 pièces d'artillerie;
"il seroit très important d'envelopper ce corps, et le détruire, avant
"qu'il puisse faire sa jonction avec quelqu'autre corps que Napoleon
"pût lui envoyer de renfort. Si V. E. se détermine à cette entre-
"prise, je ferai un mouvement avec 9 à 10 mille hommes, qui est
"tout ce que je pourrois rassembler de mieux habillés et armés; tout
"le reste se trouvant presque nud et mal equipé.

"Si V. E. me donne une réponse prompte, je sortirai demain; mais
"j'ai l'honneur de lui faire observer, que le coup donné, il faudra
"rentrer dans mes quartiers d'hiver, faute d'habillement et fourni-
"tures pour les troupes. Cependant nous laisserons à parler de cela à
"notre entrevue, comme également à concerter le plan d'operations à
"suivre. Je suis persuadé que l'Ennemi n'est pas en force, et que
"tous les désastres dont nous sommes temoins n'ont eu lieu que faute
"de combinaisons dans les opérations de nos armées. Par un Officier
"d'Ingenieurs que m'a remis la Junta de Zamora, pour avoir
"trouvé sa conduite un peu suspecte; j'ai été informé que l'armée de

" Palafox n'a reçu aucun echec comme les Ennemis le publioient, mais
" qu'il a été obligé de se replier sur Saragosse, à cause que l'armée
" de Castanos avoit quitté la position de Logrono, qu'il n' avoit jamais
" dû abandonner : il donne des détails très circonstanciés de l' armée
" Françoise sur Madrid, de l'Empereur, de la Division de Junot, et
" enfin des nouvelles que je crois très nécessaire que V. E. en aye
" connoissance, et d'après lesquelles il me semble que nous devons
" absolument avoir une entrevue.

    " J'ai l' honneur de renouveller à V. E. l'hommage de mon sincère
                " et respectueux attachement,

                                    " Le Mᵗ de la Romana."

Complete concert was thus established between the British and one
Spanish army. The number of the Spaniards which could be brought
forward, was less than the half of what had been originally stated;
and the assistance that could be expected from these troops may be
judged of from the report of Colonel Symes, who continued with the
Marquis. In a letter from him dated Leon, December 22nd, he
says, " The troops here, although they cannot be relied on to influ-
" ence materially the result of a general action, yet may be brought
" into use *as auxiliaries*, to engage the attention of a part of the
" Enemy's force ; and, in the event of the Enemy being broken, may
" prove an active instrument to complete his destruction. When I
" say this much, I say all that can possibly be expected from them,
" under the present appearance."

Early in the morning of the 23rd Sir John sent off the following
letter to the Marquis of Romana, signifying the movement he wished
him to make.

*Sir John Moore to the Marquis of Romana.*

" SIR,                                       *Sahagun, 23 December,* 1808.

" I HAD the honour to write to you yesterday; and this
" morning I received your Excellency's letter of the 21st. I shall
" march this night to Carrion, where, I have reason to believe,
" some of the Enemy are collected. To-morrow I shall march on
" Saldana. If your Excellency would march from Mansilla, either
" direct on Saldana, or pass the river a little above it, whilst I march
" on from Carrion, I think it would distract the attention of the
" Enemy, and considerably aid my attack. My march from Carrion
" will probably be in the night. Any information of your movement
" I shall thank you to address to me at Carrion, where I shall be at
" day-light to-morrow. I enclose a letter and a printed paper, sent
" to me by Mr. Frere, and which I received yesterday.
            " I have the honour to be, &c. &c.
                                    " JOHN MOORE."

Every arrangement was now completed for the attack of the
Enemy. The British were collected between Sahagun, Grahal,
and Villada, consisting of twenty-five thousand four hundred men.

The Duke of Dalmatia, after the defeat of his cavalry at Sahagun,
had withdrawn a detachment from Guarda, and concentrated his troops
to the amount of eighteen thousand behind the river Carrion. Seven
thousand were posted at Saldana, and five thousand at the town of
Carrion; and detachments were placed to guard the fords and bridges.
It was also known that the head columns of Junot's corps (the 8th)
were between Vittoria and Burgos.

Before this period, Sir John Moore had been able to establish
many excellent channels of intelligence, upon which he could, in

some measure, depend. Expresses were continually arriving with reports of every important circumstance.

He now answered Mr. Frere's last letters, and communicated to him his plan; and it appears, from this letter, how just a view the General had of his situation.

*Sir John Moore to Mr. Frere.*

" SIR,                                                           *Sahagun, 23d Dec.* 1808.

" I HAD the honour to receive yesterday your letters of " the 14th and 16th, with inclosures, which shall be forwarded by the " first opportunity.

" As you acknowledge only the receipt of my letter to you of the " 10th instant, I send you a duplicate of two letters which I addressed " to you on the 6th, and which I sent by a messenger who, perhaps, " was intercepted.

" With respect to your letter, delivered to me at Toro by Mr. " Stuart, I shall not remark upon it. It is in the style of the two " which were brought to me by Colonel Charmilly, and, consequently, " was answered by my letters of the 6th, of which I send you a du- " plicate: that subject is, I hope, at rest.

" I am in communication with the Marquis de la Romana. I " march this night to Carrion, and the next day to Saldana, to at- " tack the corps under Marshal Soult †.

" Buonaparte is dating his proclamations from Madrid; and as to " the British army, if it were in a neutral, or Enemy's country, it

† Some remarks on the Spanish co-operation are omitted.

" could not be more completely left to itself. If the Spaniards are
" enthusiasts, or much interested in this cause, their conduct is the
" most extraordinary that ever was exhibited.

" The movement I am making is of the most dangerous kind. I
" not only risk to be surrounded every moment by superior forces,
" but to have my communication intercepted with the Galicias. I
" wish it to be apparent to the whole world, as it is to every indivi-
" dual of the army, that we have done every thing in our power in
" support of the Spanish cause; and that we do not abandon it, until
" long after the Spaniards had abandoned us.

" I have the honour to be, &c.

" JOHN MOORE."

The army were now in complete preparation; the disposition for
an attack was made, and the Generals had received their instructions.
But, in the course of this day, messenger after messenger brought
unpleasant reports.

Certain information was received, that a strong reinforcement had
arrived at Carrion from Palentia; and that a large quantity of provisions and forage were preparing in the villages in front of that town.

A Courier next arrived from Los Santos, bringing information
that the French corps, which was marching to the South, had been
halted at Talavera: and several other messengers arrived, bringing
reports that the Enemy were advancing from Madrid.

Towards the evening an express arrived from the Marquis of
Romana.

*Du Marquis de la Romana à son Excellence Sir J. Moore, K. B.*

" SIR,                                           " *Leon*, 22 *Decembre*, 1808.

        " U<small>N</small> Confident que j'ai sur la rivière Duero me donne
" avis sous date de 18 courant, qu'on lui a assuré que les Ennemis
" qui se trouvoient à l'Escurial ont fait un mouvement vers ce côté-ci.
" Il m' ajoutoit que si la personne qui lui donnoit cet avis n' arrivoit
" pas ce jour même, il alloit lui de sa personne se transporter à Villa-
" castin (douze lieues éloigné de Madrid) pour être en observation
" des deux chemins, celui qui passe par Zamora, et l'autre qui va par
" Segovie.

    " Je m'empresse à donner cet avis à V. E. pour les mesures qu' elle
" jugera convenables à prendre.

                " J'ai l'honneur, &c.

                        " L<small>E</small> M<small>ARQUIS</small> <small>DE LA</small> R<small>OMANA</small>."


Sir John Moore saw at once the import of the various intelligence
he had received. He perceived that his movement and design were
discovered by Buonaparte, who was now marching a superior force
against him. This was what he had all along expected, and was
prepared for.

The forward march of the troops was instantly countermanded.

Soon after a second note arrived from the Marquis.

*Du Marquis de la Romana à son Excellence Sir J. Moore, K. B.*

" SIR,                  *Mansilla* 23 *Decembre*
*à trois heures du soir.*

" J'AI l'honneur de vous annoncer mon arrivée ici avec les troupes
" que je compte employer dans le mouvement auxiliaire. Je n'ai pu
" tirer q'environ sept milles hommes d'infanterie, 120 chevaux, et
" huit piéces d'artillerie. Les troupes sont cantonnées dans une cir-
" conférence à une lieue et quart de cette ville en avant vers
" Saldanha, excepté un corps que j'ai envoyé à trois lieues d'ici à un
" village nommé Villarmimio éloigné trois petites lieues de Cea.
" J'attends vos rapports pour me mettre en mouvement, que je ne
" ferai q'après que V. E. m'aura communiqué ses plans et ses inten-
" tions. Je desirerais avoir une réponse positive pour expédier les
" ordres de bonne heure au corps.

" J'ai l' honneur, &c.

" LE MARQUIS DE LA ROMANA."

An answer was instantly sent back.

*Sir John Moore to the Marquis of Romana.*

" SIR, .             *Sahagun,* 23d *Dec.* 1808.

" I HAD the honour to receive your Excellency's letter
" of the 22d this afternoon, and have to thank you for the informa-
" tion which it contains; the probability of its truth is confirmed to
" me, by information which reached me this morning, that a consi-
" derable quantity of provisions and forage had been ordered to be
" prepared in the villages on this side of Palencia. I also know that
" the intended march of a corps of the French to Badajos has been

" stopped, when its advanced guard had reached Talavera de la
" Reina.

" Your Excellency knows my object in marching in this direction,
" was to endeavour to free you from a troublesome neighbour, and to
" strike a blow at a corps of the Enemy, whilst it was still imagined
" that the British troops had retreated into Portugal. I was aware
" of the risk I ran, if I should be discovered, and the Enemy push on
" a corps between me and my communication.

" My movement has, in some degree, answered its object, as it
" has drawn the Enemy from other projects, and will give the South
" more time to prepare. With such a force as mine, I can pretend
" to do no more. It would only be losing this army to Spain and to
" England, to persevere in my march on Soult; who, if posted strongly,
" might wait, or, if not, would retire and draw me on until the corps
" from Madrid got behind me: in short, single-handed, I cannot
" pretend to contend with the superior numbers the French can
" bring against me.

" I received your Excellency's letter at six, and the troops were to
" have marched from this to Carrion at eight this evening. I coun-
" termanded them, and shall take immediate measures for retiring
" on Astorga. There I shall stand; as my retreat thence, if neces-
" sary, will be secure. I shall be in the way to receive the supplies
" and the reinforcements which I expect from England. At the
" worst, I can maintain myself, and, with your Excellency's aid,
" defend the Galicias, and give time for the formation of the armies
" of the South, and that which you command to be prepared, when
" a joint effort may be made, which can alone be efficacious. It is
" playing the Enemy's game to draw him to attack our armies in
" rotation.

" I hope this plan will meet your approbation; you may rest
" assured that I shall not retreat a foot beyond what is necessary

" to secure my supplies from being intercepted; and that I desire
" nothing more than to meet the Enemy upon any thing like equal
" terms.

" I have the honour to be, &c.

" JOHN MOORE."

" P. S. I had finished my letter, and was writing one to Colonel
" Symes, both of which I meant to dispatch to your Excellency in
" the morning; when I received your letter from Mansilla of this
" date.

" Your Excellency will see, that in consequence of the information
" contained in your letter of yesterday, I have countermanded my
" march to Carrion. I am sensible of the zeal and activity your
" Excellency has displayed, in thus hastening to co-operate with me;
" but, for the reasons contained in the former part of this letter, I
" believe the attempt no longer advisable. It will, however, be of
" use, and will blind the Enemy, should you continue with your
" corps a few days at Mansilla.

" You will, of course, not mention my intentions of falling back.
" If I am followed, I shall stop and offer battle; and though you
" should be at a distance, yet the knowledge that you are within
" reach will distract his attention, and act as a diversion.

" I shall be happy to hear again from you what are your intentions.
" I shall, I think, fall back on Benavente.

" I have the honour to be, &c.

" JOHN MOORE."

It is now requisite to point out the plan which was adopted by
Buonaparte. The particulars were disclosed by his movements; but
exact information has also been obtained through Major Napier of
the 50th regiment. This Officer at the battle of Corunna was stabbed
in the body by a bayonet, and wounded in the head by a sword, yet
he defended his life till quarter was promised him. When a prisoner

he was treated most handsomely by the Duke of Dalmatia. He dined with Marshal Ney frequently, who as well as General La Borde, the Chief of l'Etat Major, and other Officers of rank, frankly told him the design and sentiments of the Emperor. When Buonaparte received intelligence that the British were moving to the Duero, he said, " Moore is the only General now fit to contend with me ; I " shall advance against him in person."

Orders were then sent to the Duke of Dalmatia to give way, if attacked, and to decoy the British to Burgos, or as far Eastward as possible ; and at the same time to push on a corps towards Leon, on their left flank. And should they attempt to retreat, he was ordered to impede this by every means in his power. The corps on the road to Badajos was stopt, and ordered to proceed towards Salamanca ; while he himself moved rapidly with all the disposable force at Madrid, and the Escurial, directly to Benavente. Neither Buonaparte nor any of his Generals had the least doubt of surrounding the British with between 60 and 70,000 men before they could reach Galicia.

Sir John Moore, as appears both by his letters and his conduct, saw clearly the whole of this plan : he had prepared for the danger ; calculated the time ; and has acquired the glory of being the first General who has frustrated Buonaparte.

After having fully concerted the scheme of his retreat, he wrote again to the Marquis.

### Sir John Moore to the Marquis of Romana.

" SIR, *Sahagun, Dec. 24th*, 1808.

" My information this morning states that the French " have received reinforcements. I shall begin my retreat to-morrow " morning with a part of the infantry ; the rest will follow with the

" Cavalry the day after. It is of great importance to me, that you
" should keep a strong corps at Mansilla, to defend the bridge there,
" whilst I march in two divisions on Valencia and Benavente. The
" corps which passes at Valencia will remain on the opposite side to
" guard the Ferry, until the corps which marches on Benavente has
" passed the bridge at that place. Sir David Baird commands the
" division which goes to Valencia: I shall march with the other to
" Benavente. My hopes are to cross the river Eslar before I am in-
" terrupted: when once across, my communications with the Galicias
" will be secure; and, if pressed then, I shall have no objection to
" try an action.

" I have thought it right to make this communication to your Ex-
" cellency. You will, I suppose, think it right when I am passed,
" to order the boats upon the river to be destroyed. I have only to
" repeat my request, that Astorga and its neighbourhood may be
" left for the British troops, together with the passage into the Gali-
" cias; and not occupied by those under your Excellency's command.
" You will find no inclination in me to abandon the Spanish cause;
" but, on the contrary, every desire to co-operate with you for the
" general good.

" I have the honour to be, &c.

" JOHN MOORE."

On the 24th of December Sir John Moore was silently, but busily
occupied in preparing to retire; which, in the presence of an enemy,
is the most difficult of all military operations. But, to judge of it on
this occasion, the Map of Spain with the relative positions of the
French army, should be examined.

The Duke of Dalmatia received strong reinforcements from the
22nd to the 24th; so that his army alone was much superior to the
British. It was posted behind the river Carrion, between Carrion
and Saldana.

The Duke of Abrantes had advanced from Burgos to Palentia, and threatened the right flank of the British.

Buonaparte pushed on the corps at the Escurial, and marched from Madrid on the 18th in person, with an army consisting of 32,000 infantry and 8000 cavalry. The advanced-guard of this cavalry passed through Tordesillas on the 24th; the same day the van of the British left Sahagun; and both moved to the same point — Benavente.

There was another corps on the road to Badajos commanded by the Duke of Dantzic: this had advanced to Talavera de la Reina; and had pushed on as far as Arzo-Bispo, in pursuit of the Spanish General Galuzo. This was likewise counter-marched, and was directed towards Salamanca. Even the division under the Duke of Trevise, which was proceeding to Saragossa, was stopt: and the long, meditated vengeance against that heroic city was deferred.

In fine, the whole disposable force of the French army, forming an irregular crescent, was marching in radii with rapid steps to environ the British. To accomplish this favourite object, Buonaparte stopt his victorious career to the South, where there was nothing capable of resisting him. Lisbon and Cadiz would have yielded as easily as Madrid\*; and those must be sanguine indeed, who can believe that any further resistance would have been made by Spain.

---

\* In confirmation of this, the following is an extract of a letter from a person in the confidence of Government, to Sir John Moore.

*" Seville, Jan. 10th, 1809.*

" ALTHOUGH the Junta are daily pushed to induce them to give orders for " the advance of every thing South of Madrid towards the Capital, I do not ob- " serve that this measure appears hitherto to have taken up the attention of the " Enemy, who are steadily determined to attend to no other object until he shall " have measured his strength with your army: which is now certainly the only hope " of this country. For it is merely the time and breath they gain during this effort " of Buonaparte, which will enable them to bring together a force fit to continue " the contest."

The bold measures, adopted by Sir John Moore, arrested the immediate subjugation of this country. It remains to be seen how he extricated his army from its perilous situation.

The intelligence he had got was sufficiently founded to induce him to retire; but he had not yet learned the whole amount of the force that was marching against him, and was resolved not to be alarmed into a false step, nor retreat one step farther than was absolutely necessary. He wished to defend the Galicias, if possible.

His first object was to pass the river Eslar without interruption. There are three routes across this river: the first is by Mansilla, where there is a good bridge; the second is by Valencia where there was only a ferry; and the third is by Castro Gonsalo, where there is also a bridge; this last road leads to Benavente. It was impossible to go by Mansilla, as the Marquis of Romana's troops were there, and the country was completely exhausted by them. There were great objections to the whole army attempting the passage by the ferry at Valencia: for the intelligence received was, that the river was rapidly increasing, so that the ford would probably be too deep, and the boats were few. These circumstances would render the passage of the whole army very tedious at this point. And besides, an adequate supply of food could not be found; nor could covering, which was necessary at this season, be had for the whole army on one route.

It was, however, quite requisite to secure Valencia to stop the Enemy. Sir David Baird was, therefore, directed to take that route; and it was resolved that the rest of the army should proceed by Castro Gonsalo.

By this division of the army also the magazines and stores, which were deposited at Benavente and Zamora, were effectually covered.

The road by Leon was necessarily left to the troops of the Marquis of Romana: who, in consequence of the request of Sir John Moore to defend the passage of the river, left three thousand men there, and four pieces of cannon, and then retreated to Leon. He wrote a few lines to express a wish for a conference with Sir John Moore; to which note the following answer was returned.

*Sir John Moore to the Marquis of Romana.*

" SIR, *Sahagun, Dec.* 24, 1808.

" I HAD the honour to receive your Excellency's letter of " this date. There is nothing I wish so much as to have a personal " interview with you : but in the present situation of this army it " is impossible for me to leave it for a moment. Once across the " Eslar, and I will ride any distance to have the honour of meet- " ing you. I shall remain here with the Cavalry until the after- " noon to-morrow, and shall leave them to join the division of the " Infantry in the evening, which will be at Majorga.

" If your Excellency can make it convenient to come there, you " will make me very happy : but if this be inconvenient, I shall go " to you when I reach Benavente. The French continue to receive " reinforcements. A considerable number arrived at Palencia this " morning.

" I have the honour to be, &c.

" JOHN MOORE."

Two of the roads over the Eslar were thus occupied by the British and one by the Spanish army. But, as the latter was the nearest route to Astorga, it was of great importance that the Enemy should be retarded there. The Bridge of Mansilla and the City of Leon, were points to defend : and the following letter from Col. Symes will shew the expectations that were held out of defending Leon.

*Colonel Symes to Sir John Moore.*

" SIR,                                   *Mansilla, Dec. 25, 1808, One o'Clock.*

" I HAD the honour of your note early this morning,
" and am fully aware of the necessity which prevents a meeting be-
" tween your Excellency and the Marquis, at present.  The Mar-
" quis, for reasons of the same nature, cannot leave his troops:
" indeed, his presence is indispensibly requisite, for he has no second
" to whom he can confide his charge.  General Blake is at Leon.
" The Marquis says, that wherever else he may go, it is impossible
" for him to send any part of his troops into the Asturias, as the
" roads are now impassable ; the snow has fallen in unusual quantity.
" The Marquis's idea seems to be that of retiring on Astorga, but not
" precipitately : to put Leon in the best possible state of defence, and
" to leave there 2000 men and some guns.  These troops, when added
" to the armed inhabitants and the volunteers who are armed and under
" a sort of training, may impede the progress of an Enemy — give
" him much trouble, and afford protection to your left flank.  The
" Volunteers of Leon, including the students, are estimated at from
" 12 to 1500 men ; the rabble are numerous.

" The City of Leon is very extensive ; it is surrounded by a high
" wall, in some places ruinous.  There are old Moorish Towers at
" irregular distances ; several gateways without gates, but a little
" trouble may repair the chasms, and blockade the gateways.  The
" suburbs embrace the wall, which, in some parts, forms a back for
" long rows of mean houses.  The city is not commanded — there is
" some rising ground about a mile and a half distant, to the East and
" North ; excepting this, the country seems to be an uninterrupted

" plain for many miles.   Between Leon and Astorga it is a continued
" flat, without enclosure or obstacle to oppose the advance of troops
" from any direction.   Leon, if disputed vigorously, may prove very
" embarrassing to the Enemy, and it is a kind of warfare for which
" the Spaniards seem adapted.   The Marquis appears rather dis-
" posed to risk a general action ; but he says, what is too true, that
" his army, *in effect*, is no army.   He thinks that his artillery will
" be well served — it may be so, but I doubt.   Two howitzers and
" eighteen field-pieces compose the number of guns with us.   We
" move to Leon to-day.   The Marquis communicates to your Excel-
" lency the intelligence he has received.   Mansilla is not capable of
" defence; and breaking the bridge, the Marquis thinks, will not be
" any material obstacle to the Enemy.   In the present state of the
" weather I think it would impede his progress.

" I am, Sir, with great respect,

" Your faithful humble servant,

" M. SYMES."

According to the arrangement which was made, General Fraser, followed by General Hope, marched with their divisions on the 24th of December to Valderos and Majorga; and Sir David Baird proceeded with his to Valencia.   To conceal this movement Lord Paget was ordered to push on strong patroles of Cavalry close to the advanced posts of the Enemy.

The reserve, with two light corps, did not retire from Sahagun till the morning of the 25th; they followed General Hope.   Lord Paget was ordered to remain with the cavalry until the evening, and then follow the reserve.   Sir John accompanied these last corps.

The retreat commenced in this deliberate manner.   On the 26th of December Sir David Baird reached the Eslar, and passed the ferry with less difficulty than was expected.   He took post, according to his orders, at Valencia, and wrote to the Marquis of Romana urging him to blow up the bridge of Mansilla.

The other divisions of Infantry proceeded unmolested to Castro Gonsalo.

On the 24th of December the advanced guard of Buonaparte's army marched from Tordesillas, which is a hundred and twenty miles from Madrid, and fifty from Benavente; and strong detachments of Cavalry had been pushed forward to Villalpando and Majorga. On the 26th Lord Paget fell in with one of those detachments at the latter place. His Lordship immediately ordered Colonel Leigh, with two squadrons of the 10th Hussars, to attack this corps, which had halted on the summit of a steep hill. One of Colonel Leigh's squadrons was kept in reserve; the other rode briskly up the hill: on approaching the top, where the ground was rugged, the Colonel judiciously reined-in to refresh the horses, though exposed to a severe fire from the Enemy. When he had nearly gained the summit, and the horses had recovered their breath, he charged boldly and overthrew the Enemy: many of whom were killed and wounded, and above a hundred surrendered prisoners.

Nothing could exceed the coolness and gallantry displayed by the British Cavalry on this occasion. The 18th Dragoons had signalized themselves in several former skirmishes; they were successful in six different attacks. Captain Jones, when at Palencia, had even ventured to charge a hundred French Dragoons with only thirty British; fourteen of the Enemy were killed, and six taken prisoners.

The cavalry, the horse-artillery, and a light corps remained on the night of the 26th at Castro Gonsalo; and the divisions under Generals Hope and Fraser marched to Benavente.

On the 27th the rear-guard crossed the Eslar, and followed the same route, after completely blowing up the bridge.

It now becomes requisite to make a very painful confession. The army, which, during the advance, had been distinguished for regularity and good conduct, began to display on the retreat a very opposite behaviour. This may in part be imputed to inattention in the Spanish Magistrates; who, instead of exerting themselves to procure lodgings and necessaries for the troops, sometimes fled or hid themselves. But another cause of these disorders was, undoubtedly, the independent character of Britons; who always submit to military discipline with great reluctance. They were indignant at the little assistance afforded them by the Spaniards; and took the opportunity which the retreat afforded them, of throwing off restraint, of displaying their native humours, and of acting too much as they pleased.

But, whatever was the cause, the General was most desirous to stop this misconduct; both from humanity to the Spaniards, and for the safety of his own army. He, therefore, issued out the following order.

#### " GENERAL ORDERS.

*Head Quarters, Benavente, 27th Dec.*

" THE Commander of the Forces has observed with con-
" cern, the extreme bad conduct of the troops at a moment when
" they are about to come into contact with the Enemy, and when the
" greatest regularity and the best conduct are the most requisite. He
" is the more concerned at this, as, until lately, the behaviour of that
" part of the army, at least, which was under his own immediate com-
" mand, was exemplary, and did them much honour.

" The misbehaviour of the troops in the column which marched by
" Valderas to this place, exceeds what he could have believed of Bri-
" tish soldiers. It is disgraceful to the Officers; as it strongly marks
" their negligence and inattention.

" The Commander of the Forces refers to the General Orders of the
" 15th of October, and of the 11th of November. He desires that
" they may be again read at the head of every company of the army:

" he can add nothing but his determination to execute them to the
" fullest extent. He can feel no mercy towards Officers who neglect
" in times like these essential duties, or towards Soldiers who injure
" the country they are sent to protect. The Spanish Forces have
" been overpowered; and until such time as they are re-assembled,
" and ready again to come forward, the situation of the army must be
" arduous, and such as to call for the exertion of qualities the most
" rare and valuable in a military body. These are not bravery alone,
" but patience and constancy under fatigue and hardship, obedience
" to command, sobriety, firmness, and resolution, in every different
" situation in which they may be placed. It is by the display of such
" qualities alone, that the army can expect to deserve the name of
" Soldiers; that they can be able to withstand the forces opposed to
" them, or to fulfil the expectations of their Country.

" It is impossible for the General to explain to his army the motive
" for the movement he directs. The Commander of the Forces can,
" however, assure the army that he has made none since he left Sala-
" manca which he did not foresee, and was not prepared for; and,
" as far as he is a judge, they have answered the purposes for which
" they were intended.

" When it is proper to fight a battle he will do it; and he will
" choose the time and place he thinks most fit: in the mean time he
" begs the Officers and Soldiers of the army to attend diligently to
" discharge their parts, and to leave to him and to the General Officers
" the decision of measures which belong to them alone.

" The army may rest assured, that there is nothing he has more at
" heart than their honour—and that of their Country."

The latter part of the above order alluded to a number of Officers
having been indiscreetly free in their criticisms of the Military operations. This licence is characteristic of Englishmen: but in the pre-

sent situation of the army it had a most mischievous tendency. Besides, as Sir John Moore kept all his intelligence extremely secret, it was impossible for the officers to judge of the propriety of the movements.

Sir John Moore endeavoured to remove one of the causes of the irregular conduct by this letter to the Marquis.

*Sir John Moore to the Marquis of Romana.*

" SIR, *Benavente, 27 Dec.* 1808.

  " I HAD the honour to receive yesterday, on my arri-
" val here, your Excellency's letter from Mansilla, of the 25th.
" The Enemy are advancing; but I believe their main body only
" reached Valladolid yesterday. The movement I made to Sahagun
" has answered every purpose I had a right to expect. A little more
" good fortune would have enabled me to cut up Soult's corps; but
" the attention of the Enemy has at last been attracted from other
" objects. His march on Badajos has been stopped, and the forces
" in the South will have time to be formed, and to come forward.
" I shall continue my movement on Astorga. It is there, or behind
" it, we should fight a battle, if at all. If the Enemy follows so far,
" he will leave himself the more open to the efforts of the South.
" My opinion is, that a battle is the game of Buonaparte, not our's.
" We should, if followed, take defensive positions in the mountains,
" where his cavalry can be of no use to him; and there either engage
" him in an unequal contest with us, oblige him to employ a consi-
" derable corps to watch us, or to retire upon Madrid: in which last
" case we should again come forth into the plain. In this manner
" we give time for the arrival of reinforcements from England,—
" your army to be formed and equipped,—and that of the South to

" come forth. In short, the game of Spain and of England,
" which must always be the same, is to procrastinate and to gain
" time; and not, if it can be helped, to place the whole stake upon
" the hazard of a battle.

" The people of this part of Spain seem to be less well-disposed
" than those I have hitherto met with. They perhaps think that we
" mean to abandon them. It would have a good effect if you ex-
" plained to them, in a proclamation, that this was by no means
" either your intention, or that of the British army; and call upon
" the Alcaides and Corregidors to remain at their posts, and to be of
" all the use in their power to the different armies both Spanish and
" British. Some of them of late have run away from the towns;
" which has been the unavoidable cause of irregularities having been
" committed by the troops; for, when the Magistrates are not present
" to give regularly, the soldier must take, and this produces a mis-
" chievous habit.

" I have the honour to be, &c.

" JOHN MOORE."

During the march to Benavente a confidential person, whose
intelligence had always been correct, came up with the General at
Fuentes. He had passed Buonaparte and his army, who were making forced marches to overtake the British.

And it appeared from several accounts, that, in contradiction to
the declarations and information so repeatedly transmitted from
the Central Junta and Mr. Frere, not the slightest movement was
made by the Spanish armies; who permitted the various divisions
of the Enemy's army to traverse Spain, in every direction, with as
much tranquillity as France; with this essential difference, that the
Spaniards furnished them with every supply for nothing, whereas in
France they must have paid for what they wanted.

A A

Notwithstanding this unfavourable intelligence, Sir John Moore had still some expectations of being able to maintain a footing in Spain *. He hoped that the Spaniards, after all their declarations and promises, would rouse themselves to make some effort; and perhaps want of provisions for so large an army might stop the advance of the French. It was his earnest wish to maintain himself in the mountains of Galicia; and not to retire to the coast, unless compelled by great superiority of numbers.

There are two roads to Vigo; but that by Orense, though the shortest, is neither practicable for artillery, nor for any species of waggon; consequently the British army took the road by Astorga; and orders were now sent to Sir David Baird, who was still at Valentia, to march to that point; while on the 28th of December Generals Hope and Fraser proceeded with their divisions to La Banessa.

Next morning, at day-break, after near two days' rest, Sir John Moore followed with the reserve; and Lord Paget, as before, was ordered to bring up the rear with the cavalry.

But at nine o'clock in the morning, before his Lordship had moved, some of the Enemy's cavalry were observed trying a ford near the bridge which had been blown up; and presently between five and six hundred of the Imperial Guards of Buonaparte plunged into the river, and crossed over.

They were immediately opposed by the British piquets, who had been much divided to watch the different fords; but were quickly assembled by Colonel Otway. When united they amounted only to two hundred and twenty men. They retired slowly before such superior numbers, bravely disputing every inch of ground with the Enemy. The front squadrons repeatedly charged each other; and

* Vide Appendix, E E.

however, did not come up in time. Le Febvre owned to Sir John Moore, that when he saw nothing but the cavalry piquets, he concluded that all the rest of the army had left Benavente. This induced him to cross the river; and, when once over, he could not, he said, without fighting, retreat with such a corps as he commanded, with men who had put to flight thirty thousand Russians at Austerlitz.

As the soldier to whom he had surrendered had taken from him his sword, the General presented him with a fine East-Indian sabre.

Towards the evening the Enemy brought up some field-pieces, and cannonaded the piquets from the heights on the opposite side of the river; but without the least effect.

Lord Paget drew off the Cavalry at night, and followed the Reserve to La Banessa. As the intelligence and circumstances were still not so decisive as to enable Sir John Moore to determine whether he should in the last resource retire upon Vigo or Corunna, it was of importance that he should retain the power of choosing that port which would best suit his purposes. He, therefore, found it necessary to detach a light corps on the road to Orense, which is the shortest route to Vigo; foreseeing, that if he neglected this precaution, the Enemy might seize the road by one of their light detachments, precede the columns of the British by forced marches, and deprive them of the choice of Vigo; or, by seizing some of the passes in front, retard and embarrass the retreat exceedingly.

Besides these strong motives, provisions had become extremely deficient, and it was doubtful if the whole army could be tolerably subsisted on one road.

For these reasons General Craufurd was detached, with three thousand men lightly equipped, on the road to Orense. If pursued, he could take up a strong position behind the river Minho, and there check for some time the advance of the French.

The rest of the army proceeded to Astorga; and Sir David Baird's column, coming from Valencia, again united there with Sir John Moore; who was extremely disconcerted to find that the town was preoccupied, and filled with the troops of the Marquis of Romana.

This General did not destroy the bridge of Mansilla, as had been requested. The guard he left there was charged by a party of Soult's cavalry; and the Spaniards fled, or surrendered themselves prisoners.

The Duke of Dalmatia then advanced on this road to Leon; which City, instead of making the obstinate defence that was expected, opened its gates at once to the Enemy, and furnished them with as many rations as they required.

Thus was Sir John Moore perpetually disappointed in every assistance that was expected from the Spaniards. He had repeatedly requested the Marquis of Romana to leave the roads to Galicia clear for the British; and wished the Marquis to fall back upon the Asturias; because, when the Enemy proceeded towards Galicia, this Spanish army might have interrupted the French convoys, or compelled them to employ large detachments for their protection. In the Asturias they could certainly be eminently useful, and quite safe. But all remonstrances were in vain; the Marquis entertained a different opinion, and resolved to push across to Orense, in front of the British. Thus the Spanish army, instead of being of the slightest utility to the English, by consuming the provisions, and filling the roads with their mules and carts, were a most serious impediment.

The appearance of this army was extremely melancholy: it was ill armed, wretchedly clothed, and very sickly. But no reproach ought to be thrown upon these troops for the little resistance they made: their native courage is undoubted; and they endured the most cruel privations with the utmost patience. But their deplorable, almost famished condition, and the total want of officers, would have disheartened the bravest people.

Astorga was one of the depôts which had been formed for warlike stores, with the view of offensive operations in conjunction with the Spanish armies; which gave an opportunity of supplying the Marquis's troops with musquets, and as much ammunition as they could carry off. The rest was necessarily destroyed.

The corps under Sir David Baird had brought their camp equipage from Corunna to Astorga, and had deposited it there. But this was no country for such conveniences: there were no means of removing it, and the whole was ordered to be consumed. Many officers had brought along with them a considerable quantity of baggage, and the overloaded mules fell behind. But the General would not suffer a soldier to be detained by the baggage; and gave strict orders, that every horse or mule that could not keep up with the columns should be abandoned.

Being most anxious for the good conduct of the Troops, he issued the following encouraging order.

### " GENERAL ORDERS.

" *Head Quarters, Astorga,* 30*th Dec.* 1808.

" THE present is a moment when the Army is neces-" sarily called upon to make great efforts, and to submit to pri-" vations, the bearing cheerfully with which is a quality not less " estimable than valour.

" The good-will of the inhabitants will be particularly useful to " the Army, and can only be obtained by good conduct on the part " of the Troops.

" The Commander of the Forces cannot impress too strongly on " the whole Army the necessity of this; and he trusts that the

" Generals and the Commanding Officers will adopt such measures,
" both on the march and in the cantonments, as will ensure it.

" It is very probable that the Army will shortly have to meet the
" Enemy; and the Commander of the Forces has no doubt that they
" will eagerly imitate the worthy example which has been set them
" by the Cavalry, on several recent occasions, and particularly in the
" affair of yesterday; in which Brigadier-general Stuart, with an
" inferior force, charged and overthrew one of the best corps of
" Cavalry in the French Army.

" The Generals will immediately inspect the baggage of the bri-
" gades and divisions. They are held responsible that it does not
" exceed the proportion fixed by the General Orders."

It is known that Buonaparte had fully expected to have reached
Benavente as soon as, or before, the British; and the Duke of Dalmatia hoped, that they would be so much retarded by Buonaparte's
attacks, that he might, by forced marches through Leon, precede
them at Astorga. The little resistance made by the Spaniards at
Mansilla, and the immediate submission of Leon, facilitated this
plan. Had either been in time, the British would have been surrounded. But Buonaparte was anticipated in both his projects; and,
while a part of his cavalry was repulsed by Lord Paget, the van of the
British Army, under General Fraser, entered and secured Astorga.

The advanced guard, and the main body of the British Army, on
the 30th of December, moved on to Villa Franca; and Sir John Moore,
with General Paget and the reserve, followed on the 31st. They
marched to Camberos that evening; and the cavalry followed at
night. The piquets on the road from La Beneza, who were posted
to watch Buonaparte's cavalry, and those at the bridge at Orbigo
to attend to Soult's, retired as the Enemy advanced. The cavalry
reached Camberos at midnight; when immediately the reserve pro-

ceeded, and arrived next morning (Jan. 1) at Bembydre, precisely as the preceding divisions were marching off to Villa Franca.

The scene of drunkenness that presented itself here was disgusting. The stragglers from the preceding divisions so crowded the houses, that there was hardly accommodation for the reserve: while groups of the half-naked and unfortunate peasants belonging to the Marquis of Romana completed the confusion. The Marquis was moving towards Orense; but his troops were dispersed in all directions, filling the neighbouring towns.

The French were following so close, that their patroles, during the night, fell in with the cavalry piquets.

When Buonaparte reached Astorga he was joined by the Duke of Dalmatia. The whole Army that was assembled there amounted to near 70,000 men, independently of other corps, which were countermanded from their former destination, though not yet come up. It is natural to imagine that a man so accustomed to succeed in all his plans must have been bitterly disappointed to find that, notwithstanding his exertions, the British were beyond his reach. He here reviewed this immense force; and perceiving, by the masterly arrangements of his Enemy, that it was no longer possible to intercept him, he halted to watch the event. Three Marshals of France, with as many divisions, were commanded to follow the British closely, and to destroy them, either before or during their embarkation. And some other corps followed those divisions, to support them.

Although the Enemy had hitherto been completely frustrated, yet a multitude of severe distresses were now accumulating upon the British, which the prudence of their Leader could not avert. Deluges of cold rain fell, chilling and drenching the soldiers, who were wading in bad roads deep with mud. It was often difficult to procure shelter when they halted; or fuel to dry their clothes, or to dress their food. The provisions were often scanty, and irregularly procured; for the baggage, magazines, and stores, were transported on carts, drawn chiefly by Spanish mules and bullocks; but the drivers, terrified by the approach and attacks of the French cavalry, often ran away in the night-time, leaving their waggons; persuaded, that if they fell into the hands of the French they would be massacred. The bullocks and mules, unfortunately, could not be made to move, except by the native drivers. Thus provisions and stores were frequently obliged to be destroyed, to prevent their falling into the possession of the Enemy; and, for the same reason, the weak, the sick, and the wounded, were necessarily left behind.

Truth makes it necessary to mention, that the inhabitants of Spain gave little aid to their persevering Allies, who were encountering every evil for them, and made no attempt to annoy, or to retard the Enemy. Had the armed Spaniards harassed the flanks and rear of the French Army, they might, with little danger to themselves, have retarded their advance, and diminished their numbers; instead of which, they never fired a musket at a Frenchman; and often fled from their houses at the approach of the English; barring their doors, and carrying off mules, carts, oxen, forage, and provisions; in short, whatever could lessen the distresses, or contribute to the comfort of their friends. This conduct on the part of the Spaniards excited much animosity in the breasts of the English, and was the cause of many disorders. But I have no doubt that the passive conduct of the peasantry was owing to their rulers never organising them, nor leading them forward. Sir John Moore always entertained this opinion. In his Journal and letters he praises the people, and deprecates the apathy and weakness of their Chiefs; for he was not aware that there were traitors among them, who paralysed the Nation.

It has been mentioned, that, on the 1st of January, the General found the little town of Bembydre filled with stragglers of the preceding divisions. And when he marched with the reserve and the cavalry to Villafranca on the morning of the 2nd, he left Colonel Ross with the 20th regiment, and a small detachment of cavalry, to cover the town, while parties were sent to warn the stragglers, amounting to near a thousand men, of their danger, and to drive them, if possible, out of the houses. Some few were prevailed upon to move on; but neither threats, nor the approach of the Enemy, could induce the greater number to quit the houses. At length the rear-guard was compelled to march and leave these senseless people to their fate: yet a small detachment of cavalry covered the whole, and only quitted the town on the approach of the Enemy: then, from the immediate danger, the road was filled with Spanish and British stragglers (armed and unarmed), mules, carts, women and children, all mingled in strange confusion.

Four or five squadrons of French Cavalry were seen moving from Bembydre, their advanced-guard firing at a patrole of the 15th Hussars. On their approach the detachment in the rear was compelled to retire, and were closely pursued for several miles. As the French dragoons galloped through the long line of stragglers, they slashed them with their swords mercilessly to the right and left: and these men were so insensible from liquor, as neither to make resistance nor get out of the road. The pursuit continued till checked by General Paget with the reserve, who repulsed them.

The reserve halted at Cacabelos, and the greatest part of the cavalry at Villafranca. On arriving at this town the General heard with vexation, that great irregularities had also been committed there by the preceding divisions. The Commissaries reported that the Magazines had been plundered, stores of wine had been broke open, and a great quantity of forage and provisions spoiled. One man who was detected in committing these atrocities was made an example of, in the hope of preventing such crimes in future: and, to convince the soldiers of the miserable consequences of their drunkenness, and of quitting their corps, some of those stragglers who had been shockingly mangled by the cavalry, were shewn through the ranks. Thus every measure was adopted that prudence could devise, to put a stop to this bad conduct.

On the 3rd of January four or five thousand French cavalry were seen (at one o'clock in the forenoon) advancing cautiously within a league of Cacabelos. The 95th and a detachment of British cavalry occupied a hill about half a league in front of the town, through which a shallow river ran, and part of the reserve was posted on the opposite bank.

Sir John Moore commanded the 95th to retire through the town and over a bridge. But while the two rear companies were passing along a narrow street, the cavalry piquet retreated precipitately through them, and the Enemy's cavalry pursued so closely that some few soldiers of the 95th were made prisoners. The Enemy's dismounted chasseurs immediately advanced rapidly, crossed the river in great force, and attacked the 95th, the cavalry joining in the onset.

The 95th were directed to retreat up some hills among vineyards; which they did slowly in a very gallant manner, galling the Enemy with a well-aimed fire from their rifles.

The French cavalry charged up the road, but were driven back with considerable slaughter by the 95th. General Colbert, who commanded the advanced-guard of the French, was among the slain.

A large column of the Enemy were next observed descending the hill on the opposite side of the river. Immediately the artillery attached to the reserve opened upon this column a severe fire, which stopt their movement. In this attack the Enemy suffered much. Sir John Moore towards the evening withdrew the reserve to Villafranca; and being aware that the greater part of the Enemy's army were very near, he resolved to make a night march to Herrerias.

The country now being inclosed and mountainous, the cavalry were sent on before to Lugo; the reserve did not quit Villafranca till ten o'clock at night, and arrived at Herrerias at midnight.

The General here received a favourable description of the ground in front of Lugo; and as he perceived that the Enemy were pressing hard upon him, he conceived that it would be more advantageous to fight them there, than to suffer his troops to be continually harassed on the march.

He therefore came to the determination to offer battle at Lugo; and wrote dispatches to Sir David, who was far in front, to halt there. He inclosed in the packet letters to be forwarded, with similar orders, to Generals Hope and Fraser who commanded the advanced divisions.

This dispatch being of the utmost importance, Sir John Moore sent it by his Aid-de-Camp (Captain Napier), accompanied by an orderly dragoon. Capt. Napier reached Nogales, and delivered it with the inclosures to Sir David Baird, who forwarded them to the respective officers. The orderly dragoon who was entrusted with these last letters got drunk on the road, and lost them.

By this unlucky accident General Fraser, with his division, proceeded a full day's journey towards Vigo, the original destination, and was countermarched next day. The weather was dreadful; so that this division instead of comfortably resting these two days at Lugo, as was intended, were excessively harassed, and lost many men from fatigue.

Accounts were this day (January 4th) received from Engineers, and others, respecting Vigo and Corunna. The report respecting the peninsula of Betanzos was the most favourable; and as Vigo was three long marches more distant, Sir John Moore determined to retreat towards Corunna, in preference to Vigo. He sent off immediately two expresses, by different routes, to Rear-Admiral Sir Samuel Hood, to request he would send round the transports to Corunna. To this place letters were likewise sent, that provisions might be forwarded, and preparations made for the reception of the troops.

While the reserve were marching towards Nogales, they found between thirty and forty waggons with stores for the Marquis of Romana's army. These waggons were filled with arms, ammunition, shoes, and clothing from England: for by the arrangement that the Spaniards observed, their army was left destitute of every necessary, and abundant supplies were now moving on the road — precisely at the time the French were advancing. No stronger presumptive proof could be brought of treason having deeply pervaded the Spanish councils.

There were no means of carrying back these stores: some of the shoes, and such things as could be made use of, were distributed to the troops as they passed, and the rest were destroyed.

On a hill above Nogales there were some artillery waggons belonging to the Spaniards which had been abandoned: and two soldiers and a woman, who had drunk to excess, were lying dead in the snow. This was a shocking scene. The reserve reached Nogales in the afternoon, and here Sir John learnt the provoking loss of his dispatch, and the march of General Fraser's division on the Vigo road.

On the morning of the 5th of January the reserve left Nogales; the Enemy entering the town soon after the rear quitted it. There was a bridge here, which for want of a sufficiency of proper tools was not completely destroyed; but this was of little importance as the river was fordable. There were some Officers who criticised, occasionally, the operations that were adopted, in a manner injurious to the service; and this subject of blowing up bridges was one of those upon which they chiefly dwelt. General Paget at length mentioned this to Sir John Moore, and pressed him to destroy more bridges.

Sir John, in answer, requested him to look around and examine with him more particularly the nature of the rivers over which these bridges were thrown. He pointed out to him, that both infantry and cavalry could usually pass a little above or below the bridge: and that the obstruction to artillery would be quickly repaired by an army constituted like the French. That it must likewise be recollected, that the destruction of these strong bridges could not be soon effected; and that the troops must halt during that time. So that when this loss was deducted, it would be found that the advantage was much less considerable than was imagined. Whenever any important advantage could arise from blowing up a bridge, he thought it certainly should be done: but he was persuaded that General Paget would agree with him, that when the advantage was less, it was a cruel measure to do such lasting mischief to those allies we came to benefit, as to ruin, for a length of time, the communications of their country.

This was the defence that Sir John Moore made, for what some, perhaps, thought a neglect; but which increased General Paget's esteem for his friend and commander.

The Rifle Corps, which always marched with the reserve, covered the rear; and the Enemy being close at hand it was engaged nearly the whole of this day. In such circumstances it was impossible to suffer any thing to retard the march of the column: whatever could not keep up was therefore destroyed.

There were even two carts with dollars to the amount of five and twenty thousand pounds, which fell behind. This money had been brought forward from Corunna with Sir David Baird's corps, and was under the charge of Mr. Courtney belonging to the Paymaster-general's department. The means provided for its conveyance were insufficient; for the carts were drawn by tardy bullocks who were quite exhausted by fatigue, and could not be got on. After every effort was made in vain, the casks were at length rolled down a precipice on the side of the road, and the advanced-guard of the French passed the place in five minutes afterwards. It was afterwards learnt by some prisoners, that this money was found by the Spanish peasants.

There is a hill above Constantino, and the General feared that in descending the column would be severely annoyed. To protect it he halted the Rifle Corps and Horse Artillery at the top of the hill; and as the road was winding and exposed, their position was good. In the mean time the remainder of the reserve retired over the hill. The Enemy perceiving that if they advanced they would be saluted with the guns, halted their column for more than half an hour behind another hill: and, as soon as the rear of the reserve had nearly reached the bridge of Constantino, and were in safety, the Artillery and Rifle Corps suddenly retired also, and the whole passed over without loss.

Upon this occasion the Enemy acted with excess of caution, but afterwards poured down the hill. General Paget was then ordered to defend the bridge and the banks of the river, with the 28th and 95th; while Sir John Moore drew up the 52nd, 20th, and 91st regiments on a strong position on the top of a hill near the river: the Horse-artillery were likewise well posted. This position was hardly taken when the attack commenced. The Enemy's cavalry and dismounted chasseurs attempted to pass the bridge, but the well-directed fire of the artillery and of the rear-guard drove them quickly back. They repeatedly advanced, for the skirmishing continued till night, the Enemy's numbers always augmenting; but General Paget maintained the bridge, and preserved his position.

At eleven at night General Paget received orders to retire to Lugo, while the remainder of the reserve were under arms to protect him. The reserve were much fatigued by their exertions, and were quartered near Lugo. The following Order was issued next day.

## GENERAL ORDERS.

" *Head Quarters, Lugo, 6th January,* 1809.

" Generals and Commanding Officers of Corps must be as
"sensible as the Commander of the Forces, of the complete disorga-
" nization of the army.

" The advanced-guard of the French is already close to us, and it
" is to be presumed that the main body is not far distant; an action
" may, therefore, be hourly expected. If the Generals and Command-
" ing Officers of Regiments (feeling for the honour of their country
" and of the British arms) wish to give the army a fair chance of
" success, they will exert themselves to restore order and discipline
" in the regiments, brigades, and divisions which they command.

" The Commander of the Forces is tired of giving Orders which
" are never attended to: he therefore appeals to the honour and feel-
" ings of the Army he commands; and if those are not sufficient to
" induce them to do their duty, he must despair of succeeding by any
" other means. He was forced to order one soldier to be shot at
" Villafranca, and he will order all others to be executed who are
" guilty of similar enormities: but he considers that there would be
" no occasion to proceed to such extremities if the Officers did their
" duty: as it is chiefly from their negligence, and from the want of
" proper regulations in the regiments, that crimes and irregularities
" are committed, in quarters and upon the march."

The remarks in this Order are extremely severe; but this was not a
moment to employ flattery. It was undoubtedly right to adopt whatever measure would succeed best to restore order; and it was expected
that the appeal to the honour of the Officers was most likely to stimu-

late them to make every exertion. Nor was the Commander disappointed.

On examining the ground near Lugo, a position was found on which he would have been happy to have engaged. The Enemy appeared about mid-day, but nothing serious occurred.

Next morning (January 7th) the French planted four pieces of artillery on the front of the British, and commenced a cannonade. The fire was returned by the British Artillery, who dismounted one of the Enemy's guns. Towards the evening some French regiments attacked the right of the British, and were chiefly opposed by the Guards and General Leith's brigade.

Sir John Moore then observed the Enemy moving to his left, his light troops skirmishing with the piquets. He conceived that the principal attack would be made on that point, and the proper orders were immediately given.

The divisions were all at their posts, and he gallopped to the spot.

A part of the 76th regiment at first retired before a strong column of the Enemy, at the head of which was their much-esteemed 2nd light infantry battalion, which advanced rapidly.

The General, by accident, found himself in front of the 51st regiment, in which he had served as an Ensign. He addressed them in an animated tone, and commanded them to advance : when the light company of the 76th rushed forward with charged bayonets, and drove the Enemy down the hill with considerable loss.

In this sharp skirmish Captain Roberts of the 51st was shot in the hand, but before the Frenchman could recover his musket he was transfixed by a soldier of the 76th named Canner. This brave fellow bayoneted two other Frenchmen, and was rewarded by promotion.

The General having witnessed this gallant attack, bestowed deserved praises upon the 76th.

The Enemy after this repulse returned no more : and Sir John thence conjectured that Marshal Soult's design had been to reconnoitre his position, previously to an attack which he expected to be made next morning.

To prepare and animate the army he threw out this Order.

## " GENERAL ORDERS.

"*Near Lugo, 7th January,* 1809.

" THE Army must see that the moment is now come
" when, after the hardships and fatiguing marches they have under-
" gone, they will have the opportunity of bringing the Enemy to ac-
" tion.  The Commander of the Forces has the most perfect confi-
" dence in their valour, and that it is only necessary to bring them to
" close contact with the Enemy in order to defeat them ; and a defeat,
" if it be complete, as he trusts it will be, will, in a great measure,
" end their labours.

" The General has no other caution to give them, than not to
" throw away their fire at the Enemy's skirmishers, merely because
" they fire at them ; but to reserve it till they can give it with effect."

The General had received certain intelligence that three divisions of the French army were now in his front; which, though a force considerably superior to his own, he wished to engage.  He knew he could not get rid of them, and he conceived it more advantageous to fight in his present position, than either at Betanzos or in the act of embarking.

The artillery, under the excellent direction of Colonel Harding, was drawn into the field with great labour, and judiciously planted. The preparations for the reception of the Enemy continued till night.

It is proper now to recal to the reader's recollection, the positive assurance given by the Central Junta to Sir John Moore, on the 8th of December, that in a month 44,000 Spanish soldiers should be united to his army. And to stamp this engagement with complete validity, they deputed a Member of the Junta to confirm it *.

Mr. Frere, being determined that every thing should be done to give full authority to this mission, and to convince the General that implicit reliance ought to be placed on the Spanish Declaration, deputed also Charles Stuart, Esq. the diplomatic agent, to introduce the Spanish Deputy, and to present Mr. Frere's letter from Truxillo. It appears from that letter that Mr. Frere stifled his feelings to avoid giving offence to Sir John Moore, but thought proper to mention to him, that, if he persisted in his own measures, he would bring indelible disgrace upon his Country, and do the utmost possible mischief to the cause of Spain, exclusive of attacking the Spanish army.

It was hardly possible to doubt the fulfilment of an engagement voluntarily contracted by the Spanish Government, confirmed by the British Minister, and presented with so much solemnity. But the month is now expired, and not a Spanish soldier is to be seen. The British army has been followed and assailed by all the disposable French army, and is totally abandoned by the Spaniards; who neither unite with them, according to their own stipulation, nor has a single Spanish Corps advanced to attack, or even to threaten the French posts, now weakened by the absence of their army.

Thus was Sir John Moore again deceived by a mission from the Spanish Government and the British Minister; and his devoted troops had nothing to trust to but their arms, and their General.

* Vide page 134 to 139.

Early in the morning of the 8th of January the army was marshalled in array, and offered battle to the Enemy. The Commander rode through the ranks, and had the pleasure of finding that, in consequence of the Orders he had issued, of the exertions of the officers, and, above all, of the hopes of an action, regularity was restored. The artillery, cavalry, and reserve, who had been so often engaged, were envied by the other divisions, who wished also to have their share of fighting. When the General perceived that the troops were obedient to command, and full of confidence, he was satisfied, and longed for the advance of the Enemy.

But Marshal Soult stirred not from his post. He had now experienced the talents of the General, and the intrepidity of the troops he had to encounter.

From this backwardness it was concluded, that his intention was to harass the British as much as possible during their march, and to defer his attack till the embarkation.

On the other hand the British Commander perceived, that it would be equally imprudent for him to attack the strong position of the French, or to remain longer in his own.

If he advanced, Marshal Soult was posted on formidable heights, protected by enclosures, and could not be approached without great loss. He might engage partially, and retire when he pleased: if such an attack failed, the army was undone; and even if it succeeded, the situation of the British would only be rendered worse; for reinforcements would soon join the Enemy; the retreat must be resumed, and every wounded man left behind.

It was also deemed impossible to remain in their present position; for the numbers of the French would soon become too great to be withstood; or they might push on corps on either flank by the lateral roads, cut off the communication with the coast, and surround the British. But, even if these dangers could have been hazarded, it was impossible to remain two days, from the want of provisions. The country could furnish nothing more, and adequate means for conveying supplies from Corunna were wanting. The Commissariat was by no means on a scale for such measures, and the British army was too weak to guard the convoys.

To retreat to the coast was, therefore, indispensable; and to avoid the annoyance of attacks on the rear-guard, and to elude the Enemy, the General resolved to march off that night.

The different brigades were directed to quit the ground at ten o'clock at night, leaving fires burning to deceive the Enemy. But, owing to the darkness of the night, the badness of the roads, and mistakes of the guides, some of the columns did not reach the walls of Lugo till two o'clock in the morning. They, however, proceeded, though it rained the whole night, and the following day.

Before the reserve left Lugo the General published another warning, to repress the irregularities of the march.

## " GENERAL ORDERS.

*" Head Quarters, Lugo, 9th January, 1809.*

" It is evident that the Enemy will not fight this " Army, notwithstanding the superiority of his numbers; but will " endeavour to harass and tease it upon its march.

" The Commander of the Forces requests that it may be carefully " explained to the Soldiers, that their safety depends solely upon " their keeping their divisions, and marching with their regiments; " that those who stop in villages, or straggle on the march, will " inevitably be cut off by the French cavalry; who have hitherto " shewn little mercy even to the feeble and infirm, who have fallen " into their hands.

" The army has still eleven leagues to march, the soldiers must
" make an exertion to accomplish them; the rear-guard cannot stop,
" and those who fall behind must take their fate."

Unfortunately, no attempt to preserve regularity on the march
was altogether effectual. The corps in which there was the least
straggling were, the Artillery, the Guards, and the Reserve. The
Artillery consist of peculiarly well-behaved men; the Guards were
the strongest body of men in the army, and consequently suffered least
from fatigue: besides, they are strictly disciplined, and their non-
commissioned officers are excellent. The Reserve was commanded
by an indefatigable Officer, and the regiments that composed it were
admirable.

On this day's march, the first halt was at Valmeda; and, as
there was no shelter, they were obliged to remain exposed to a
torrent of rain. The different columns were ordered to be again
under arms early in the evening; but many of the regiments had
been severely harassed, by being called out by their commanding
officers, on false alarms. The fatigue sustained and the hardships
suffered were very great, and scarcely to be endured by the weak.
Sore feet afflicted many, and rendered it impossible for them to keep
their ranks; but others left them from the love of wine, and perhaps
from worse motives.

Marshal Soult was, however, able to take little advantage of these
circumstances. The mortifying checks he had received on the 5th
and 7th of January, and the menacing attitude of the Army on the
8th, had alarmed him; and, by the sudden retreat of the British, so
much ground was gained, that he was completely baffled. For the
French did not discover the retreat till long after day-light; and
their cavalry were not prepared to leave Lugo till after nine in the
morning of the 9th.

This gave much time, and the only difficulty was the protection of the loiterers. The advanced-guard of the Enemy at length came up in the evening, and hung upon the rear. And General Paget, with the reserve, was ordered to take up a position, for the protection of the stragglers, some miles from Betanzos, where he remained all night.

It was found preferable that the soldiers should endure the cold and rain of a severe night, rather than be exposed to the irresistible temptation of the wine-houses in the town. The other divisions of the army were quartered in Betanzos.

So much fatigue had been endured, in the march from Lugo, that Sir John Moore halted, on the 10th, to give the soldiers repose. He there published a fresh Order, being unwearied in exertions to diminish the irregularities, though he could not entirely restore discipline.

## " GENERAL ORDERS.

*"Head Quarters, Betanzos, 10th Jan. 1809.*

" A GREAT.deal of irregularity has arisen from the
" practice of some Commanding Officers allowing Soldiers, who pre-
" tend to be bad marchers, to precede their corps. Men of this
" description, whom commanding officers may think expedient to
" send forward, must be placed under an officer, who is held respon-
" sible for their conduct.

### (*Memorandum for General Officers.*)

" To prevent the renewal of the same scene which the march of
" last night presented, the Commander of the Forces directs that,
" previously to the march to-morrow morning, the General Officers

" will see their divisions and brigades properly formed; that they
" wheel them by sections; and that, during the march, they pay
" constant attention to the preservation of that order."

A letter was received on the 11th of January from Mr. Frere, who
is endeavouring to be of use.

*Mr. Frere to Sir John Moore.*

" SIR,                                    *Seville, Dec. 28th, at night,* 1808.

" THE inclosed intelligence appears to me of such
" importance, that, though I should hope that there could be little
" doubt of your having already received it from other quarters, I
" have thought it right to send off a courier with it, with the pro-
" mise of a reward in proportion to his dispatch.

" There is nothing in the state of things here which can make it
" worth while to detain him. I am endeavouring to persuade the
" Government to take some steps for securing the great towns in
" this province, instead of relying upon the defence of military posi-
" tions, with peasants dressed in uniform. There are 10,000 in
" Despena Penos; of whom 6000 only are armed. You will see that
" the siege of Barcelona has been raised. The beaten army have,
" however, re-assembled at a very short distance.

" In La Mancha there seems to be a beginning of something like
" enterprize, and a disposition to worry the Enemy as far as is in
" their power. I am not yet able to make any report upon the sub-
" ject of the dispatches of the 10th, from Lord Castlereagh's Office.
" Orders are sent, as you desire, to the Juntas of Ciudad Rodrigo,
" Salamanca, and Zamora, for putting those towns in a state of
" temporary defence, and arming the inhabitants.

" I have proposed (I hope with your approbation) that the same
" measure should be extended to Toro, and even to Astorga.

" Believe me, with great truth and respect,

" Sir,

" Your most obedient humble servant,

" J. H. FRERE."

Here we perceive Mr. Frere striving, a little too late, to check
the progress of the Enemy, by fortifying the provincial towns, and
by raising up the formidable obstacles which he described in such
energetic terms in his letter from Merida. He expected, I suppose,
that this plan would now be realized. Salamanca, Zamora, Toro,
and Astorga, are to be surrounded with bulwarks; and not to be
overcome by the French but at the price of their blood. For
Mr. Frere had certainly forgotten he was in Spain in the nineteenth
century; and, by a poetical flight, had transported himself to Greece
during the invasion of Xerxes. When he awakened from this trance,
he must have been astonished to learn that not one of these towns
ever made the least shew of resistance, but most servilely opened
their gates, and the inhabitants bowed their heads, at the approach
of the first French patrole.

To give a just idea of the real state of the country, we shall tran-
scribe a passage of a letter from a very sensible Officer of Engineers,
who was sent by Sir John Moore to survey the roads in Carabria,
and to endeavour to rouse up the people there to make an effort.
The letter is a Report to the General from the Capital of the district,
dated La Puebla, 1st January 1809.

" With respect to the defence of this place, which I am instructed
" to promote, I can give your Excellency no reason to expect that

D D

" any will be made. There is no artillery, no garrison, nor arms
" for the townsmen. The Spanish soldiers now here (about 700)
" are merely on their way to the Marquis de la Romana; and as to
" any neighbouring passes, there are no people whom I can call
" upon to occupy them, or should expect to defend them, however
" naturally strong they may be; for I see no people who are think-
" ing of the Enemy's advance with any sentiments beyond passive
" dislike, and hopes of protection from God and the English Army."

This is a natural description of the dispositions of the Spaniards,
from an observing man.

On the 11th of January the Army marched from Betanzos, which
was the last day's journey. There was a bridge at the outside of the
town, which was attempted to be blown up. The Enemy's cavalry
tried to interrupt this; but they were driven back by the 28th regiment.

Sir John Moore, being anxious to examine the positions near
Corunna, left the Reserve under General Paget, and proceeded from
Betanzos with the main body of the Army. He passed every regiment, and addressed the Commanding Officer of each; observing to
them, that there was no particular post for a Commanding Officer,
who ought to range on the front, flank, and rear of his regiment;
that his eye should be every where; and that all straggling should
be prevented by the activity of the Officers.

This march was conducted with much more regularity than on
former occasions; yet eight or nine stragglers were detected, who
had preceded the column, and had taken possession of a house, and
the wine contained in it. They were seized, and brought prisoners
to the General: on which he halted the Army; and the Commanding Officers of the regiments, and the Captains of the companies, to
which the prisoners belonged, were sent for. Their haversacks were

searched, to discover if they contained plunder; and he enquired how long the men had been absent from their regiments.

An Officer replied to Sir John, that one of the prisoners, not being able to march with the column, had been sent on before, according to the General's Orders.

Sir John answered, "that when he gave out Orders he considered " that he addressed them to Military men; for, were he to write " every detail, no Orderly Book could contain them; that the man-" ner of obeying such an Order was, to form up such men as were " unable to march with the regiment, and place them under the " charge of an officer or a non-commissioned officer; but, undoubtedly, " they should not have been sent by themselves, to follow their own " discretion. Sir," continued he, " had I found plunder in the pos-" session of this man, he must have been condemned to death; and " you would have been the cause of his guilt."

Sir John rode on to Corunna, and viewed all the positions in the neighbourhood. The Guards and General Fraser's brigade were quartered in the town; General Hope's division in the suburbs; and General Paget, with the reserve, at El-Burgo, near the bridge of the Mero, and in the villages on the St. Jago road.

This bridge was destroyed; and it was thought proper to destroy another, higher up the river; but, by an unfortunate accident, the superintending Officer of Engineers lost his life by the explosion of the mine.

The Army had now reached the sea-port from which they were to embark; but adverse winds had detained the transports, or the whole would have been quickly on board in safety. Only a few ships lay in the harbour; in which some sick men, and some stragglers, who preceded the Army, calling themselves sick, immediately embarked.

The British Army thus arrived at Corunna entire and unbroken; and, in a military point of view, the operation was successful and splendid. Nearly 70,000 Frenchmen, led by Buonaparte, with a great superiority of cavalry, had endeavoured in vain to surround or to rout 26,000 British. Two hundred and fifty miles of country had been traversed; mountains, defiles, and rivers, had been crossed, in daily contact with their Enemy. Though often engaged, even their rear-guard was never beaten, nor thrown into confusion; but was victorious in every encounter.

Much baggage undoubtedly was lost, and some three-pounders were abandoned; but nothing was taken by force. What was left was owing to the death of waggon-horses and mules, and not to their escort ever being defeated. The courage and menacing attitude maintained by the cavalry and reserve were sufficient always to repel and overawe the advanced-guard of the Enemy; and at Lugo battle was offered by this handful of British to three divisions of French, commanded by their Marshals. This challenge was declined; and the impression it made, enabled the British to terminate their march almost undisturbed.

In fine, neither Napoleon nor the Duke of Dalmatia won a piece of artillery, a standard, or a single military trophy, from the British Army.

The greatest danger was still to be incurred: the position at Corunna was found to be extremely bad, the transports were not arrived, and the Enemy were appearing on the heights. Some experienced General Officers, of excellent judgment and distinguished valour, were so impressed with the melancholy aspect of affairs, as to consider the state of the Army almost desperate. They thought it their duty to represent to the Commander of the Forces the little probability there was of being able to resist the attacks of an Enemy cannonading and pouring upon them from the hills, while they were waiting for shipping. And even should the transports arrive, to embark in the face of a superior Enemy could not be accomplished without an enormous loss. From these considerations they counselled Sir John Moore to send to the Duke of Dalmatia, and propose to enter into terms with him, to permit the British army to embark unmolested.

Sir John Moore without a moment's hesitation rejected this advice.

It has excited a natural surprise, why the British army did not retire upon Ferrol, and endeavour to save, at least, the Spanish Fleet from falling into the hands of the French? Unfortunately, there was not that mutual cordiality between the two nations to admit of such a measure. It was well known that the Spaniards would not admit the British within the gates of Ferrol, nor into any other Naval arsenal. This put it out of the question. But had the Spaniards been better disposed, the harbour of Ferrol is so winding and commanded by such high grounds, that the transports could never have got out.

The French were seen next morning (January 12) moving in force on the opposite side of the river Mero. They took up a position near the village Perillo on the left flank, and occupied the houses along the river: while Sir John was incessantly occupied in preparing for the defence of his post, and making every arrangement for the embarkation of the troops. The Generals, and every Officer of the army, were now in full exertion to restore discipline and regularity to the troops, which were receiving such refreshments as could be procured in that place, and some repose from their toils.

On the 13th of January Sir David Baird marched out of Corunna with his division, to occupy the position on the swelling grounds, and to remain out all night.

Sir John now completed his examination of every plot of ground in the neighbourhood.

Had the army consisted of double its force, by occupying the range of hills situated about four miles from Corunna, they could have defended themselves against very superior numbers. But this position was found much too extensive; for the right and left flanks must have been exposed to be turned; and the Enemy could have penetrated to Corunna, especially by the right flank. The possession of these high hills was therefore obliged to be given up to the Enemy; and the British were under the necessity of occupying a second range of much inferior heights. Disadvantageous as this position was, it was preferable to leaving it also to the Enemy, and contracting the posts close round the town. For, had that been done, the Enemy would have approached so near the shore that every movement would have been seen, and the embarkation would have been rendered quite impossible.

Sir John Moore therefore determined, that one division under General Hope should occupy a hill on the left, which commanded the road to Betanzos, but the height of which decreased gradually towards the village of Elvina, taking a curved direction. Sir David Baird's division commenced at this village and bending to the right, the whole formed nearly a semi-circle. The rifle corps on the right of Sir David Baird formed a chain across a valley, and communicated with General Fraser's division, which was drawn up near the road to Vigo, and about half a mile from Corunna. The reserve under Major-General Paget occupied a village on the Betanzos road, about half a mile in the rear of General Hope.

Sir John Moore had been on horseback from day-break to make every arrangement for battle. He returned about eleven in the forenoon, exhausted with fatigue, and sent for Brigadier-General Stuart, and desired him to proceed to England, and explain to Ministers the situation of the army.

He said a vessel would convey him, but he was so tired he was incapable of writing; but that General Stuart being a competent judge of every thing, required no letter.

He then rested, and took some refreshment; and, two hours afterwards, the vessel not being quite ready, nor General Stuart gone, he called for paper and wrote off his last dispatch to Government *.

On the 14th of January the Enemy commenced a cannonade on the left, near the road to El-Burgo; the British Artillery returned this fire with great effect, and at last compelled the Enemy to draw off their guns.

There was found on a hill on the outside of the British posts a magazine of 4000 barrels of gunpowder, which had been brought from England, and was uselessly left in store, while the Spanish armies were without ammunition. The General ordered that as many barrels as possible should be conveyed to Corunna, which, for want of carts and mules, was a small portion, and that the rest should be blown up. The explosion was tremendous, and shook Corunna like an earthquake.

In the evening the transports from Vigo hove in sight, which gave the troops the agreeable prospect of being again enabled to return to their native shore.

January 15th the Enemy advanced to the height where the magazine had been blown up, and opposite to the position of the British.

The rifle corps skirmished with the Enemy's light troops on the right.

In the evening Colonel Mackenzie of the 5th, commanding the advanced post on the left, perceived two of the Enemy's cannon not far distant. He imagined that by a sudden attack he might surprise them. He accordingly rushed forward gallantly with a part of his

* Vide Appendix, F F.

regiment; but in crossing a field this enterprising officer was shot, and the attack failed.

In forming the disposition for action, Sir John found that from the nature of the ground much artillery could not be employed. He directed that seven six-pounders and one howitzer should be placed along the line, and four Spanish guns were kept as a reserve, to be advanced to any point where they might be useful. The rest of the artillery were all embarked this day.

When the out-posts became quiet, the General was busily occupied with Colonel Murray, Quarter-Master General; Lieutenant-Colonel Anderson *, of the Adjutant-General's department; and the Naval Officers, in making arrangements for the embarkation; which was fixed for the next evening. But both on this day and on the 14th the sick, artillery, dismounted cavalry, and horses were incessantly embarking.

Sir John Moore had this day the pleasure of receiving another letter from Mr. Frere, communicating the efforts he had made to check the advance of the French.

### Mr. Frere to Sir John Moore.

" SIR, *Seville, Jan. 2nd,* 1809.

" Upon the receipt of your letter of the 23d, inform-
" ing me of your march upon Carrion, I wrote to the Duke of Infan-
" tado, who was at Cuenca with a force superior to that which the
" French had left in Madrid, urging him, in the most pressing man-
" ner, to make a forward movement upon that capital. I left this
" letter with the Junta, by whom it was agreed that corresponding

---

* Brigadier General Clinton, Adjutant-General, fell sick, and Lieutenant-Colonel Anderson acted in his stead.

" instructions should be sent to the Duke by the Minister of War.
" It was likewise agreed, that similar orders should be forwarded at
" the same time to the Marquis of Palacios.

" I have the honour to transmit a copy of them, which has been
" since communicated to me; and, though I find them by no means
" so pressing as I could have wished and expected, I have still thought
" they were of sufficient importance to justify my forwarding them
" to you.

" I have the honour to be, with great truth and respect, Sir,

" Your most obedient humble servant,

" J. H. FRERE."

There is no letter of Mr. Frere's undeserving of attention; this is
distinguished by urbanity in the expression, and energy in the matter.

It is here announced, that he has written to the Duke of Infantado
to urge him to march towards Madrid.

This was unquestionably done with the view of relieving the British
army: for as Sir John Moore by threatening the communications
of Madrid had drawn upon himself the whole French force; so Mr.
Frere, by writing to the Duke of Infantado to threaten Madrid itself,
might hope to recal part of that force from the British army.

But there was a material difference between the activity of Mr.
Frere and Buonaparte, in their proceedings. For Buonaparte was
informed of the advance of the British on the 16th of December: on
the 18th his troops were in motion, and on the 2nd of January he
had reached Astorga, with above 65,000 men; having marched 300
miles to surround the British.

Mr. Frere, on the other hand, got the same intelligence something
sooner; and on the 2nd of January, when Buonaparte had reached
his destination, he wrote a letter to the Spanish General with a view
to stop him. Mr. Frere's letter had certainly little influence in check-

E E

ing the Emperor; but it might persuade the Secretary of State that he had done his utmost.

On the morning of the 16th of January the French posted on the hills were apparently quiet; no firing was heard: and the preparations for embarking the army being now completed, the General resolved to accomplish it that night.

Orders were given that the transports should receive on board the troops of every corps, as fast as the boats came along side. It was intended to sail to Vigo, and there shift the troops into their proper ships.

This last Order was then issued out.

" GENERAL ORDERS.

"*Head Quarters, Corunna*, 16*th January*, 1809.

" THE Commander of the Forces directs that Com-
" manding Officers of Regiments will, as soon as possible after they
" embark, make themselves acquainted with the names of the ships
" in which the men of their regiments are embarked, both sick and
" convalescent: and that they will make out the most correct states
" of their respective corps: that they will state the number of sick
" present, also those left at different places: and mention at the back
" of the return where the men returned on command are employed."

About noon the General sent for Colonel Anderson, to communicate his final instructions respecting the embarkation. He directed that he must continue to send sick men, horses, and baggage aboard the ship as quickly as possible: but that he wished all the boats to be disengaged at four in the afternoon; for he intended, if the French did not move, to begin embarking the reserve at that hour. And that he would go out himself, as soon as it was dark, to send in the troops by brigades in the order he wished them to embark. He continued transacting business until a little after one o'clock, when his horse was brought. He then took leave of Colonel Anderson, saying, " Remember, I depend upon your paying particular attention " to every thing that concerns the embarkation ; and let there be as " little confusion as possible."

He mounted his horse in good spirits, and set off to visit the outposts, and to explain his design to the General Officers.

He had not proceeded far on the road towards the position of the army, when he received a report from General Hope, " that the " Enemy's line were getting under arms ;" which was confirmed by a deserter who came in at that moment. Sir John expressed the highest satisfaction at this intelligence ; and only regretted that there would not be day-light enough to profit sufficiently from the advantages he anticipated as certain.

He struck spurs into his horse, and flew to the field. The advanced piquets were already beginning to fire at the Enemy's light troops, who were pouring rapidly down the hill on the right wing of the British.

The army was drawn up in the order of battle he had planned three days before, and was filled with ardour. The General surveyed them with pleasure ; and examined carefully the movements of the French columns. In a few minutes he dispatched almost all his Staff Officers with orders to the Generals at the different points.

General Fraser, whose brigade was in the rear, was commanded to move up, and take his position on the right ; and General Paget was ordered to advance with the reserve to support Lord William Bentinck.

The Enemy now commenced a destructive cannonade from eleven heavy guns, advantageously planted on the hills.

Four strong columns of French were seen moving from their position. One advanced from a wood, the other skirted its edge, and both were directed towards the right wing, which was the weakest point.

A third column approached the centre; and the fourth was advancing slowly upon the left along the road from El-Burgo. Besides these, there was a fifth corps which remained half way down the hill, towards the left.

It was the opinion of Sir John Moore, that the presence of the Chief in Command near to the point where the great struggle occurs, is often most useful *. He probably thought it peculiarly requisite to follow this rule here, as the position of his right wing was bad; and if the troops on that point gave way, the ruin of the army was inevitable.

Lord William Bentinck's brigade, consisting of three incomparable regiments, the 4th, the 42d, and 50th, maintained this dangerous post. The Guards were in their rear; and, to prevent the right being turned, Captain Napier was dispatched to desire General Paget to bring up the reserve to the right of Lord William Bentinck.

Sir David Baird leading on his division had his arm shattered with a musket ball; and was forced to leave the field.

The French artillery plunged from the heights, and the two hostile lines of infantry mutually advanced, beneath a shower of balls.

They were still separated from each other by stone walls and hedges, which intersected the ground: but as they closed it was perceived that the French line extended beyond the right flank of the

* Perhaps Sir John Moore learnt this doctrine from the practice of one of his Masters in the art of War, Sir Ralph Abercrombie, under whom he commanded the reserve in Egypt; and though he possessed his full confidence, yet he told the author, that in the hottest fire he usually found Sir Ralph at his elbow.

British; and a body of the Enemy were observed moving up the valley to turn it. An order was instantly given, and the half of the 4th Regiment, which formed this flank, fell back, refusing their right, and making an obtuse angle with the other half. In this position they commenced a heavy flanking fire; and the General, watching the manœuvre, called out to them, " That was exactly what I wanted to " be done."

He then rode up to the 50th regiment, commanded by Majors Napier and Stanhope; who got over an inclosure in their front, and charged most gallantly. The General, ever an admirer of valour, exclaimed, " Well done the fiftieth! well done, my Majors* !" They drove the Enemy out of the village of Elvina, with great slaughter. In this conflict Major Napier, advancing too far, was wounded in several places, and taken prisoner; and Major Stanhope unfortunately received a mortal wound.

Sir John Moore proceeded to the 42d, addressing them in these words, " Highlanders, remember Egypt." They rushed on, driving the French before them, till they were stopped by a wall. Sir John accompanied them in this charge, and told the soldiers that he was " well pleased with their conduct."

He sent Captain Hardinge to order up a battalion of Guards to the left flank of the Highlanders; upon which the officer commanding the light company conceived that, as their ammunition was nearly expended, they were to be relieved by the Guards, and began to fall back; but Sir John, discovering the mistake, said to them, " My " brave 42d, join your comrades, ammunition is coming, and you have " your bayonets." They instantly obeyed; and all moved forward.

* Sir John used this expression from having recommended them for the military rank they held. The Honourable Major Stanhope was second son to Earl Stanhope, and nephew to the late Mr. Pitt. The General entertained a sincere friendship for him.

Captain Hardinge now returned, to report that the Guards were advancing. While he was speaking, and pointing out the situation of the battalion, a hot fire was kept up, and the Enemy's artillery played incessantly on the spot. Sir John Moore was too conspicuous. A cannon-ball struck his left shoulder, and beat him to the ground.

He raised himself, and sat up with an unaltered countenance, looking intently at the Highlanders, who were warmly engaged. Captain Hardinge threw himself from his horse, and took him by the hand ; then, observing his anxiety, he told him the 42d were advancing ; upon which his countenance immediately brightened.

His friend Colonel Graham now dismounted, to assist him ; and, from the composure of his features, entertained hopes that he was not even wounded ; but, observing the horrid laceration and effusion of blood, he rode off for surgeons.

The General was carried from the field on a blanket, by a serjeant of the 42d, and some soldiers. On the way he ordered Captain Hardinge to report his wound to General Hope, who assumed the command.

Many of the soldiers knew that their two Chiefs were carried off, yet they continued the fight undaunted.

General Paget, conformably to his orders, hastened to the right with the reserve. Colonel Beckwith dashed on with the rifle corps, repelling the Enemy, and advancing on their flank. They penetrated so far, as nearly to carry one of their cannon ; but were at length forced to retire, before a much superior corps, who were moving up the valley. General Paget attacked this corps with the 52d, and some more of the reserve, and quickly repelled it. He pressed on to a great distance, dispersing every thing in his front ;

till the Enemy, perceiving their left wing quite exposed, drew it entirely back.

The French then advanced upon the centre, where Generals Manningham and Leith successfully resisted their onset. The ground there being more elevated, and favourable for artillery, the guns were of great utility. An effort was likewise made on the left, which was very unavailing; for the position on that side was strong. But a corps of French took possession of a village on the road to Betanzos, from which they continued to fire. On which Lieut.-Col. Nichols boldly attacked the village with some companies of the 14th, and beat out the Enemy with loss.

Light now began to fail, and the French had fallen back on every point; yet the roaring of cannon, and report of musketry, continued till dark.

The victory was complete, and gained under many disadvantages. The British had been much reduced by the multitude of sick, by the loss of stragglers, and by those employed in necessary duties; and General Craufurd's detachment was now at Vigo; so that not quite 15,000 men were brought into the field. The French also were greatly diminished by the length of the march, the severity of the weather, and their losses in the various defeats they had previously sustained; yet, according to the report of the prisoners, their three divisions amounted to full 20,000 men. Besides this great superiority of numbers, their position was far more favourable, and their cannon was of much heavier metal; which, being planted on the hills, fired down on the British with great advantage. Yet, by the daring courage of the troops, by the skilful disposition of the army, and by the manœuvres during the action, the French were entirely discomfited.

The loss of the British in killed and wounded was between seven and eight hundred men; and General Hope conjectured that the Enemy had lost about double that number; but Major Napier, when a

prisoner, learnt from the French Generals, that their loss was upwards of three thousand men. This was owing to the quick firing
and steady aim of the British troops; the French veteran officers
declaring, they had never been in such a fire in their lives.

The darkness of the night made it impossible to pursue the Enemy;
and General Hope, weighing the circumstances under which the
British Army was placed, and the reinforcements which could soon
be sent to the French, considered that it would be impossible to retain his position long. A succession of attacks from fresh troops
must ultimately overwhelm the British. He, therefore, judged
that the only prudent step that could be taken was to proceed to
embark the Army.

At ten o'clock at night he ordered the troops, by brigades, to
move from the field, and march to Corunna. Strong piquets were
left to guard the ground, and to give notice if the Enemy approached.

Major-General Beresford commanded the rear-guard, of about
2000 men, to cover the embarkation. He occupied the lines in front
of the town. And Major General Hill was stationed, with a corps
of reserve, on a promontory behind the town.

The boats were all in readiness, and the previous measures had
been so well concerted, that nearly the whole Army were embarked
during the night.

The piquets were withdrawn before day-light, and immediately
carried on board the ships also; so that nothing remained ashore
except the rear-guard.

The French had no disposition to renew the engagement; but
when the morning rose, and they saw that the British were gone,
they pushed on their light troops to the heights of St. Lucia.

In the forenoon (January 17th) they got up some cannon to a
rising ground near the harbour, and fired at the transports. Several

of the masters were so much frightened, that they cut their cables, and four of the ships ran aground. The troops of these ships were put on board others, and the stranded vessels were burnt. The rest of the fleet quitted the harbour.

At two o'clock General Hill's brigade embarked under the citadel; and during that night, and the following morning, General Beresford sent off all the sick and wounded, whose condition admitted of their being removed; and, lastly, the rear-guard got into the boats, without the slightest effort being made by the Enemy to interrupt it.

The whole of this difficult operation was so well conducted as to reflect much credit upon the superintending Officers, both of the Navy and Army.

As many will receive a melancholy gratification from reading the particulars of the last moments of the life of Sir John Moore, such incidents as are authentic shall be communicated.

The following letter from Captain Hardinge describes his fall.

" The circumstances which took place immediately after the fatal " blow which deprived the Army of its gallant Commander, Sir John " Moore, are of too interesting a nature not to be made public, for " the admiration of his countrymen. But I trust that the instances " of fortitude and heroism of which I was a witness may also have " another effect, that of affording some consolation to his relatives " and friends.

" With this feeling I have great satisfaction in committing to paper, " according to your desire, the following relation.

F F

" I had been ordered by the Commander in Chief to desire a bat-
" talion of the Guards to advance; which battalion was at one time
" intended to have dislodged a corps of the Enemy from a large
" house and garden on the opposite side of the valley; and I was
" pointing out to the General the situation of the battalion, and our
" horses were touching, at the very moment that a cannon-shot
" from the Enemy's battery carried away his left shoulder and part
" of the collar-bone, leaving the arm hanging by the flesh.

" The violence of the stroke threw him off his horse, on his back.
" Not a muscle of his face altered, nor did a sigh betray the least
" sensation of pain.

" I dismounted, and, taking his hand, he pressed mine forcibly,
" casting his eyes very anxiously towards the 42d regiment, which
" was hotly engaged; and his countenance expressed satisfaction
" when I informed him that the regiment was advancing.

" Assisted by a soldier of the 42d, he was removed a few yards
" behind the shelter of a wall.

" Colonel Graham Balgowan and Captain Woodford about this
" time came up; and, perceiving the state of Sir John's wound, in-
" stantly rode off for a surgeon.

" The blood flowed fast; but the attempt to stop it with my
" sash was useless, from the size of the wound.

" Sir John assented to being removed in a blanket to the rear.
" In raising him for that purpose, his sword, hanging on the
" wounded side, touched his arm, and became entangled between
" his legs. I perceived the inconvenience, and was in the act of
" unbuckling it from his waist, when he said, in his usual tone
" and manner, and in a very distinct voice, '*It is as well as it is. I*
" *had rather it should go out of the field with me.*'

" Here I feel that it would be improper for my pen to venture
" to express the admiration with which I am penetrated in thus

" faithfully recording this instance of the invincible fortitude, and
" military delicacy, of this great man.

" He was borne by six soldiers of the 42d and Guards, my sash
" supporting him in an easy posture.

" Observing the resolution and composure of his features, I caught
" at the hope that I might be mistaken in my fears of the wound
" being mortal; and remarked, that I trusted when the surgeons
" dressed the wound, that he would be spared to us, and recover.—
" He then turned his head round, and, looking steadfastly at the
" wound for a few seconds, said, '*No, Hardinge, I feel that to be
" impossible.*'

" I wished to accompany him to the rear, when he said, '*You need
" not go with me. Report to General Hope that I am wounded,
" and carried to the rear.*'

" A serjeant of the 42d, and two spare files, in case of accident,
" were ordered to conduct their brave General to Corunna; and I
" hastened to report to General Hope.

" I have the honour to be, &c. &c.

" H. HARDINGE."

The tidings of this disaster were brought to Sir David Baird when
the surgeons were dressing his shattered arm. He instantly commanded them to desist, and run to attend on Sir John Moore. When
they arrived, and offered their assistance, he said to them, " *You
" can be of no service to me, go to the soldiers, to whom you may
" be useful.*"

As the soldiers were carrying him slowly along, he made them
turn him round frequently, to view the field of battle, and to listen
to the firing; and was well pleased when the sound grew fainter.

A spring waggon bearing Colonel Wynch wounded from the
battle came up. The Colonel asked, " who was in the blanket?"

and being told it was Sir John Moore, he wished him to be placed in the waggon. The General asked one of the Highlanders, whether he thought the waggon or the blanket best; who answered, that the blanket would not shake him so much, as he and the other soldiers would keep the step, and carry him easy. Sir John said, " I think so too." So they proceeded with him to his lodgings in Corunna, the soldiers shedding tears as they went.

In carrying him through the passage of the house he saw his faithful servant François, who was stunned at the spectacle. Sir John said to him, smiling, " *My Friend, this is nothing.*"

Colonel Anderson, for one-and-twenty years the friend and companion in arms of Sir John Moore, wrote the morning following this account, while the circumstances were fresh in his memory.

" I met the General, in the evening of the 16th, bringing in " a blanket and sashes. He knew me immediately, though it was " almost dark, squeezed me by the hand, and said, ' *Anderson,* " *don't leave me.*'

" He spoke to the Surgeons on their examining his wound, but " was in such pain he could say little.

" After some time, he seemed very anxious to speak to me, " and at intervals got out as follows : ' *Anderson, you know* " *that I have always wished to die this way.*' He then asked, " ' *Are the French beaten ?*' which he repeated to every one he " knew, as they came in. ' *I hope the People of England will* " *be satisfied ! — I hope my Country will do me justice !*' — " *Anderson, — you will see my friends as soon as you can. — Tell* " *them—every thing. — Say to my mother.*" — Here his voice quite " failed, and he was excessively agitated. — ' *Hope—Hope—I have* " *much to say to him, — but — cannot get it out — Are Colonel Gra-* " *ham—and all my Aides-de-Camp well ?* (a private sign was made

" by Colonel Anderson not to inform him that Captain Burrard *,
" one of his Aides-de-camp, was wounded in the action.) — ' *I have*
" *made my will, and have remembered my servants.—Colborne has*
" *my will, — and all my papers.*'

" Major Colborne then came into the room. He spoke most
" kindly to him, and then said to me, ' *Anderson, remember you go*
" *to —— and tell him it is my request, and that I expect he will give*
" *Major Colborne a Lieutenant-Colonelcy.—He has been long with*
" *me,—and I know him most worthy of it.*' He then asked Major
" Colborne, ' *if the French were beaten?*'. And, on being told they
" were on every point, he said, ' *It's a great satisfaction for me to*
" *know we have beaten the French. — Is Paget in the room?*' On
" my telling him, no; he said, '*Remember me to him.—It's General*
" *Paget I mean—he is a fine fellow.—I feel myself so strong—I*
" *fear I shall be long dying. — It is great uneasiness — It is great*
" *pain.—Every thing Francois says—is right.—I have the greatest*
" *confidence in him.*"

" He thanked the Surgeons for their trouble. Captains Percy and
" Stanhope, two of his Aides-de-camp, then came into the room.
" He spoke kindly to both, and asked Percy †, *if all his Aides-de-*
" *camp were well?*

" After some interval he said, ' *Stanhope‡—remember me to your*
" *sister.*' He pressed my hand close to his body, and in a few mi-
" nutes died without a struggle.

" This was every syllable he uttered, as far as I can recollect,
" except asking occasionally to be placed in an easier posture.

" P. ANDERSON, Lieut.-Col."

---

* Son of Sir Harry Burrard, a promising young officer, who died two days afterwards of his wound.

† The Honourable Captain Percy, son of Lord Beverley.

‡ The Honourable Captain Stanhope, third son to Earl Stanhope, and nephew to the late Mr. Pitt.

From a sentiment of veneration that has been felt in every age, the corpse of a man who has excited admiration cannot be neglected as common clay. This impression leads mankind sometimes to treat an inanimate body with peculiar respect; and even to bestow upon it unfelt honours.

This was now the subject of deliberation among the military friends of Sir John Moore, who had survived the engagement; when Colonel Anderson informed them, that he had heard the General repeatedly declare, " that, if he was killed in battle, he wished to be " buried where he had fallen!" General Hope and Colonel Graham immediately acceded to this suggestion: and it was determined that the body should be interred on the rampart of the Citadel of Corunna.

At twelve o'clock at night the remains of Sir John Moore were accordingly carried to the Citadel by Colonel Graham, Major Colborne, and the Aides-de-Camp, and deposited in Colonel Graham's quarters.

A grave was dug by a party of the 9th Regiment, the Aides-de-Camp attending by turns. No coffin could be procured, and the body was never undressed, but wrapt up by the Officers of his Staff in a military cloak and blankets.

Towards eight o'clock in the morning some firing was heard. It was then resolved to finish the interment, lest a serious attack should be made; on which the Officers would be ordered away, and not suffered to pay the last duties to their General.

The officers of his family bore the body to the grave; the funeral service was read by the Chaplain, and the corpse was covered with earth.

It is not for a brother to delineate a character where the warmest affections were united with such a grandeur of soul as to create a delusion in his family, and almost to persuade them that his mind, like the forms of Grecian sculpture, approached to ideal excellence.

Their testimony cannot be received. But the high estimation he was held in by the most celebrated Generals and Statesmen of the period in which he lived, mark him to have been an extraordinary man.

Those who have run their course, but who live in our memories, shall alone be cited.

That eminent soldier Sir Charles Stuart, first remarked the conspicuous valour and abilities of Lieutenant Colonel Moore, and pointed him out to his Sovereign and his Country.

Sir Ralph Abercrombie next selected him for his friend, and wielded him as his sword.

Then Marquis Cornwallis, when serving in Ireland, conferred upon him (though one of his youngest Generals) the most important command in his army. Thus did three of the greatest British Generals of the age intrust Sir John Moore to achieve those enterprises which demanded the most daring resolution and consummate military knowledge; and, by an uninterrupted train of success, he surpassed their expectations.

He never courted Ministers, nor sought for pre-eminence by mean solicitations. But when sent for, or employed by them, he behaved with the deference due to their station, and expressed his opinions with the candour that was becoming himself.

Mr. Pitt was struck with his actions, and solicited his acquaintance. The esteem he had pre-conceived augmented in proportion to the intimacy that was formed. He consulted him on Military affairs, and on several important occasions yielded to his judgment. This confidential intercourse continued till the death of that statesman. Had he lived, and still continued to superintend the Councils of Government, the reasons which drew forth this work never could have existed; for his conduct towards the Naval and Military Commanders whom he made choice of, was always just and noble.

During the short time Mr. Fox was Minister, he likewise expressed, in his energetic manner, the highest consideration for this General.

When it was in agitation to appoint him Commander in Chief in India, Mr. Fox sent for him; and with characteristic frankness told him, " he could not give his consent: that it was impossible for him, " in the state in which Europe then was, to send to such a distance " a General in whom he had such entire confidence."

Mr. Fox did not survive long: but those distinguished Noblemen and Commoners who belonged to that administration, or who were politically attached to that Minister, have emulously and most eloquently exerted themselves, that due honours might be paid to the memory of the chosen General of Mr. Pitt.

The guardian solicitude with which the King watches over the honour and interest of his Army, has been conspicuous through the whole of his reign. Moore was an Officer whom his Majesty noticed early, and cherished constantly; and when he was assailed by powerful undermining intrigues, ever afforded him his Royal Protection.

The ungenerous persecution continues beyond the Grave: but his Sovereign bewails his death with deep sorrow; defends his Fame, which he valued above life; and holds him up by proclamation as an example to the British army. For as soon as the troops returned from Spain, the following address was promulgated.

## " GENERAL ORDERS.

" THE benefits derived to an army from the example
" of a distinguished Commander do not terminate at his death;
" his virtues live in the recollection of his associates, and his fame
" remains the strongest incentive to great and glorious actions.

" In this view, the Commander in Chief, amidst the deep and uni-
" versal regret which the death of Lieutenant-General Sir John
" Moore has occasioned, recalls to the troops the Military career of
" that illustrious Officer for their instruction and imitation.

" Sir John Moore, from his youth, embraced the profession with
" the feelings and sentiments of a soldier; he felt, that a perfect
" knowledge, and an exact performance of the humble, but important
" duties of a Subaltern Officer are the best foundations for subsequent
" Military fame; and his ardent mind, while it looked forward to
" those brilliant achievements for which it was formed, applied itself
" with energy and exemplary assiduity to the duties of that station.

" In the school of regimental duty, he obtained that correct know-
" ledge of his profession so essential to the proper direction of the
" gallant spirit of the soldier; and he was enabled to establish a cha-
" racteristic order and regularity of conduct, because the troops found
" in their leader a striking example of the discipline which he en-
" forced on others.

" Having risen to command, he signalized his name in the West
" Indies, in Holland, and in Egypt *. The unremitting attention

* In enumerating the scenes where Sir John Moore conspicuously distinguished himself, Corsica and Ireland have been forgotten.

In Corsica he stormed the Convention Fort, and the outworks of Calvi, which was followed by the conquest of the Island.

In Ireland he gained the battle of Wexford, which was the prelude to the suppression of the Rebellion.

" with which he devoted himself to the duties of every branch of his
" profession obtained him the confidence of Sir Ralph Abercrombie ;
" and he became the companion in arms of that illustrious Officer,
" who fell at the head of his victorious troops, in an action which
" maintained our national superiority over the arms of France.

" Thus Sir John Moore at an early period obtained, with.general
" approbation, that conspicuous station in which he gloriously termi-
" nated his useful and honourable life.

" In a Military character, obtained amidst the dangers of climate,
" the privations incident to service, and the sufferings of repeated
" wounds, it is difficult to select any one point as a preferable subject
" for praise : it exhibits, however, one feature so particularly charac-
" teristic of the man, and so important to the best interests of the ser-
" vice, that the Commander in Chief is pleased to mark it with his
" peculiar approbation.

" The life of Sir John Moore was spent among the troops.

" During the season of repose, his time was devoted to the care
" and instruction of the Officer and Soldier ; in war, he courted ser-
" vice in every quarter of the globe. Regardless of personal con-
" siderations, he esteemed that to which his Country called him the
" post of honour, and by his undaunted spirit, and unconquerable
" perseverance, he pointed the way to victory.

" His Country, the object of his latest solicitude, will rear a Mo-
" nument to his lamented memory; and the Commander in Chief
" feels he is paying the best tribute to his fame by thus holding him
" forth as an example to the Army.

" By order of his Royal Highness the Commander in Chief,

" HARRY CALVERT, Adj.-Gen.

" *Horse Guards, Feb.* 1, 1809."

LONDON GAZETTE EXTRAORDINARY.

---

*Downing Street, January* 24, 1809.

THE Honourable Captain Hope arrived late last night, with a Dispatch from Lieutenant-General Sir David Baird to Lord Viscount Castlereagh, one of His Majesty's Principal Secretaries of State, of which the following is a Copy.

" MY LORD, *His Majesty's Ship Ville de Paris,*
*at Sea, January* 18, 1809.

" BY the much-lamented death of Lieutenant-
" General Sir John Moore, who fell in action with the Enemy on
" the 16th instant, it has become my duty to acquaint your Lord-
" ship, that the French army attacked the British troops in the posi-
" tion they occupied in front of Corunna, at about two o'clock in the
" afternoon of that day.

" A severe wound, which compelled me to quit the field a short
" time previous to the fall of Sir John Moore, obliges me to refer
" your Lordship for the particulars of the action, which was long
" and obstinately contested, to the inclosed report of Lieutenant-
" General Hope, who succeeded to the command of the army, and
" to whose ability and exertions in direction of the ardent zeal and
" unconquerable valour of his Majesty's troops, is to be attributed,
" under Providence, the success of the day, which terminated in the
" complete and entire repulse and defeat of the Enemy at every point
" of attack.

" The Honourable Captain Gordon, my Aide-de-Camp, will have
" the honour of delivering this dispatch, and will be able to give
" your Lordship any further information which may be required.

" I have the honour to be, &c.

" D. BAIRD, Lieut.-Gen.

" *Right Hon. Lord Viscount Castlereagh.*

———

" SIR,

*His Majesty's Ship Audacious, off Corunna,*
*January* 18, 1809.

" IN compliance with the desire contained in your
" communication of yesterday, I avail myself of the first moment I
" have been able to command, to detail to you the occurrences of the
" action which took place in front of Corunna on the 16th instant.

" It will be in your recollection, that about one in the afternoon of
" that day the Enemy, who had in the morning received reinforce-
" ments, and who had placed some guns in front of the right and left
" of his line, was observed to be moving troops towards his left flank,
" and forming various columns of attack at that extremity of the strong
" and commanding position which on the morning of the 15th he had
" taken in our immediate front.

" This indication of his intention was immediately succeeded by
" the rapid and determined attack which he made upon your division
" which occupied the right of our position. The events which oc-
" curred during that period of the action you are fully acquainted
" with. The first effort of the Enemy was met by the Commander of
" the Forces, and by yourself, at the head of the 42nd regiment, and
" the brigade under Major-General Lord William Bentinck.

" The village on your right became an object of obstinate contest.

" I lament to say, that soon after the severe wound which deprived
" the army of your services, Lieutenant-General Sir John Moore,
" who had just directed the most able disposition, fell by a cannon
" shot. The troops, though not unacquainted with the irreparable
" loss they had sustained, were not dismayed, but by the most deter-
" mined bravery not only repelled every attempt of the Enemy to gain
" ground, but actually forced him to retire, although he had brought
" up fresh troops in support of those originally engaged.

" The Enemy, finding himself foiled in every attempt to force the
" right of the position, endeavoured by numbers to turn it. A judi-
" cious and well-timed movement which was made by Major-General
" Paget, with the reserve, which corps had moved out of its canton-
" ments to support the right of the army, by a vigorous attack, de-
" feated this intention. The Major-General, having pushed forward
" the 95th (rifle corps) and 1st battalion 52d regiments, drove the
" Enemy before him, and in his rapid and judicious advance, threatened
" the left of the Enemy's position. This circumstance, with the
" position of Lieutenant-General Fraser's division, (calculated to
" give still further security to the right of the line) induced the Enemy
" to relax his efforts in that quarter.

" They were however more forcibly directed towards the centre,
" where they were again successfully resisted by the brigade under
" Major-General Manningham, forming the left of your division,
" and a part of that under Major-General Leith, forming the right
" of the division under my orders. Upon the left, the Enemy at first
" contented himself with an attack upon our piquets, which however
" in general maintained their ground. Finding however his efforts
" unavailing on the right and centre, he seemed determined to render
" the attack upon the left more serious, and had succeeded in obtain-
" ing possession of the village through which the great road to Ma-
" drid passes, and which was situated in front of that part of the line.

" From this post, however, he was soon expelled, with considerable
" loss, by a gallant attack of some companies of the 2nd battalion
" 14th regiment, under Lieutenant-Colonel Nicholls; before five in
" the evening, we had not only successfully repelled every attack
" made upon the position, but had gained ground in almost all points,
" and occupied a more forward line than at the commencement of
" the action, whilst the Enemy confined his operations to a cannonade,
" and the fire of his light troops, with a view to draw off his other
" corps. At six the firing ceased. The different brigades were re-
" assembled on the ground they occupied in the morning, and the
" piquets and advanced posts resumed their original stations.

" Notwithstanding the decided and marked superiority which at
" this moment the gallantry of the troops had given them over an
" Enemy, who from his numbers and the commanding advantages of
" his position, no doubt expected an easy victory, I did not, on re-
" viewing all circumstances, conceive that I should be warranted in
" departing from what I knew was the fixed and previous determina-
" tion of the late Commander of the Forces, to withdraw the army on
" the evening of the 16th, for the purpose of embarkation, the pre-
" vious arrangements for which had already been made by his order,
" and were in fact far advanced at the commencement of the action.
" The troops quitted their position about ten at night, with a degree
" of order that did them credit. The whole of the artillery that re-
" mained unembarked, having been withdrawn, the troops followed
" in the order prescribed, and marched to their respective points of
" embarkation in the town and neighbourhood of Corunna. The
" piquets remained at their posts until five on the morning of the 17th,
" when they were also withdrawn with similar orders, and without
" the Enemy having discovered the movement.

" By the unremitted exertions of Captains the Honourable H. Cur-
" zon, Gosselin, Boys, Rainier, Serret, Hawkins, Digby, Carden,

" and Mackenzie, of the Royal Navy, who, in pursuance of the or-
" ders of Rear Admiral de Courcy, were entrusted with the service
" of embarking the army; and in consequence of the arrangements
" made by Commissioner Bowen, Captains Bowen and Shepherd, and
" the other Agents for Transports, the whole of the army was em-
" barked with an expedition which has seldom been equalled. With
" the exception of the Brigades under Major-Generals Hill and
" Beresford, which were destined to remain on shore, until the move-
" ments of the Enemy should become manifest, the whole was afloat
" before day-light.

" The brigade of Major-General Beresford, which was alternately
" to form our rear-guard, occupied the land front of the town of Co-
" runna; that under Major-General Hill was stationed in reserve on
" the Promontory in rear of the town.

" The Enemy pushed his light troops towards the town soon after
" eight o'clock in the morning of the 17th, and shortly after occupied
" the heights of St. Lucia, which command the harbour. But, not-
" withstanding this circumstance, and the manifold defects of the
" place; there being no apprehension that the rear-guard could be
" forced, and the disposition of the Spaniards appearing to be good,
" the embarkation of Major-General Hill's brigade was commenced
" and completed by three in the afternoon; Major-General Beresford,
" with that zeal and ability which is so well known to yourself and
" the whole army, having fully explained, to the satisfaction of the
" Spanish Governor, the nature of our movement, and having made
" every previous arrangement, withdrew his corps from the land-front
" of the town soon after dark, and was, with all the wounded that
" had not been previously moved, embarked before one this morning.

" Circumstances forbid us to indulge the hope, that the victory
" with which it has pleased Providence to crown the efforts of the
" army, can be attended with any very brilliant consequences to Great

" Britain. It is clouded by the loss of one of her best Soldiers. It
" has been atchieved at the termination of a long and harassing ser-
" vice. The superior numbers, and advantageous position of the
" Enemy, not less than the actual situation of this army, did not ad-
" mit of any advantage being reaped from success. It must be how-
" ever to you, to the army, and to our Country, the sweetest reflec-
" tion that the lustre of the British arms has been maintained, amidst
" many disadvantageous circumstances. The army which had en-
" tered Spain, amidst the fairest prospects, had no sooner completed
" its junction, than owing to the multiplied disasters that dispersed
" the native armies around us, it was left to its own resources. The
" advance of the British corps from the Duero, afforded the best hope
" that the South of Spain might be relieved, but this generous effort
" to save the unfortunate people, also afforded the Enemy the oppor-
" tunity of directing every effort of his numerous troops, and concen-
" trating all his principal resources, for the destruction of the only
" regular force in the North of Spain.

" You are well aware with what diligence this system has been
" pursued.

" These circumstances produced the necessity of rapid and harass-
" ing marches, which had diminished the numbers, exhausted the
" strength, and impaired the equipment of the army. Notwithstand-
" ing all these disadvantages, and those more immediately attached
" to a defensive position, which the imperious necessity of covering
" the harbour of Corunna for a time had rendered indispensable to
" assume, the native and undaunted valour of British troops was
" never more conspicuous, and must have exceeded what even your
" own experience of that invaluable quality, so inherent in them, may
" have taught you to expect. When every one that had an opportu-
" nity seemed to vie in improving it, it is difficult for me, in making
" this report, to select particular instances for your approbation.

" The corps chiefly engaged were the brigades under Major-Generals
" Lord William Bentinck, and Manningham and Leith; and the
" brigade of Guards under Major-General Warde.

" To these officers, and the troops under their immediate orders,
" the greatest praise is due.   Major-General Hill and Colonel Catlin
" Crauford, with their brigades on the left of the position, ably sup-
" ported their advanced posts.   The brunt of the action fell upon the
" 4th, 42d, 50th, and 81st regiments, with parts of the brigade of
" Guards, and the 26th regiment.   From Lieutenant-Colonel Mur-
" ray, Quarter-Master-General, and the Officers of the General
" Staff, I received the most marked assistance.   I had reason to re-
" gret, that the illness of Brigadier-General Clinton, Adjutant-Gene-
" ral, deprived me of his aid.   I was indebted to Brigadier-General
" Slade during the action, for a zealous offer of his personal services,
" although the cavalry were embarked.

" The greater part of the fleet having gone to sea yesterday even-
" ing, the whole being under weigh, and the corps in the embarka-
" tion necessarily much mixed on board, it is impossible at present to
" lay before you a return of our casualties.   I hope the loss in num-
" bers is not so considerable as might have been expected.   If I was
" obliged to form an estimate, I should say, that I believe it did not
" exceed in killed and wounded from seven to eight hundred; that of
" the Enemy must remain unknown, but many circumstances induce
" me to rate it at nearly double the above number.   We have some
" prisoners, but I have not been able to obtain an account of the
" number; it is not, however, considerable.   Several Officers of
" rank have fallen or been wounded, among whom I am only at pre-
" sent enabled to state the names of Lieutenant-Colonel Napier, 92d
" regiment, Majors Napier and Stanhope, 50th regiment, killed;
" Lieutenant-Colonel Winch, 4th regiment, Lieutenant-Colonel
" Maxwell, 26th regiment, Lieutenant-Colonel Fane, 59th regiment,

H H

" Lieutenant-Colonel Griffith, guards, Majors Miller and Williams,
" 81st regiment, wounded.

" To you, who are well acquainted with the excellent qualities of
" Lieutenant-General Sir John Moore, I need not expatiate on the
" loss the army and his Country have sustained by his death. His
" fall has deprived me of a valuable friend, to whom long experience
" of his worth had sincerely attached me. But it is chiefly on public
" grounds that I must lament the blow. It will be the conversation
" of every one who loved or respected his manly character, that, after
" conducting the army through an arduous retreat with consummate
" firmness, he has terminated a career of distinguished honour by a
" death that has given the Enemy additional reason to respect the
" name of a British Soldier. Like the immortal Wolfe, he is
" snatched from his Country at an early period of a life spent in her
" service; like Wolfe, his last moments were gilded by the prospect
" of success, and cheered by the acclamation of victory; like Wolfe
" also, his memory will for ever remain sacred in that Country which
" he sincerely loved, and which he had so faithfully served.

" It remains for me only to express my hope, that you will speedily
" be restored to the service of your Country, and to lament the un-
" fortunate circumstance that removed you from your station in the
" field, and threw the momentary command into far less able hands.

" I have the honour to be, &c.

" JOHN HOPE, Lieut.-Gen.

" To Lieutenant-General Sir David Baird,
&c. &c. &c."

# APPENDIX.

# APPENDIX.

---

## A.

*From Lord Castlereagh to Sir John Moore, K. B. &c. &c. &c.*

SIR, *Downing Street, 25th September, 1808.*

His MAJESTY having determined to employ a corps of his troops, of not less than 30,000 infantry and 5,000 cavalry, in the North of Spain, to co-operate with the Spanish armies in the expulsion of the French from that kingdom, has been graciously pleased to entrust to you the Command in Chief of this Force.

The Officer commanding His Majesty's forces in Portugal is directed to detach, under your orders, a corps of 20,000 infantry, together with the Eighteenth and King's German Regiment of Light Dragoons, now at Lisbon, and a due proportion of artillery; to be joined by a corps of above 10,000 men which are now assembling at Falmouth; the detail of which you will receive herewith enclosed.

The Cavalry will be sent from hence, upon the return of the horse-transports from the Tagus, some time since ordered; and it may be expected to arrive before the rest of the corps can be assembled and equipped to take the field.

It has been determined to assemble this force in the North of Spain, as the quarter where they can be most speedily brought together, and that to which the exertions of the Enemy appear at present to be principally directed.

As it will require considerable arrangements before a force of this magnitude can be enabled to take the field, and as it is not deemed advisable that it should be partially committed against the Enemy, before the whole can be assembled and rendered completely moveable, it has been thought prudent to send that part of this army which is to proceed from hence to Corunna, rather than to disembark any part of it, in the first instance, at any position more advanced towards the Enemy.

It will be for you to consider on what points in Gallicia, or on the borders of Leon, the troops can be most advantageously assembled and equipped for service, from whence they may move forward as early as circumstances shall permit; and it is left to your judgment to decide whether the whole of the infantry and artillery shall be transported from Lisbon by sea to Corunna, or whether a proportion shall be marched through Portugal to that destination.

The Cavalry you will of course direct to move by land; and if the horses for the artillery can take the same route, so as to admit of the whole of the horse-transports being returned to England, it will tend much to accelerate the arrival of the cavalry from hence.

It will be necessary to concert with the Commissary General (Mr. Erskine), who will be attached to the service of your army, the best means of assembling an adequate supply of horses and mules for rendering your army moveable. And that this may be effected with more dispatch, it may be advisable to draw your supplies from different parts of Spain, and not altogether to depend upon Gallicia; which has been considerably drained of its resources by the equipment of General Blake's army.

A Deputy Commissary (Mr. Assiotti) has been dispatched with Colonel Hamilton of the Waggon-train into the Asturias, to procure such horses and mules as that Country can furnish; and he is directed to report the progress of his purchases to you. When you have ascertained the number of draft-cattle of different descriptions that you will require for rendering your army moveable (which you will feel it important to restrict within the narrowest compass, consistent with the efficiency of your corps), you will be enabled to regulate the purchases made by the several agents; and should you deem it necessary to procure the support of His Majesty's Minister (Mr. Frere) who is now proceeding to the Central Government, to facilitate these purchases, you will address yourself to him on this subject; or to any of His Majesty's Civil or Military agents now employed in the respective provinces of Spain.

I inclose for your information, a statement of the various equipments which have proceeded with the respective corps now on service in Portugal, which, subject to the waste that has since taken place, will enable you to judge of the means immediately within your reach, for the equipment of your army.

I also send a similar statement with respect to the corps assembling at Falmouth, under the orders of Lieutenant-General Sir David Baird; whatever supplies you may wish to receive, not therein included, will be immediately forwarded from hence.

With respect to provisions, the principle upon which I have acted has been to send three months' provisions in victuallers with every corps that has moved; exclusive of the provisions in their transports, which may be averaged at about ten weeks' additional consumption.

This supply, aided by the cattle to be procured for the troops when on shore, may be deemed as considerably exceeding a supply for six months; and as provisions for 20,000 men for three months are ordered to be embarked, and constantly kept up as a depôt here, there will be no difficulty in sending you, at the shortest notice, such supplies as you may think may be more conveniently introduced by Sea, and for which you may not think it prudent to depend on the resources of the country. A large proportion of biscuit has been sent in the victuallers, that you may be relieved from the inconvenience of baking when the troops are in motion.

With respect to the plan of operations on which it may be most expedient to employ your troops, when assembled and ready for service, there will be full time before your equipments can be completed for concerting this with the Commanders of the Spanish armies.

I shall lose no time in forwarding to you from hence, such information as I may have been enabled to collect. And I am to recommend that you will take the necessary measures for opening a communication with the Spanish authorities for the purpose of framing the plan of the campaign, on which it may be advisable that the respective armies should act in concert.

His Majesty has been pleased to direct, that the command on which you are employed should be considered as a distinct and separate one, from that of Portugal: but you will continue to communicate with the Officer in the Chief Command at Lisbon, and act in concert with him as may be most for the advantage of His Majesty's service.

I have the honour to be,

Sir,

Your most obedient humble servant,

CASTLEREAGH.

*To Lieutenant-General*
*Sir John Moore, K.B. &c. &c. &c.*

B.

*Letter from Lord Castlereagh to Lord William Bentinck.*

MY LORD,                                        *London, 30th Sept. 1808.*

As the dispatches received from Sir Hew Dalrymple yesterday, leave me no room to doubt, that this letter will find you out at Madrid, I deem it advisable that you should be apprised of the arrangements that are in progress for affording military succours to the Spanish nation.

Mr. Frere, who proceeds as Minister to the Central Government in a few days, will be directed to make a formal communication on this subject; but you will, in the mean time, make such use of the information I send you, as you may think fit, to make the Spaniards feel how eagerly His Majesty desires to contribute to their deliverance.

The amount of force which it is proposed to employ in Spain will fall very little short of 40,000 men: it is to consist of 30,000 infantry, rank and file; 5,000 cavalry, and the necessary proportion of foot and horse artillery, waggon train, &c.: the whole to be assembled under the orders of Sir John Moore, on the borders of Gallicia and Leon; from whence they may operate in the open country, as soon as the necessary proportion of horses and mules can be procured to render them moveable, leaving it to the Spanish armies, not having a due proportion of cavalry, to act on their flanks in the mountains.

Sir David Baird, with 12,000 men, is ordered to sail for Corunna;—Sir John Moore is to move the remainder of the force required to complete the 30,000 infantry from Portugal, either by land or sea, as he may find most convenient, sending the two regiments of cavalry, under my brother,

I I

through the interior; the rest of the cavalry will be sent from hence as speedily as circumstances will permit.

It would have been more satisfactory, had our army been equipped for service, to have disembarked at St. Andero, or some other point nearer the Enemy; but, as it is of equal importance to the Spaniards as it is to us, that this army should not be partially committed or brought into contact with the Enemy, till the means of moving and following up an advantage are secured; and as the navigation on the coast of Asturias becomes extremely precarious towards the close of the year, it was the decided opinion of all military men, and of none more than the Marquis de la Romana, whose sentiments on this subject are stated in the accompanying memorandum, and will be expressed on his arrival in Spain, as fully approving of the decision that has been taken to make Corunna our principal Depôt, and to operate from thence. To render the Northern provinces the more secure whilst our army is assembling, and to co-operate with the other Spanish armies in circumscribing the Enemy's positions on the Ebro, the Marquis has determined to proceed with his own corps, amounting nearly to 10,000 men, to St. Andero; and he proposes, on his arrival there, by the incorporation of the armed peasantry of the Asturias and the Montagna, to augment their numbers to, at least, 20,000 men; which, with the Asturian army and Blake's, will carry the force in that quarter to 60 or 70,000 men, exclusive of the armies operating towards the front or left of the Enemy's line. I am not enabled to send you any precise calculation of the number of horses and mules we shall want. The cavalry, artillery, and waggon train will be provided from hence; the stores and baggage of the army, the Commissariat, &c. must be equipped in Spain. I have sent a Commissary into the Northern provinces to collect what can be had. Sir David Baird is directed, on his arrival, to equip his corps, if possible, from the resources of Gallicia and the North of Portugal. Sir John Moore, when he has arranged the movement of his army from Portugal, will, probably, superintend in person the equipment on the spot. I have only, in the mean time, to request you will communicate with those in authority, on the best means of rendering this important force serviceable as early as possible; that you will furnish Sir John Moore with every information and assistance; and that you will cause orders to be sent into the provinces of Gallicia, and to facilitate the equipment of the army, and ensure them a good reception.

The Marquis of Romana has written to make his Government perfectly understand the principles upon which our decision has been taken, and to explain to them why they must not expect the British troops to take the field in detached corps.

I have the honour to be, &c.

CASTLEREAGH.

*Major General*
*Lord William Bentinck.*

---

## C.

*Letter from Sir John Moore to Lord Castlereagh.*

MY LORD, *Lisbon, 9th October, 1808.*

I HAD the honour to receive, on the evening of the 6th instant, your Lordship's letter of the 25th September, communicating to me, that His Majesty had been graciously pleased to entrust to me the Command in Chief of a corps of troops, not less than 30,000 infantry and 5,000 cavalry, which His Majesty had determined to employ in the North of Spain. I beg your Lordship will convey to His Majesty the high sense I have of the honour conferred upon me; and that you will assure His Majesty, that I have nothing more at heart than the good of the service, that my best exertions shall not be wanting to promote its success, and I can only be happy in proportion as I shall be able to fulfil his Majesty's wishes, and to justify, in any degree, the trust he has been graciously pleased to repose in me.

I shall take an early opportunity to communicate with your Lordship on the various matters contained in your last dispatches, dated the 25th and 26th September. At present I can do little more than to acknowledge their receipt, and to state that it is my intention, as it was that of Sir Harry Burrard, to move with the troops from this on Almeida and Ciudad Rodrigo; this, your Lordship will observe by Lord William Bentinck's letter of the 2d October, is recommended by the Spanish Generals; and I think it preferable, for many reasons, to a movement by sea to Corunna, which at this season would be tedious and uncertain; and where the country, already exhausted by General Blake's army, will, perhaps, scarcely be able to supply the equipment required, to enable the corps, under Sir David Baird, when landed, to move forward.

The march from this will be by three routes, Coimbra, Guarda, and Alcantara; one regiment will begin its march the day after to-morrow in the direction of Coimbra, and all may be forwarded to a short distance, in their different routes, in the course of a week or ten days; but when they will be able to proceed further, or to pass the frontier of Portugal, it is impossible for me, at this instant, to say; it depends upon a knowledge of country which I am still without, and upon Commissariat arrangements yet unmade; but every effort shall be made by me, and those under me, to accomplish so desirable an object before the rains set in. I cannot conclude without mentioning the very great assistance I receive from Sir Harry Burrard, who acts with a degree of candour, of which few people would be capable under such circumstances. He seems, on this occasion, to put himself aside, and to give every thing to me, and to a service he thinks the most important, with as much liberality as if he himself were personally concerned in the conduct of it.

I have the honour to be, &c.

JOHN MOORE.

# D.

*Letter from Sir John Moore to Lord Castlereagh.*

*Lisbon, 9th Oct. 1808.*

I AM honoured with your Lordship's letter, private, which accompanied the public dispatch of the 25th September. I am very sensible of your Lordship's attention to me on this occasion. I shall avail myself of the permission you are kind enough to give me to correspond with you unofficially, and shall communicate, without reserve, every thing that can give you pleasure, or, in any degree, contribute to promote the public service. The great object at present is to get the troops out of Portugal before the rains set in; but, at this instant, the army is without equipment of any kind, either for the carriage of the light baggage of regiments, artillery stores, Commissariat stores, or other appendages of an army; and not a magazine is formed in any of the routes by which we are to march. The few days which Sir Harry Burrard held the command only enabled him to ascertain his wants, but not to remedy them. I mention this circumstance in the first place, because it is a truth; and in the next, to prevent your Lordship from being too sanguine, as to the probable period of my reaching the North of Spain. It is my intention to forward from this to Almeida as much ammunition and artillery stores as I can; and to form there also a depôt of provisions and other stores. Whatever comes with Sir David Baird, and from England, may be landed, or remain on board a ship at Corunna, to be forwarded from thence to such place, in that line, as may hereafter be judged most fit; but as yet I have no information from Madrid, but what is contained in Lord William Bentinck's letter of the 2d October.

I shall, probably, have an opportunity of writing to you very soon; but I hope your Lordship will have the goodness to excuse me for not entering upon further details at present, occupied, as I must necessarily be, in entering upon a command of such importance, and in the necessary arrangements for the march I am about to undertake.

I have the honour to be, &c.

JOHN MOORE.

----

E.

*Letter from Sir John Moore to Lord Castlereagh.*

MY LORD,                                   *Lisbon, 18th October, 1808.*

SINCE I had the honour to address your Lordship on the 9th instant, I have received your Lordship's letter, marked private, of the 30th September, inclosing copies of your instructions to Sir David Baird, and of your letter to Lord William Bentinck; a statement of transports, and a paper of the Marquis of Romana upon the line of march from Corunna into Castile. I immediately wrote to Sir David Baird, to inform him of my intention to march the whole of the troops by land, and to prevent his sending round the transports from St. Andero to Corunna; but had I wished to send any part of the army by sea, I could have done it without the aid of these transports, as there still remains here, after the embarkation of the French, tonnage for 12,000 men. I have received letters within these two days from Lord William Bentinck, from Madrid, of the 8th instant, in which he mentioned that the Spanish Government had been thrown into a considerable degree of alarm, in consequence of a letter intercepted from the Government of Bayonne to Marshal Jourdan, informing him, that between the 16th of

October and 16th November, 66,000 infantry, and from 5 to 7,000 cavalry would enter Spain. Lord William seems to consider this alarm, upon the whole, as salutary, although he gives credit to the contents of the letter; as the former supineness of the Central Council, its confidence and indifference to the existing danger, had been succeeded by a state of great activity. The troops from Madrid had been ordered to advance by double marches. General Castanos was sent to the army; and a determination was come to appoint Mr. Morla of Cadiz, Minister for the War department, a man, from whose ability and energy of character, much benefit was to be expected. A letter was also written to Mr. Stuart, by Count Florida Branca, to press the immediate junction of the British force. The letters which I wrote, both to Lord William and Mr. Stuart, on the 10th, would inform them of the succours coming from England, and the measures I was taking to accelerate the march of the troops.

It is impossible to be more anxious than I am to get forward; but it is needless to take forward troops without the means to enable them to act; and however light the equipment I have fixed, yet the difficulty of procuring it is very considerable; add to this, a Commissariat extremely zealous, but quite new and inexperienced in the important duties which it now falls to their lot to execute. I am, however, sufficiently aware of the importance of even the name of a British army in Spain, and I am hurrying as much as possible. The greatest part of the troops are in motion; in the course of this week all will, I hope, be clear of Lisbon. As soon as they are placed on their different routes, and I have concluded the arrangements here, I shall leave the conduct of the marches to the Generals conducting the different columns, and shall proceed myself direct to Almeida, to determine their further movement.

I have received no report yet of the arrival of Sir David Baird. I expect it daily, and have already sent two Staff Officers to join him.

I have the honour to be, &c.

JOHN MOORE.

F.

*Letter from Sir John Moore to Lord Castlereagh.*

MY LORD,                                              *Lisbon, 18th October, 1808.*

   I wish I could announce to your Lordship a greater progress, and that this letter had been addressed from any where but from Lisbon. All I can assure you of is, that I am labouring in my vocation, and if each day does not produce all the effect I could wish, or which, perhaps, I have a right to expect; yet there is no day which has not produced some, and we are accordingly getting on. In none of the departments is there any want of zeal; but in some of the important ones there is much want of experience, * * * * * * This remark applies particularly to the Commissariat, few of whose members have even seen an army in the field. The short maritime expeditions in which they have been employed, require but middling talents, and give them but little or no experience of the operations they are now called upon to perform. I have no complaint to make. Mr. Erskine is a clever man, of strict integrity; but still his habits have not been such of late, as to prepare him for a situation, to fill which so much ability and energy should be united. Mr. Erskine's character for integrity and honour may be of much use at the head of the department. * *
* * * * * * * * * * *

I have only touched upon this subject in my official letter; but I take the liberty you have given me to address you privately, to impress it seriously upon your Lordship's attention, as one of the greatest importance. The department itself must not be looked to; in it, I am persuaded, proper Officers will not be found; but men of business and of resource are to be found in London; and it is such men only who are fit for the higher branches of the Commissariat.

I have no hope of getting forward at present with more than the light baggage of the troops, the ammunition immediately necessary for the service of the artillery, and a very scanty supply of medicines. The depôt which I wish to establish at Almeida, I cannot wait for; but I hope the experience which is acquired in setting the troops in motion, will enable the Commissariat, when we are gone, to forward what is wanted for Almeida.

The Officers proposed to be sent from Madrid and the Spanish army, are not yet arrived; but, upon the information I have, I shall proceed, and am retarded only by my own arrangement. Money and shoes are the two articles we shall be principally in want of; and with respect to shoes, whatever quantities are sent, I should wish they were carefully inspected, as in general they are very bad. B. Gen. Sontag came here some time ago from Oporto. He shewed me your Lordship's instructions, to be employed in the South of Spain; but the Spaniards have expressed a dislike to have foreigners sent amongst them, though they are pleased to see any Englishmen. I should, therefore, upon this ground, have thought it proper to stop General Sontag; but it appears to me no longer necessary to employ Officers in the distant provinces, since the Central Government is formed at Madrid; with which I shall be henceforward in direct communication. I have, therefore, also put an end to Major Cox's mission at Seville, and have ordered him to return to his regiment at Gibraltar; and I believe it will be equally necessary soon to call in the other Officers employed in this manner with the different Spanish armies. I understand that Colonel Doyle received at first, from some of the provincial Governments, the rank of B. General; and he has now got, from General Blake, that of Marshal de Camp, or Major General. It strikes me as an impropriety in British Officers to take rank in a foreign service without the King's permission; and dangerous in another view, as the hope of such promotion may tempt them to forget the interest of the service for which they were sent, and their duty as British Officers. At any rate, I see no good purpose it can answer; and when the armies join it may be troublesome.

I have the honour to be, &c.

JOHN MOORE.

K K

P. S. I propose to employ B. General Sonttag in taking charge of the sick left at Lisbon, and in forwarding them to the army when recovered; and in assisting in forwarding the different articles for the use of the army, and the depôt at Almeida.

---

## G.

*Letter from Sir John Moore to Lord Castlereagh.*

MY LORD,                                                      *Lisbon, 27th October, 1808.*

EVERY thing is now clear of Lisbon, except two regiments which march to-morrow and the day following; and I shall myself leave it in a couple of hours.

I am under the necessity of sending General Hope with the artillery, cavalry, and a corps of infantry, in all about 6,000 men, by the great road leading from Badajos to Madrid; as every information agreed, that no other was fit for the artillery, or could be recommended for the cavalry. This is a great round, and will separate the corps, for a time, from the rest of the army; but there is no help for it; the road turns to the left a short distance from Madrid, and leads upon Espinar, from whence it can be directed on Valladolid and Burgos, or whatever other place may be judged hereafter best for the assembling of the army.

Sir David Baird arrived at Corunna on the 13th instant; but as it had not been previously notified to the Provincial Junta, he was not permitted to land his troops until an answer was received from Madrid. I have not heard from Sir David since that answer was returned; but I conclude that he landed on the 21st. I have written to him to march upon Astorga as soon as his corps is equipped. With the infantry which marched from this direct upon Almeida and Ciudad Rodrigo, I shall not advance beyond Salamanca; until the corps under Baird and Hope approach Astorga and Espinar, but shall collect them in Almeida, Ciudad Rodrigo, and Salamanca. This, at least, is my intention at present; and I shall consider myself fortunate if they reach those places before the first rains, which, in general, last six or eight days, and fall so heavy, that, during their continuance, the troops must halt.

I have directed Sir David Baird to form a small depôt of provisions and ammunition at Astorga. I am endeavouring to form one at Almeida; but the difficulty of carriage through Portugal is such, that it is extremely doubtful whether it will be formed in time to be of much use. As we advance, Corunna must be the place from whence our supplies from England are drawn; Lisbon and Portugal become then of no use to us. I have, however, under present circumstances, and until the army is united, thought it right to request Sir Charles Cotton not to send home the transports; and to this he has consented, unless he should be otherwise directed from England. Some ordnance and other ships should, at any rate, be left at Lisbon, for the conveyance of such stores and provisions as may be wanted to Corunna.

Colonel Lopez, the Officer sent to me from Madrid, was with me two days; he is now gone to aid General Hope's march. He is very confident we shall not want supplies; and it is upon this general assurance of the Spanish Government that I am leading the army into Spain without any established magazines. In this situation nothing is more essentially requisite than money; and, unfortunately, we have been able to procure here very little. Sir David Baird has come without any, and his troops paid only to the 24th September; and from this we could only send him £.8,000. Mr. Erskine has, I believe, written upon this subject, and I should hope that a supply was now on its passage. It is my intention as soon as I have made the necessary arrangements for the troops at Almeida and Rodrigo, &c. to go for a few days to Madrid. No Commander in Chief is yet named, and I fear the consequences, should the French, reinforced, be able to act offensively, and the different Spanish armies continue to be directed by a Council residing at Madrid.

I have the honour to be, &c.

JOHN MOORE.

———

## H.

*Resolution of a Council of War of Spanish Generals.*

*Tudela, 5th Nov. 1808.*

ATTENTION being had to the actual state of penury and want, which the Army of the Centre, destitute of the most necessary means, is suffering; considering also that their effective force is much less than had been supposed, it is agreed that in the present moment, it cannot be of assistance to the Army of the Left, notwithstanding the conviction of the urgency of such assistance. But it is agreed that the Estremadura troops, which ought to arrive at Burgos on the 6th or 7th of the present month, should pass towards Ona and Frias to support the right of General Blake; and that then the army of the Centre, leaving a flying corps of observation on the right bank of the Ebro towards Calaorra, should unite itself to the army of Arragon, for the purpose of acting offensively, as circumstances may require; this being the best means of remedying the actual state of weakness, and of accomplishing that system of movements which the comparative state of ours and of the Enemy's force requires.

## I.

### To H. E. Charles Stuart.

SIR,

THE Supreme Central Junta is assured that nothing is more necessary in the actual state of affairs than to unite against the common Enemy the greatest military force possible, to dislodge him without the least delay from the Spanish territory, and that it is expedient that the British auxiliary troops unite, with the greatest expedition, with the Spanish army, in order to co-operate with it; and anxious that the British troops should march with the celerity that circumstances and the interests of the two governments require, I am directed by the Supreme Junta to acquaint your Excellency with its wishes, so that the march and union of the English troops with our armies may be accelerated, as highly favourable to the common cause we defend; requesting your Excellency to take the necessary steps to effectuate this, the Supreme Junta is ready to contribute most powerfully on its part to remove every obstacle, and render every assistance possible, and is persuaded that Y. E. on your part will effectually labour for the same purpose.

I have the honour, &c.

6 *Nov. Aranjuez.*

PEDRO CEVALLOS.

---

MUY SENIOR MIO,

LA Suprema Junta Central reconoce que en la situacion actual nada es tan necessario como reunir contra el Enemigo comun la mayor fuerza armada posibile, p[r] desalofarle sin perder momento del territorio Español, y que conviene que las tropas Britanicas auxiliares se reunan ala mayor brebedad al Exercito Nacional con quien have obrar de concierto; y descarido que las tropas Britanicas marchen con la celeridad que exigen las circumstancias y los interezes de ambos Goviernos, tengo orden de S. M. la Suprema Junta de manifestar a V. S. sus deseos deque se accelero la marcha y reunion de las tropas Inglesas con nuestros exercitos, como seumamente conducente al bien dela cauza que defendemos; convidando a V. S. atomar de comun acuerdo las providencias correspondientes al efecto, p̃ la Suprema Junta esta pronta contriviun poderosamente por su parte ala remocion de todo embarazo, y a facilitan todos los auxilios oportunos que esten en su arbitrio, al paso que se luongea deque V. S. p̃ su parte con airrira eficarmente al mismo intento. Tengo el honor de ofrecer a V. S. mis deseos de complacerlo y serverle. Dios gue a V. S. m. aᵉ. Aranjuez 6 de Noviembre del 1808. B. L. M. de V. S. su al Seg. Ser.

PEDRO CEVALLOS.

*Sᵒʳ Stuart.*

---

## K.

*Letter from Viscount Castlereagh to Lieutenant-General Sir John Moore.*

SIR,                                            *Downing Street,* 14 *Nov.* 1808.

WITH the exception of the four regiments of cavalry and two troops of horse artillery, which are under orders to embark upon the return of the horse transports from Corunna, your army, consisting of the numbers stated in the margin *, will, I trust, by the time this dispatch shall reach you, have assembled on such points of the Spanish frontier as have been concerted with the Spanish Government, and be preparing to advance.

* From Portugal 23,745.—From England 14,561.—Cavalry, &c. to go 2,760.—Total, 41,066.

In entering upon service in Spain you will keep in mind that the British army is sent by His Majesty as an auxiliary force, to support the Spanish Nation against the attempts of Buonaparte to effect their subjugation.

You will use your utmost exertions to assist the Spanish armies in subduing and expelling the Enemy from the Peninsula; and in the conduct of your command you will conform to the regulations hereafter stated with respect to the question of military rank, and your intercourse with the Government of Spain.

In framing these Instructions it is necessary distinctly to provide first, for the case of the Spanish Government having entrusted the command of their armies to a Generalissimo, or Commander in Chief; and secondly, for the case which has hitherto existed, of distinct armies, each commanded by its own General.

Should the Spanish Government appoint a Commander in Chief of all their armies (the necessity of which appointment every day's experience appears to demonstrate) you will consider yourself as placed under the orders of that officer.

If the armies of Spain should remain as they have hitherto done, under their respective chiefs, the co-operation of the British army must, in that case, remain to be settled as a matter of concert by you with the commanders of the respective armies of Spain, in connection with whom you may be carrying on operations.

When the officers of the British and Spanish armies meet in service, they must take rank according to the dates of their respective commissions, without reference to the powers from whom those commissions are derived, provided such commissions are at present acknowledged by the Supreme Government of Spain.

You are to consider that the British force under your command is intended to act as a field army, to be kept together as far as the circumstances of the war will permit; and that all orders from the Commander in Chief, proceeding either directly or through his staff, are to be given to the British army through you as its immediate Commander; that it is not to be separated into detachments, nor any detachment to be made from it but with your entire concurrence, and by your express order. It is not to be employed in garrisons, whereby a material diminution would be made of its effective strength in the field, nor to be occupied in sieges without your particular consent.

Whenever you shall have occasion to make any communication to the Spanish Government, you are to correspond with it through the Minister at Madrid, and all communications from the Spanish Government are to be made to you through the same channel; and although communications either from the Spanish Government or the British Minister are not to be considered by you as in the nature of orders, you will nevertheless receive such requisitions or representations upon all occasions with the utmost deference and attention; and in case you shall feel it your duty to dissent from them, you will take care to represent in the fullest manner your reasons for so doing, as well to the British Minister, for the information of the Spanish Government, as to the Government at home.

You are also to keep up a constant and intimate correspondence with the British Minister, and to co-operate in the most cordial manner with him in carrying on the public service.

Should any difference of opinion arise on important military subjects between you and the Spanish Commander in Chief, you are to consider it your duty to pay obedience in the first instance to the orders you may receive; but you will, if you shall think it necessary, make a representation thereupon, through the British Minister, to the Supreme Government of Spain, as also to me for His Majesty's information.

As it is of peculiar importance, at the present moment, that His Majesty's Government should receive early, regular, and detailed reports of your proceedings, I am to desire that you will make it a rule to address a dispatch to me at least once in every week, or as much oftener as any occurrence of sufficient importance may arise, always being careful to send duplicates of the preceding dispatch by the subsequent conveyance.

It will be most grateful to His Majesty to find that the intercourse between the British army and the Spaniards has been invariably distinguished by marks of reciprocal confidence and kindness. His Majesty cannot doubt that the most exemplary discipline will be observed ; and His Majesty commands me particularly to enjoin, that the utmost respect and deference should be shewn by his troops upon all occasions towards the manners and customs of the Spanish Nation. His Majesty trusts that the example and influence of the officers will be directed to inspire this sentiment throughout every branch of the army.

I have the honor to be, &c.<br>CASTLEREAGH.

*To Lieut.-General Sir John Moore, K. B. &c. &c. &c.*

## L.

*Letter from Sir John Moore to Lord Castlereagh.*

MY LORD, *Salamanca, 24th Nov. 1808.*

I HAD the honour upon the 17th instant to receive your Lordship's dispatches of the 2d, conveyed to me by a King's Messenger.

My Letter from Lisbon of the 27th October would apprize your Lordship, that having concluded every arrangement there, I was about to follow the troops then already upon their march into Spain. As I travelled with my own horses, and was necessarily detained by business, at different places upon the road, I did not reach Salamanca until the 13th. On the day following the regiments began to arrive, and continued daily to come in by corps in succession. The three divisions of infantry, which marched under

Lieut.-Gen. Fraser, Major-Generals Paget and Beresford, are now all here; together with one brigade of artillery, which, with infinite difficulty, followed the road by Abrantes and Castle Branco. One brigade of infantry, which left Lisbon last, is still absent. It is employed in the escort of the ordnance, and the other stores which are forwarding for the service of the Army.

The troops have performed their march well, in spite of very bad weather, and the worst roads I ever saw. Their appearance now is as good, and their fitness for service much better, than when they left Lisbon. Their conduct upon the march, and since their arrival here, has been exemplary. All this does them honour, and marks strongly the care and attention of the Generals and Officers who conducted the marches, and who are in the immediate command of the troops.

Lieut.-General Hope, with the corps which marched from Badajos, in the direction of Madrid, will arrive, with the head of that division, at Arevalo, on the 25th; where I have ordered it to halt, and to close up. The first of the troops under Sir David Baird, from Corunna, reached Astorga on the 13th; and the whole, including the 7th, 10th, and 15th dragoons, will be assembled there about the fifth of December; before which time General Hope's corps will also be collected at Arevalo.

If we are not interrupted, the junction of the Army will be effected early in the next month. But the French, after beating the army of Estremadura, are advanced to Burgos. Gen. Blake's army in Biscay has been defeated, dispersed, and its officers and soldiers are flying in every direction; and the armies of Castanos and Palafox, on the Ebro and Alagon, are at too great a distance to render me the smallest assistance. Under such circumstances the junction of this Army becomes exceedingly precarious, and requires to be conducted with much circumspection. Should the French advance upon us before it is effected, Sir David Baird must retire upon Corunna, and I shall be forced to fall back upon Portugal, or to join General Hope, and retire upon Madrid.

The information which your Lordship must already be in possession of, renders it perhaps less necessary for me to dwell upon the state of affairs in Spain, so different from that which was to be expected, from the reports of the officers employed at the head quarters of the different Spanish armies. They seem all of them to have been most miserably deceived; for until lately, and since the arrival of Mr. Stuart and Lord William Bentinck at Madrid, and of Colonel Graham at the Central Army, no just representation seems ever to have been transmitted. Had the real strength and composition of the Spanish armies been known, the defenceless state of the country, and the character of the Central Government, I conceive that Cadiz, not Corunna, would have been chosen for the disembarkation of the troops from England; and Seville or Cordova, not Salamanca, would have been selected for the proper place for the assembling of this Army.

The Spanish Government do not seem ever to have contemplated the possibility of a second attack, and are certainly quite unprepared to meet that which is now made upon them. Their armies are inferior even in number to the French. That which Blake commanded, including Romana's corps, did not exceed 37,000. A great proportion of these were peasantry. The armies of Castaños and Palafox united do not now exceed 40,000, and are not, I suspect, of a better description; and until lately they were much weaker.

In the provinces no armed force whatever exists, either for immediate protection, or to reinforce the armies. The French cavalry from Burgos, in small detachments, are over-running the province of Leon, raising contributions, to which the inhabitants submit without the least resistance. The enthusiasm, of which we heard so much, no where appears; whatever good-will there is (and I believe amongst the lower order there is a great deal) is taken no advantage of.

I am at this moment in no communication with any of the Generals commanding the Spanish armies. I am ignorant of their plans, or of those of the Government. General Castanos, with whom, after repeated application, I was desired to communicate, for the purpose of combining the operations of the British Army, was deprived of his command at the moment I had begun my correspondence with him. The Marquis of Romana, who is appointed his successor, is still at Santander. Whatever weight the Marquis may have, when he assumes the command, General Castanos had very little; the Generals intrigued against him, and civil Commissaries sent by the Supreme Junta, without any plan of their own, served no other purpose but to excite dissention, and to controul his actions. In this state of things it is difficult for me to form any plan for myself, beyond the assembling of the Army. I shall then be in a state to undertake something; and if the Spaniards, roused by their misfortunes, assemble round us, and become once more enthusiastic and determined, there may still be hopes of repelling the French. It is my wish to lay before your Lordship, for the information of Government, things exactly as they are: it answers no good purpose to represent them otherwise, for it is thus that we must meet them. I feel no despondency in myself, nor do I wish to excite any in others, but our situation is likely soon to become an arduous one.

Reverses must be expected—and, though I am confident this Army will always do its duty, yet ultimate success will depend more upon the Spaniards themselves, and their enthusiastic devotion to their cause, than on the efforts of the British; who, without such aid, are not sufficiently numerous to resist the armies which will be immediately opposed to them.

I have the honour, &c.

JOHN MOORE.

---

*Letter from Sir John Moore to Lord Castlereagh.*

MY LORD,                                          *Salamanca, Nov. 24, 1808.*

I HAVE been so much occupied with the business of the Army, that I have trusted to Mr. Frere, Mr. Stuart, and Lord W. Bentinck, to convey to your Lordship a just representation of the state, civil and military, of this Country. This army is certainly too much adventured, and risks to be brought into action before it is united, and before its stores, ammunition, &c. are brought forward to enable it to act. I never understood the meaning of the Spanish Generals, in separating their armies, beyond communication, on each flank of the French; but I gave them credit that their plans were calculated upon their strength, and framed upon a knowledge of country, and other circumstances of which I was ignorant; and as they proposed Burgos, I certainly thought I was perfectly safe in assembling the army at Salamanca; but if I had had sooner a conception of the weakness of the Spanish armies, the defenceless state of the country, the apparent apathy of the people, and the selfish imbecility of the Government, I should certainly have been in no haste to enter Spain, or to have approached the scene of action, until the army was united, and every preparatory arrangement made for its advance; after I was here, and the troops were landed at Corunna, it was too late to retire, though I fear it may prove the wisest thing I could have done; for I see nothing that has a chance of resisting the force that is now brought against this country. There seems neither to be an army, generals, nor a government. I cannot calculate the power of a whole people determined and enthusiastic, if persons are brought forward with ability to direct it; but at present nothing of this kind appears, and yet I see no other chance Spain has of resistance. We are here by ourselves, left to manage the best way we can, without communication with any other army; no knowledge of the strength or position of the Enemy, but what we can pick up in a country where we are strangers, and in complete ignorance of the plans or wishes of the Spanish Government. Indeed, as far as I can learn, the Junta, alarmed at their situation which they might have foreseen and obviated, are incapable of forming any plan, or of coming to any fixed determination. I have of course communicated my sentiments to Mr. Frere, and in a late letter have plainly told him, that the ruin of the Spanish cause seemed to me so inevitable, that it would very soon become my duty to consider alone the safety of the British army, and withdraw it from a contest which risked its destruction, without the prospect of doing the least good. In the mean time, I am in constant communication with Sir David Baird and General Hope. Every thing is forwarding from Corunna and Lisbon that we can want, as fast as the natural difficulties of the countries through which they pass, and the scanty means of conveyance they afford, will allow. Every effort shall be exerted on my part, and that of the officers with me, to unite the army. But your Lordship must be prepared to hear that we have failed; for situated as we are, success cannot be commanded by any efforts we can make, if the Enemy are prepared to oppose us. I am without a shilling of money to pay the army their subsistence, and I am in daily apprehension that from the want of it, our supplies will be stopped. The 500,000 dollars your Lordship mentions, Sir David Baird considered as sent to him; he detained them, and has nearly expended them. The money which it is possible to procure at Madrid and in other towns of Spain is quite trifling, and it is impossible to describe the embarrassment we are thrown into from the want of this essential article; nothing but abundance of money, and prompt payments, will compensate when we begin to move, for the want of experience and ability of our Commissariat. Mr. Erskine is still at Lisbon, confined to his bed with the gout. There must be a change in the head of this department: your Lordship seems to have misunderstood me; assistants can easily be procured every where, but it is a man of ability to direct, that is wanted. And believe me, my Lord, that it is essentially necessary to find one if this army is kept together, even if to do it, you deviate from the common line, and place a man as the head, who has never before been in the department; but I beg to be understood, that, unless the change is essentially for the better, it will do more harm than good. The changes which have already taken place have only tended to puzzle us the more, for Mr. Kennedy is a very respectable man, and is at least as good as any of his colleagues in the department. I have transmitted to Mr. Erskine, copies of Mr. Harrison's and Mr. Burgman's letters, which accompanied your dispatches, but I doubt if money to any considerable amount can be procured in any part of Spain, and your Lordship must be prepared to supply it from England. Provisions can be of no use to us, unless we were acting upon the coast; it would be impossible, when at a distance, to have them conveyed to us, or to find the means of their accompanying the movement of the troops.

It is my intention to make the troops find their own meat, and to call upon the Commissary for bread, wine, and forage only. This would be attended with many good effects, besides easing the Commissariat. The troops would be satisfied with less meat, and would gradually learn to live upon what the country produced in greatest abundance ; but to adopt this plan, I must be certain of money to pay them, which at present I am not. With respect to the officers employed with the armies, I cannot help thinking, though probably not intentionally, that they have done harm, as the intelligence they have conveyed has tended to deceive; for nothing can differ more from the real state of Spain, the strength, condition, and composition of its armies, than all the representations I have ever read, which they had sent.

Major-General Leith is an old acquaintance of mine, and he perfectly deserves the character you give of him ; although from letters I have seen from him, I think he has in some instances mistaken the purposes of his mission. At present he can be of little use with a dispersed army; and as from the General Officers who left us, we are in want of Officers to command the brigades, I trust you will approve of my having ordered him to join Sir David Baird ; he will leave one of the officers attached to him to carry on the correspondence.

\*　　\*　　\*　　\*　　\*　　\*

\*　　\*　　\*　　\*　　\*　　\*

*[This passage contains observations on the abilities of several individuals, Spanish and British, very important for Ministers, but not proper for the public eye.]*· \*　　\*　　\*　　\*　　\*

\*　　\*　　\*　　\*　　\*　　\*

\*　　\*　　\*　　\*　　\*　　\*

The British officers employed with the Spanish armies should confine themselves to their duty to transmit faithful statements of all that passes, but should keep aloof from all cabals or intrigues. I have no uneasiness about the relative rank I should hold when serving with the Spanish Generals, though perhaps it will be right for the British Government to stipulate something upon this head. My situation at the head of so large a British force will always give me sufficient influence. The tone of my letter to General Castanos was conciliatory, and tending to convey that I considered

him as chief of the Spanish army, the person whose wishes I desired to follow, and begged him to communicate them to me. I shall adopt the same style in my correspondence with the Marquis of Romana. I perfectly feel the power I have as commanding an auxiliary force, to depart from any plan I disapprove; but this need not be produced unless required; it is natural that the Commander of the Spanish army should be considered as the Commander of the whole. What I have stated in my official dispatch of the conduct of the troops, is not more than they deserve: nothing can exceed their behaviour : it is the surprize and admiration of the Spaniards.     *     *     *
*     *     *     At Almeida was the only exception.     *     *
*     *     *     *     *     *     *     *     *
One of the soldiers who was sentenced to be hanged by a Court Martial, I ordered to be executed; and I spoke my mind pretty freely to both the officers and soldiers as I passed Almeida. I hope this will have a good effect; and that when they join the army, they will behave better. Brigaier-General Charles Stuart is with General Hope. I forwarded his letter to him ; and I hear good accounts both of him and of the Cavalry.

I have the honour to be, &c.

JOHN MOORE.

----

M.

*Letter from Sir John Moore to Lord Castlereagh.*

MY LORD,                                      *Salamanca, 25th Nov. 1808.*

IN answer to your Lordship's Letter, inclosing the Copy of a Warrant for the assembling a Court of Enquiry to investigate the circumstances under which the late Convention in Portugal was concluded; I have only to say, that I hope, in the middle of such operations as I am at present engaged in, I shall not be desired to send home the Adjutant and Quarter-Master Generals of the Army; the two Officers upon whom hinges the whole business of the Army. It is hardly necessary for me to dwell upon such a subject; the Members themselves must be sufficiently acquainted with the inconvenience which must attend such a measure to me; and the injury which it will occasion to the service. I trust that the Court and Parties will either dispense with the evidence of these officers, or that they will send out the questions which they wish to be answered; when they can be taken upon oath here, before the Deputy Judge Advocate of the army.

Indeed, from the nature of the evidence which Brigadier-General Clinton and Colonel Murray can give, I should think this method might be adopted with equal advantage to all the parties: but at any rate, if this cannot be, I hope the Enquiry will be put off until quieter times.

I have the honour to be, &c.

JOHN MOORE.

## N.

### Letter from Sir John Moore to Lord Castlereagh.

MY LORD, Salamanca, 25 Nov. 1808.

I HAD the honour to receive your Lordship's letter, mentioning, that it had been determined to send Sir John Craddock to command in Portugal, in consequence of Sir Harry Burrard's recall; but that his superior rank was not to interfere with my command of the army in the field, in the event of the British army falling back on Portugal. Sir Harry Burrard sent an order to Maj.-Gen. Mackenzie, now with Sir David Baird, but who belongs to the staff of Portugal, to go to Lisbon to take the command upon his departure; but, as the commotions which your Lordship mentions are long since quelled, and as Portugal is perfectly tranquil, I have taken upon me to detain Maj.-Gen. Mackenzie with Sir David Baird, who is much in want of General Officers, until the arrival of General Leith, for whom I have sent to St. Andero.

I am not prepared at this moment to answer minutely your Lordship's question respecting the defence of Portugal; but I can say generally, that the frontier of Portugal is not defensible against a superior force. It is an open frontier, all equally rugged, but all equally to be penetrated. If the French succeed in Spain, it will be vain to attempt to resist them in Portugal. The Portuguese are without a military force; and, from the experience of their conduct under Sir Arthur Wellesley, no dependence is to be placed on any aid they can give. The British must in that event, I conceive, immediately take steps to evacuate the country. Lisbon is the only port, and therefore the only place from whence the army, with its stores, can embark. Elvas and Almeida are the only fortresses on the frontier. The first is, I am told, a respectable work. Almeida is defective; and could not hold out beyond ten days against a regular attack. I have ordered a depôt of provisions, for a short consumption, to be formed thère, in case this army should be obliged to fall back. Perhaps the same should be done at Elvas. In this case we might check the progress of the Enemy, whilst the stores were embarking, and arrangements were made for taking off the Army. Beyond this the defence of Lisbon, or of Portugal, should not be thought of.

I have the honour to be, &c.

JOHN MOORE.

## O.

*Letter from Sir John Moore to Lord Castlereagh.*

MY LORD, *Salamanca, 26 Nov. 1808.*

    IT was my intention to have detained the Messenger until I should have received from Madrid Mr. Frere's dispatches; but I have received no answer from him to the letters I wrote to him on the 19th, two days after the arrival of this messenger from England. I am averse to detain him longer, thinking the matter contained in my letters of the 24th sufficiently important not to be longer detained. I was the more surprized at not receiving any from Mr. Frere, as he should be able to judge, from the state of the Junta, and of the public mind there, what efforts are likely to be made to oppose the French; and this is material to determine me whether to fall back on Portugal or Madrid, in case such measures are necessary. If I am obliged to fall back before my junction with Sir David Baird, it will, I think, be on Portugal. After the junction I am inclined to prefer Madrid; unless I plainly see that the game is up, and resistance on the part of Spain vain. If we remain in Spain, too many cavalry cannot be sent, as the French cavalry are numerous, and the Spaniards have few or none. Yesterday I received a letter from General Leith, from Leon; where he had arrived with the Marquis de Romana.

  I am in hopes of seeing the Marquis of Romana as he passes to Madrid; and think it most important that I should. General Blake is at no great distance from Leon; but I believe alone, without any part of his force, which is completely dispersed.

      I have the honour to be, &c.

             JOHN MOORE.

P.

*Letter from Sir John Moore to Lord Castlereagh.*

MY LORD,                                        *Salamanca, 29 Nov.* 1808.

I RECEIVED yesterday evening a letter from Mr. Stuart, inclosing one from Lieut.-Col. Doyle, from Aranjuez, announcing the total defeat of the army of Castanos and Palafox. My junction with Sir David Baird, which was always extremely doubtful, although I was determined to try it, is become, I conceive, quite impracticable; but if this army could be united, after the specimens we have had of the very little resistance offered by the Spaniards, what chance has this army alone, of resisting the formidable numbers which will be immediately brought against it? I conceive the British troops were sent in aid of the Spanish armies; but not singly to resist France, if the Spaniards made no efforts. By persevering longer I should certainly sacrifice the Army, without benefiting Spain. I have, therefore, determined to retire. I have ordered Sir David Baird to fall back on Corunna, and General Hope to endeavour, by forced marches, to join me at this place. I have already given your Lordship my opinion, that Portugal cannot be defended against a superior Enemy; but the Spaniards may still give the French some occupation, and the difficulties of the country, the swelling of the rivers, &c. may prevent the French from pushing us much, and enable me to stand for a time. This time can only be well employed in withdrawing the army, which can do no good here; but which, if the Spaniards rouse, and get an able man at their head, are able to collect, and to make battle from the South. If landed at Cadiz we may still be useful. I have desired Sir David, therefore, to repair, when embarked, to the Tagus; and I should hope that your Lordship will immediately order a sufficient number of transports from England to receive the Army. When I left Lisbon there was tonnage there for 12,000 men. It is by landing in the South of Spain, that now we can be of any use. The Spaniards have failed not so much from any fault, or weakness, in the people, as from the want of energy and ability in the government. If this be overset, and men of greater talent get to the head, there may still be a chance; and, by throwing in arms and ammunition, and finally with this army, their affairs may be retrieved. It is, however, impossible, after what we have seen, to be very sanguine on this subject.

I shall probably have an opportunity of writing to you again very soon; but I was anxious not to detain Mr. Vaughan, who carries this, and who brought me Mr. Stuart's letter from Madrid. I shall anxiously wait for your Lordship's answer, and hope to find that the decision I have made meets the approbation of his Majesty's Government.

I have the honour to be, &c.

JOHN MOORE.

P. S. I shall write to the General commanding in Portugal to embark immediately the stores of the Army; and to send provisions to Abrantes and Oporto for this Army. He will provision Elvas, and make dispositions to aid us in covering Lisbon.

---

Q.

*Leon, le 30 Novembre, 1808.*

*Du Marquis de la Romana à S. E. Mr. Le Gén. Sir John Moore,*<br>*Com. Gén. de l'Armée Angloise en Espagne.*

JE viens de recevoir la lettre de votre Excellence en date du 28, par laquelle je suis informé de la position que V. E. occupe, tandis que je suis ici à réorganiser cette armée du Gen. Blake, dont la fuite et la dispersion ne peut-être attribuée à autre chose qu' au défaut de subsistance. La perte dans toutes les attaques, depuis le 6 ou 7 de Nov<sup>re</sup> jusqu' au 11, ne devant monter qu' à mille cinq cents hommes entre morts et blessés et prisonniers. J' espère que dans peu nous serons en état de faire quelque mouvement; et je n' attends que les souliers pour les faire marcher, car ils sont dans un état de nudité le plus parfait qu' on puisse imaginer, mais leur esprit n' est pas abbatu, et en les nourissant bien ils iront leur train.

Je me flatte que votre corréspondence sera suivie et fréquente: en attendant j' ai l' honneur de vous faire passer une lettre qu' un Paysan a intercepté à un aide-de-camp d' un Gén¹ qui est à Carrion. Si la nouvelle est vraie, il faut prendre ses précautions pour faire notre jonction, ou la faire au plus-tot. C' est ce que je ne laisserai pas de vous avertir.

Je désire aussi que V. E. m' écrive en François; non que je n' entende pas parfaitement l'écriture Angloise, mais parcequ' ordinairement on écrit si vite que les mots m' échappent.

En attendant j' ai l' honneur de vous saluer cordialement, Mr. Le Gén¹; et je vous prie de croire aux sentimens de vraie amitié avec lesquels.

J' ai l' honneur d' être votre

Très humble et parfait Serviteur,

Le M<sup>uis</sup> DE LA ROMANA.

---

## R.

*Letter from Sir John Moore to Lord Castlereagh.*

MY LORD, *Salamanca, Dec. 5, 1808.*

I HAD the honour to address your Lordship on the 29th of November, and to inform you with the determination I had come to, in consequence of the defeat of the army of General Castanos ; and General Hope, with the division he commands, marched to Avila to avoid the superior cavalry of the Enemy in the plain, and reached Alba de Tormes, four leagues from this, yesterday ; his junction is thus secured, and I am now preparing to fall back on Ciudad Rodrigo. The Enemy has directed his whole force towards Madrid, which will probably give me time to reach Portugal unmolested. Buonaparte is at Aranda de Duero ; reinforcements join him daily. The French attacked and carried the pass of Somma Sierra on the 27th, which opens to them that of the Guardarama; and they are in possession of Segovia. The few Spanish corps opposed to them are composed of fugitives collected from the beaten armies, and they offer no resistance. I have had no communication with Madrid since the 30th of November ; the inhabitants had taken up arms, were barricading the streets, and expressed a determination to die rather than submit ; no such spirit has yet been manifested by any other force in Spain. How long the populace of a large town are likely to persevere in such a resolution, or how long they will be able to withstand the formidable attack made against them I cannot say. Your Lordship may believe that it was not without much reflection and extreme reluctance that I determined to withdraw the army from Spain, and to abandon the cause, for the success of which the Government are so much interested, and the public mind so highly exalted. My letters to your Lordship of the 25th and 26th November, containing a just representation of the state of affairs in this country, would tend to shew how much the Government and the people of England had been deceived, and would prepare your Lordship for the reverses which have since taken place. As long as there remained an army, and any hope of resistance on the part of the Spaniards, I was determined to persevere, at all risks, in the junction of the army, and then if General Castanos had received a check, or been forced to retreat, it was my intention, if nothing better offered, to march upon Madrid, from whence getting behind the Tagus, we should have given the Spaniards an opportunity of rallying around us, and have shared their fortunes. This intention I mentioned to your Lordship in my letter of the 26th, and I imparted it as a question to Mr. Frere for his opinion. But the sudden defeat of General Castanos' army, so complete, and yet accomplished after so little resistance, shewed with what little ardour the Spaniards are inspired in their country's cause—it left nothing either to aid me, or to prevent the farther progress of the Enemy. The British army was at that moment on its march to collect at this place and Astorga. General Hope with the head of his division was at Villa Castin, and from the collected manner in which it was necessary to march, he could not have joined me sooner than he has done; Sir David Baird's corps could not be collected at Astorga before the 4th of this month; it was thus impossible for this army to have been united before the 14th, or 13th; and still later before it could be ready to undertake an offensive movement. This time was more than sufficient to enable the Enemy to finish the destruction of what little Spanish force remained, and to turn the greatest part of his army against the British, which when united does not exceed 26,000 men, but which probably he would be able to attack whilst detached and separated. I had the most perfect conviction from experience, of the want of energy and ability in the Spanish Government, and of the apathy of the people, and of the unprepared state of the country, and that upon the defeat of the armies no aid was to be expected from any other quarter. I considered the British army as standing alone, that its union could not be attempted without great hazard, and, if effected, that it could not withstand the great force that would be brought against it. It was vain, I thought, that under such circumstances it could retrieve the Spanish cause; and though I knew the army would cheerfully attempt whatever I ordered, I thought my duty called upon me not to expose it to a contest in which its best efforts could not promise to be successful. It may fairly be said that the British army never reached Spain: it cannot in the true sense be called an army until it is united and prepared to act; the Spanish forces were defeated, and their cause lost, before the British so constituted could come to their assistance. I feel the weight of the responsibility fallen to me; I had nothing but difficulties to chuse; whether I have chosen the least, and that which will be the least disapproved by His Majesty and my Country, I cannot determine: my wish has been, to decide right: I reflected well upon the different duties I had to discharge, and if I have decided wrong, it can only be because I am not gifted with that judgment which was imputed to me when I was entrusted with this important command.

I have the honour to be, &c.

JOHN MOORE.

———

S.

*Letter from Sir John Moore to Lord Castlereagh.*

MY LORD, *Salamanca, 5th Dec. 1809.*

Since I had the honour to address my dispatch to you this morning, I find considerable hopes are entertained from the enthusiastic manner in which the people of Madrid resist the French. I own I cannot derive much hope from the resistance of one town against forces so formidable, unless the spark catches, and the flame becomes pretty general; and here the people remain as tranquil as if they were in profound peace.

I have however in consequence of the general opinion, which is also Mr. Frere's, ordered Sir David Baird to suspend his march, and shall continue at this place until I see farther, and shall be guided by circumstances. Unless the spirit becomes general, Madrid must soon fall. At all events, if I marched into Portugal, it would be with a view to return the moment a favourable opportunity offered. But I shall not go towards Madrid until I know with more certainty the force of the Enemy, and see something to convince me that more confidence can be placed in the steadiness of the Spaniards.

I had the honour to receive yesterday your Lordship's dispatches of the 15th November, by Mr. Windham 1st Guards.

I have the honor to be, &c.

JOHN MOORE.

N N

## T.

Ex<sup>lmo</sup> S<sup>or</sup>.

Con esta ftia digo lo que signe al S<sup>or</sup> Ministro de S. M. B. en España.

DESEANDO la Junta Suprema Gubernativa del Reyno fixar de una vez su concepto acerca de las operaciones del Exercito auxiliar Yngles, y que la continuacion de planes decididos proporcione las ventasas que devemos esperar de las fuerzas Españolas auxiliadas de las Britanicas, ha juzgado conveniente comisionar sujetos q<sup>e</sup> al caracter, conocim<sup>tos</sup>, y experiencia militar, reumesen las demas qualidades que se necesitan para encargo tan importante. Las personas q<sup>e</sup> por todas estas consideraciones ha juzgado mas aproposito son D<sup>n</sup> Bentura Escalante, Capitan General de los R<sup>s</sup> Extos y del Reyno de Granada, Presid<sup>te</sup> de Aquella Junta, y el Brigadier D<sup>n</sup> Agustin Bueno, los cuales saldrán immediatamente para Salamanca a tratar con los S. S. Generales del Exto Yngles, y conviñar con ellos quantas medidas, planes, e ideas sean oportunas, decidan sobre las operacion<sup>s</sup> militares y demas puntos q<sup>e</sup> ocurran y convenga arreglar; afin de q<sup>e</sup> las tropas de S. M. B. obren de concierto con las nuestras, y accelerando sus movimientos convinados, se eviten dilaciones tan contrarias ala noble empresa importante a ambas Naciones, cuyos lazos de amistad y de alianza van a estrechiar mas y mas riesgos comunes, y una gloria en q<sup>e</sup> ntra generosa auxiliar tendrá la may<sup>r</sup> pte.

Y lo traslado a V. E. para su gobierno y q<sup>e</sup> le conste la autorizacion de q<sup>e</sup> van revestidos el Gen<sup>l</sup> Escalante y el Brigadier Bueno.

Dios gue<sup>e</sup> a V. E. m<sup>s</sup> a<sup>s</sup>. R<sup>l</sup> Palacio de Aranjuez, 28 de Novembre de 1808.

MARTIN DE GARAY.

*S<sup>or</sup> Gen<sup>l</sup> en Xefe delas tropas de S. M. B. en Espana.*

## V.

*Ex^mo Sir Moor G^ral del Exercito de S. M. B.*

Exmo Senor.

SENOR,

Muy Señor nuestro y de nuestro mayor aprecio. La Junta Militar y Politica, formada de todas las autoridades, reunidas en nombre del Rey que Dios guarde para atender ala defensa de esta Corte que se halla amenada por los Enemigos ; tiene el honor de hacer presente a V. E. con la debida exactitud el elado de las cosas ; y se reduce, a que el Exercito del Centro que mandaba el General D^n Franc^o Xabier Castaños, y que sera como de beinte y cinco mil hombres, se viene replegando a toda priesa hacia Madrid para reunirse con su guarnicion ; y que el de Somasierra, en numero de unos diez mil hombres, viene tambien al mismo efecto a esta villa, donde se reuniran hasta quarenta mil ; cuyo numero y fuerza hace que no deba temerse el Exercito de los Enemigos que se ha presentado. En estas circumstancias, y temiendo la Junta que vengan mas fuerzas Francesas, a unirse con las actuales, espera que V. E. sino tiene Enemigos ala vista puede replegarse para unirse con nuestro Exercito, a tomar direccion a caer sobre las espaldas del Enemigo ; y creheria agrabar el notorio celo de V. E. por la causa justa y su singular actividad si dudare de modo alguno, que la rapidez de sus movimentos sera qual conviene al interes de su nacion y la nuestra. Con este motivo ofrece la Junta a V. E. su consideracion y respetos.

Dios gue a V. E. m^s a^s. Madrid, 2 de Diciembre de 1808.

EL PRINCIPE DE CASTELFRANCO,

THOMAS MORLA.

P. S. La Junta se persuade que V. E. se habra reunido ya al Exercito que mandaba D^n Joaquin Blak y estaba poca hace en Leon.

*Ex^mo S^r Moor G^ral del Exercito de S. M. B.*

## U.

*From the London Newspapers, Dec. 19th 1808.*

### "PARIS.

#### Thirteenth Bulletin of the Army in Spain.

*Saint Martin, near Madrid, Dec. 2.*

"On the 29th ult. the head-quarters of the Emperor was removed to the village of Bonquillas. On the 30th, at break of day, the duke of Belluno presented himself at the foot of the Soma-Sierra. A division of 13,000 men of the Spanish army of reserve defended the passage of the mountains. The Enemy thought themselves unattackable in that position. They were entrenched in the narrow passage called Puerto with 16 pieces of cannon. The 9th light infantry marched upon the right, the 96th upon the causeway, and the 24th followed by the side of the heights on the left. General Senarmont, with six pieces of artillery, advanced by the causeway; the action commenced by the firing of musquetry and cannon. A charge made by General Montbrun, at the head of the Polish light horse, decided the affair; it was a most brilliant one, and this regiment covered itself with glory, and proved it was worthy to form a part of the Imperial Guard. Cannons, flags, muskets, soldiers, all were taken, or cut to pieces. Eight Polish light horse were killed upon this causeway, and 16 have been wounded; among the latter is Captain Dzievanoski, who was dangerously wounded, and is almost without hopes of recovery. Major Segur, Marshal of the Emperor's household, charged among the Polish troops, and received many wounds, one of which is very severe. Sixteen pieces of cannon, ten flags, thirty covered chests, 200 waggons laden with all kinds of baggage, and the military chests of the regiments, are fruits of this brilliant affair. Among the prisoners, who are numerous, are all the Colonels, or Lieutenant-Colonels of the corps of the Spanish divisions. All the soldiers would have been taken if they had not thrown away their arms and dispersed in the mountains. On the 1st of December the head-quarters of the Emperor were at St. Augustin, and on the 2d the Duke of Istria with cavalry commanded the heights of Madrid. The infantry would not arrive before the 3d. The intelligence which we hitherto received led us to think that this town is suffering under all kinds of disorders, and that the doors are barricaded. The weather is very fine."

*Moniteur, Dec. 13th.*

## " PARIS, Dec. 13th.

*Camp at Madrid, Dec. 4th.*

" The town of Madrid has capitulated; our troops entered it to-day at noon."

*Moniteur, Dec. 14th.*

*From the London Newspapers, December 29, 1808.*

### FOURTEENTH BULLETIN OF THE ARMY IN SPAIN.

*Madrid, 5th Dec.*

THE 2d at noon his Majesty arrived in person on the heights which impend over Madrid; on which were already placed the divisions of Dragoons of Generals La Tour, Maubourg, and La Houssaye, and the Imperial Horse-Guards. The anniversary of the Coronation, that epoch which has signalised so many days for ever fortunate for France, awakened in all hearts the most agreeable recollections, and inspired all the troops with an enthusiasm which manifested itself in a thousand exclamations. The weather was beautiful, and like that enjoyed in France in the finest days in the month of May. The Marshal Duke of Istria sent to summon the Town, where a military Junta was formed, under the presidency of the Marquis Castelar; who had under his orders General Morla, Captain-General of Andalusia, and Inspector-General of Artillery. The Town contained a number of armed peasants, assembled from all quarters, 6000 troops of the line, and 100 pieces of cannon. Sixty thousand men were in arms; their cries were heard on every side; the bells of 200 churches rang altogether; and every thing presented the appearance of disorder and madness. The General of the troops of the line appeared at the advanced posts, to answer the summons of the Duke of Istria. He was accompanied by thirty men of the people, whose dress, looks, and ferocious language, recalled the recollection of the assassins of September. When the Spanish General was asked whether he meant to expose women, children, and old men, to the horrors of an assault, he manifested secretly the grief with which he was penetrated; he made known, by signs, that he, as well as all the honest men of Madrid, groaned under oppression; and, when he raised his voice, his words were dictated by the wretches who watched over him. No doubt could be entertained of the excess to which the tyranny of the multitude was carried, when they saw him minute-down all his words, and cause the record to be verified by the assassins who surrounded him. The Aide-de-camp of the Duke of Istria, who had been sent into the town, was seized by men of the lowest class of the people, and was about to be massacred, when the troops of the line, indignant at the outrage, took him under their protection, and caused him to be restored to his General. A butcher's boy from Estremadura, who commanded one of the gates, had the audacity to require that the Duke of Istria should go himself into the town with his eyes blindfolded. General Montbrun rejected this presumptuous demand with indignation. He was immediately surrounded, and effected his escape only by drawing his sword. He narrowly escaped falling a victim to the imprudence of having forgot that he had not to make war with civilized enemies. A little time after, some deserters from the Walloon Guards came to the camp. Their depositions convinced us that the people of property, and honest men, were without influence; and it was to be concluded that conciliation was altogether impossible.

The Marquis of Perales, a respectable man, who had hitherto appeared to enjoy the confidence of the people, had been on the day before this accused of putting sand in the cartridges. He was immediately strangled. It was determined that all the cartridges should be remade. 3 or 4000 monks were employed upon this work at the Retiro. All the palaces and houses were ordered to be open, to furnish provisions at discretion. The French infantry was still three leagues from Madrid. The Emperor employed the evening in reconnoitring the town, and deciding a plan of attack, consistent with the consideration due to the great number of honest people always to be found in a great capital.

To take Madrid by assault might be a military operation of little difficulty; but to engage that great city to surrender, by employing alternately force and persuasion, and by rescuing the people of property, and real good men, from the oppression under which they groaned — this was what was really difficult. All the exertions of the Emperor, during these two days, had no other end. They have been crowned with the greatest success.

At seven o'clock the division Lassisse of the corps of the Duke of Belluno arrived. The Moon shone with a brightness that seemed to prolong the day. The Emperor ordered the General of Brigade, Maison, to take possession of the Suburbs; and charged the General of Brigade, Lauriston, to support him in the enterprize with four pieces of artillery, belonging to the Guards.

The sharp-shooters of the 16th regiment took possession of some buildings, and in particular of the grand cemetery. At the first fire the Enemy shewed as much cowardice as he did of arrogance all the day. The Duke of Belluno employed all the night in placing his artillery in posts marked out for the attack. At midnight the Prince of Neufchatel sent to Madrid a Spanish Lieutenant-Colonel of Artillery, who had been taken at Somosierra, and who saw with affright the obstinacy of his fellow-citizens. He took charge of the annexed letter, No. 1. On the third, at nine in the morning, the same flag of truce returned to the Head Quarters with the letter, No. 2, But the General of Brigade Senarmont, an officer of great merit, had already placed 30 pieces of artillery, and had commenced a very smart fire; which made a breach in the walls of the Retiro. The sharp-shooters of the division of Villatte having passed the breach, their battalion followed them; and in less than a quarter of an hour 1000 men who defended the Retiro were knocked on the head. The Palace of the Retiro, the important posts of the Observatory, of the Porcelain Manufactory, of the Grand Barrack, the Hotel of Medina Celi, and all the outlets which had been fortified, were taken by our troops. On another side 20 pieces of cannon of the Guards, accompanied by light troops, threw shells, and attracted the attention of the Enemy by a false attack.

It would have been a difficulty to form a conception of the disorder that reigned in Madrid, if a greater number of prisoners, arriving in succession, had not given an account of the frightful scenes, of every description, of which that capital presented the spectacle. They have intersected the streets, erected parapets on the houses; barricades of bales of wool, and of cotton, had been formed; and the windows had been stopped with mattresses. Those of the inhabitants who despaired of a successful resistance were flying into the fields; others, who had preserved some share of reason, and who preferred appearing in the midst of their property before a generous enemy, to abandoning it to the pillage of their fellow-citizens, demanded that they should not expose themselves to an assault. Those who were strangers to the town, or who had nothing to lose, were for a defence to the last extremity, accused the troops of the line of treason, and obliged them to continue their fire.

The enemy had more than 100 pieces of cannon pointed; a more considerable number of two and three-pounders had been dug up, taken out of cellars, and tied upon carts, a grotesque train, and sufficient in itself to prove the madness of a people abandoned to itself. But all means of defence were become useless. The possessors of Retiro are always Masters of Madrid. The Emperor took all possible care to prevent the troops going from house to house. The City was ruined if many troops had been employed. Only some companies of sharp-shooters advanced, and the Emperor constantly refused to send any to sustain them. At eleven o'clock the Prince of Neufchatel wrote the annexed letter (No. 3). His Majesty, at the same time, ordered the fire to cease on all points.

At five o'clock General Morla, one of the Members of the Military Junta, and Don Bernardo Yriarte, sent from the town, repaired to the tent of his Serene Highness the Major-General. They informed him that the most intelligent persons were of opinion, that the town was destitute of resources, and that the continuation of the defence would be the height of madness; but that the lowest classes of the people, and the crowd of *men, strangers to Madrid,* wished to defend themselves, and thought they could do it with effect. They required the day of the 4th to make the people listen to reason. The Prince Major-General presented them to His Majesty the Emperor and King, who addressed them thus : " You make use of the name of the People to no
" purpose; if you cannot restore tranquillity, and appease their minds, it is
" because you have yourselves excited them—you have led them astray by
" propagating falsehoods. Assemble the Clergy, the Heads of Convents, the
" Alcades, the men of property and influence, and let the town capitulate
" by six o'clock in the morning, or it *shall cease to exist.* I will not, nor
" ought I to withdraw my troops. You have massacred the unfortunate
" French prisoners who had fallen into your hands. Only a few days ago
" you suffered two persons in the suite of the Russian Ambassador to be
" dragged along and murdered in the public streets, because they were
" Frenchmen born. The incapacity and cowardice of a General had put
" into your power troops who capitulated on the field of battle; and the
" capitulation has been violated. You, Mr. Morla, what sort of a letter did
" you write to that General? It well became you, Sir, to talk of pillage;
" you who, on entering Roussillon, carried off all the women, and distri-
" buted them as booty among your soldiers! Besides, what right had you
" to hold such language?—the capitulation precluded you from it. See what
" has been the conduct of the English, who are far from piquing themselves
" on being rigid observers of the Law of Nations. They have complained
" of the Convention of Portugal, but they have carried it into effect. To

" violate military treaties, is to renounce all civilization; it is placing Generals
" on a footing with the *Bedouins* of the desert. How dare you then pre-
" sume to solicit a capitulation, you who violated that of Baylen? See how
" injustice and bad faith always recoil upon the guilty, and operate to their
" prejudice. I had a fleet at Cadiz: it was in alliance with Spain; yet you
" directed against it the mortars of the town, where you commanded. I
" had a Spanish army in my ranks: I would have preferred seeing it embark
" on board the English ships, and being obliged to precipitate it from the
" rocks of Espinosa, than to disarm it; I preferred having 7000 more ene-
" mies to fight, rather than to be deficient in honour and good faith. Re-
" turn to Madrid: I give you till six o'clock to-morrow morning. Return
" at that hour, if you have to inform me only that they have surrendered;
" if not, you and your troops shall be all put to the sword."

On the 4th, at six in the morning, General Morla and General Don
Fernando de Vera, Governor of the Town, presented themselves at the
tent of the Prince Major-General. The discourses of the Emperor,
repeated in the midst of the persons of distinction, the certainty that he
commanded in person, the losses sustained during the foregoing day, had
carried terror and repentance into all minds. During the night the most
mutinous withdrew themselves from the danger by flight, and a part of the
troops was disbanded. At ten o'clock General Belliard took the command
of Madrid; all the posts were put into the hands of the French, and a
general pardon was proclaimed. &c."

## W.

*A Su Ex<sup>a</sup> S<sup>nor</sup> Frere.*

Ex<sup>mo</sup> So<sup>r</sup>,

Muy So<sup>r</sup> mio, Desde su Quartel Gen<sup>l</sup> en Leon dice el Marques de la Romana à la Junta Suprema Gubernativa del Reino con f<sup>ha</sup> de 2 del corriente q<sup>e</sup> havia 8 dias estaba tratando con el Gen<sup>l</sup> Ingles Sir D. Baird, q<sup>e</sup> manda las tropas de su nacion en Astorga, para que con ellas y doçe ó catorce mil hombres escogidos del Ex<sup>to</sup> de su cargo pasarán à Zamora à reunir se con el G<sup>l</sup> Sir John Moore p<sup>r</sup> la ruta q<sup>e</sup> le havia indicado, con el fin de hacer un movimiento sobre los Enemigos haciá el punto q<sup>e</sup> sea mas conveniente : pero quando se lisonjeaba de la conformidad del G<sup>l</sup> Baird, le havia respondido q<sup>e</sup> tenia orden positiva de pasar por tierra ó por mar à reunirse por Portugal con el G<sup>l</sup> Moore. Que havia repitido sus instancias à los dos Generales, y en el dia anterior le havia contestado definitivamente el Gen<sup>l</sup> Baird q<sup>e</sup> retiraba su artilleria p<sup>a</sup> embarcarla en la Coruña, y el con sus tropas pensaba dirigirse à Portugal por la costa de Galicia, ó por la provincia de Tras los Montes sobre Almeida. Que le escribia de acuerdo con el G<sup>ral</sup> Belarde, q<sup>e</sup> havia llegado aquella noche à Leon, manifestandole la consternacion en q<sup>e</sup> iba à poner aquel pais con su retirada, la imposibilidad de marchar el Marques solo sin ninguna cavalleria acia Zamora, los males à q<sup>e</sup> quedaba expuesta aquella provincia, y el riesgo q<sup>e</sup> amenazaba al Reino de Galicia.

La Junta Suprema ha sabido con la mayor sorpresa y dolor esta resolucion de los Gen<sup>les</sup> Ingleses, laqual si llegará à verificarse proporcionaria grandes ventajas à las armas Francesas, y acarreria à las Españolas las mas terribles consequencias. Los generosos y prontos socorros q<sup>e</sup> nos facilitó la Inglaterra, y las tropas con q<sup>e</sup> nos auxiliaba, aumentaron el entusiasmo de nuestros Pueblos, y alentaron la justa esperança de q<sup>e</sup> esta reunion aseguria el feliz exito de la empreza. Por lo mismo el desaliento y consternacion q<sup>e</sup> producirá ahora el ver qᵉ el Exᵗᵒ Britanico, sin obrar ni reunirse, se retira à los Puertos excitarán sentimientos y causarán efectos contrarios à la buena causa. Se debilitarán el entusiasmo y ardor qᵉ hasta ahora ha sostenido la confianza en la uniformidad de ideas y en las operaciones del Exᵗᵒ Ingles unido con nuestras tropas.

Ademas de los irreparables perjuicios qᵉ sentiriamos nosotros, el Portugal quedaria expuesto à verse segunda vez sugeto a los Franceses, qᵉ entonces desconcertaban completamente quantos planes y medidas pudieron salvar estos dos reinos aliados de la Inglaterra, la qual por ultimo resultado no habria facilitado socorros ni tropas sino para hacernos contar su ayuda efectiva, y retirarla en el momento mas critico y interesante. En efecto acaso el Enemigo nunca ha estado mas cerca de se ruina (si los Exercitos Ingleses y Españoles saben obrar con oportunidad y energia) qᵉ en el momento en qᵉ debilitado con lo qᵉ le han costado sus ultimos esfuerzos, podemos aprovechar la ventaja de ver su exercito dividido en cubrir una linea tan extendida.

Todas estas consideraciones y las funestas consequencias qᵉ politicamente acarreria el retirarse las tropas Inglesas no pueden ocultarse à la penetracion de V. E. y de los S. S. Generales de S. M. B. qᵉ con la reunion contribuian à la libertad de Portugal y la nuestra, y concluyendo asi la generosa obra à qᵉ los destinó la amiga de la España immortalizaban su nombre y el servicio qᵉ hacian à todo el continente.

Aunqᵉ nuestras tropas han tenido revezes, no hay fundamento pᵃ desmayar, antes bien el estado de los cosas ofrece en el numero de tropas qᵉ formarán Ingleses y Españolas, en el entusiasmo y confianza qᵉ producirá la union unos recursos casi indefectibles qᵉ deven asegurarnos el vencimiento.

En efecto el M. de la Romana luscará al Gˡ Sir J. Moore, se le reunirá desde luego con catorce mil hombres escogidos de su Exᵗᵒ y con las activas y energicas providencias qᵉ la Junta Suprema ha dictado, deutro de un mes aumentará su gente con treinta mil conscriptos de los Reinos de Leon, Galicia, y Asturias. S. M. como V. E. sabe ha resuelto que pase à conferenciar con Sir J. Moore uno de sus vocales que está pronto à marchar, y à quien acompañará como V. E. ha ofrecido, y contribuirá pʳ su parte al objeto el Sʳ Stuart.

Tambien espera q° V. E. movido de tan fuertes consideraciones se esfuerce en persuadir al G¹ en Gefe de las tropas Ingleses q° el entusiasmo de los Pueblos, su consuelo, la libertad de la Nacion, la seguridad del Portugal, los intereses de la Inglaterra, y los de la Europa entera dependen de q° se verifique al momento la reunion, y concertados los planes se obre del modo q° se juzgue conveniente; pues de otra forma ni se consigue el objeto de la venida, ni de ella habra resultado otra ventaja que la de malograr la mejor ocasion de destruir al Enemigo eterno de la quietud del Continente, abandonando à su suerte à la España y al Portugal en el momento en q° mas necesitaban los auxilios de su aliado.

La Junta Suprema confia en la adesion q° V. E. la ha manifestado, y en el vivo interes q° toma por nuestra causa, q° contribuirá con todo su influxo y representacion à q° no se malogre tan grande empresa : todo lo qual pongo en consideracion de V. E. de orden de S. M.

MARTIN DE GARAY.

Truxillo, 6 Dec. 1808.

## X.

*A Su Exᵃ il General en Xefe de las Tropas de S. M. B. Sᵒʳ Moore.*

EXCᴹᴼ SENOR,

La Junta de Gobierno de Toledo desea salvar la Patria, reune el Exᵗᵒ disperso, y toma las medidas y ha está ora da abiso al Sʳ Eredia qᵉ tiene esta Cap¹ endonde hallará los socorros, qᵉ pueda hᵗᵃ morir, comunica iguales partes à Aranjuez y demas puntos de reunion qᵉ ha llegado à n'tra noticia lo qᵉ se participa V. E. pᵃ qᵉ midiendo sus operaciones contras medidas tenga la satisfaccion al mismo tiempo deqᵉ la tenemos y tendremos en morir a su lado pʳ la Patria.

Dios guⁿ a V. E. mᵃ aˢ. Toledo 5 de D'bre de 1808, a la una dela mañana.

Excᵐᵒ Sʳ,

ANTONIO PEREZ DEL CASTILLO.    RAMON MARECA.
PEDRO BIOSCA.    MARTIN CELLA CERDA.
    MANUEL DE MEDINA Y CAMINO.

## Y.

THE numbers of effective fighting men in an army differ much from the total numbers of the various corps, owing to sickness, absentees, and various contingencies. The following is a correct extract from the Adjutant-General's Reports.

*Effective Soldiers who marched from Portugal under the Command of Sir John Moore.*

| Description of Troops. | Regiments. | Officers Commanding. | Numbers. Rank & File | Total. |
|---|---|---|---|---|
| Artillery - - | Royal Artillery - - - | Colonel Hardinge - - - | 686 | 686 |
| Cavalry - - - | 18th Light Dragoons - | Lieut. Col. Jones - - - | 565 | 912 |
| | 3rd Ditto, or King's German Legion - - | Major Burgwedel - - - | 347 | |
| Infantry - - | 2nd Regiment - - - | Lieut. Col. Ironmonger - | 616 | 16,933 |
| | 3rd Ditto - - - - | Lieut. Col. Blunt - - - | 815 | |
| | 4th Ditto - - - - | Lieut. Col. Wynch - - | 754 | |
| | 5th Ditto - - - - | Lieut. Col. Mackenzie - | 833 | |
| | 6th Ditto - - - - | Major Gordon - - - - | 783 | |
| | 9th Ditto - - - - | Lieut. Col. Campbell - | 607 | |
| | 20th Ditto - - - - | Lieut. Col. Ross - - - | 499 | |
| | 28th Ditto - - - - | Lieut. Col. Belson - - | 750 | |
| | 32nd Ditto - - - | Lieut. Col. Hynde - - | 756 | |
| | 36th Ditto - - - - | Lieut. Col. Burne - - - | 736 | |
| | 38th Ditto - - - - | Lieut. Col. Greville - - | 823 | |
| | 42nd Ditto - - - - | Lieut. Col. Stirling - - | 880 | |
| | 43rd Ditto - - - - | Lieut. Col. Null - - - | 411 | |
| | 50th Ditto - - - - | Major Napier - - - - | 794 | |
| | 52nd Ditto (1st battalion) | Lieut. Col. Barclay - - | 828 | |
| | 52nd Ditto (2nd ditto) | Lieut. Col. Ross - - - | 381 | |
| | 71st Ditto - - - - | Lieut. Col. Pack - - - | 724 | |
| | 79th Ditto - - - - | Lieut. Col. Cameron - - | 838 | |
| | 91st Ditto - - - - | Major Douglas - - - | 698 | |
| | 92nd Ditto - - - - | Lieut. Col. Napier - - | 900 | |
| | 95th Ditto - - - - | Lieut. Col. Beckwith - - | 467 | |
| | 95th Ditto - - - - | Major Travers - - - | 321 | |
| | Staff Corps - - - - - | Captain Leicester - - - | 61 | |
| | King's German Legion | | | |
| | 1st Light Battalion - - | Lieut. Col. Leonhart - - | 803 | |
| | 2nd Ditto - - - - | Lieut. Col. Halket - - - | 855 | |
| | | | | 18,531 |

N. B. The 3rd Regiment 815 strong, who were left on the frontiers of Portugal to keep up the communication, should be deducted, 815
The 82nd Regiment, commanded by Major Williams, and one company of the 3rd joined at Sahagun, forming together about 700, are to be added - - - - - - - - - - - - - - - - - 700

| | | | 115 | — 115 |
|---|---|---|---|---|
| | | From Portugal | | 18,416 |

*The Numbers of the Effective Soldiers that marched from Corunna under*
*Sir David Baird.*

| Description of Troops. | Regiments. | Officers Commanding. | Numbers. Rank & File | Total. |
|---|---|---|---|---|
| Artillery - - - | Horse Artillery - - - | Captain Downman - - | } 177 | } 611 |
| | Royal Artillery - - - | Captain Eveleigh - - | 434 | |
| Cavalry - - - | 7th Hussars - - - - | Lieut. Col. Vivian - - | 497 | } 1,538 |
| | 10th Ditto - - - - | Lieut. Col. Leigh - - | 514 | |
| | 15th Ditto - - - - | Lieut. Col. Grant - - | 527 | |
| Infantry - - | 1st Foot Guards (1st bat.) | Lieut. Col. Cocks - - | 1300 | } 7,401 |
| | Ditto (3rd battalion) - | Lieut. Col. Wheatley - | 1027 | |
| | 1st Regt. (3rd battalion) | Major Mullers - - - | 597 | |
| | 14th Ditto (2nd battalion) | Lieut. Col. Nichols - - | 550 | |
| | 23rd Ditto - - - - | Lieut. Col. Wyatt - - | 496 | |
| | 26th Ditto - - - - | Lieut. Col. Maxwell - | 745 | |
| | 43rd Ditto - - - - | Lieut. Col. Gifford - | 817 | |
| | 51st Ditto - - - - | Lieut. Col. Darling - | 516 | |
| | 76th Ditto - - - - | Lieut. Col. Symes - - | 654 | |
| | 95th Ditto (detachments) | Lieut. Col. Wade - - | 699 | |
| | | | | 9,550 |

From Corunna - - - 9,550
From Portugal - - - 18,416

Army 27,966

Z.

*Letter from Sir John Moore to Lord Castlereagh.*

MY LORD,                                              *Salamanca,* 8 *Dec.* 1808.

In a short letter which accompanied my dispatch of the 5th inst. I mentioned that the resistance offered by the people of Madrid had arrested the operations of the French, and gave a hope that the affairs of this country might still be recovered, desperate as they are; yet if the example of the Capital is followed, and enthusiasm becomes general, France will be forced to divide her armies, and will be no longer so formidable. The difficulty of obtaining information is very great; I have none certain with respect to Madrid, only I believe it still holds out. I have ordered Sir David Baird, who was retreating, to march back. I shall continue the arrangements I have ordered in Portugal, in case I should be obliged to fall back, but I am preparing to march to Zamora and Toro, to join Baird, whom I have ordered to advance to Benavente; when we are joined, and if the Marquis de la Romana, with the troops he is collecting at Leon are ready, I shall move towards Burgos, and the communications of the French. Your Lordship may depend upon it, that I never shall abandon the cause as long as it holds out a chance of succeeding; but you must be sensible that the ground may be in an instant cut from under me : Madrid may fall, and I be left to contend with very superior numbers indeed. I hope a better spirit exists in the Southern Provinces; here no one stirs, and yet they are well inclined. An expression in a letter intercepted, from a French officer commanding at Vittoria to the Chief of the Staff with the Army, paints the people in this part exactly :

P P

" L'esprit publique est toujours mauvais, toujours de l'incredulitè sur nos avantages, quant à la tranquillité du pays, elle est parfaite \*."

I have made no remark on the subject of your Lordship's dispatch of the 25th November, respecting my rank with the Spanish Generals : the Government has not as yet named any one to the Chief Command of their armies, every thing on that head is as loose as ever. You perceive by the manner I have already expressed myself in former letters, that I have no wish to be tenacious on this subject ; but I confess I have heard of none of their Generals yet, under whom it would be safe to place the command of the British troops. I shall certainly always be inclined to pay great deference to the wishes of whatever General commands any Spanish army with which I am acting ; yet, until some one appears very different from any we have heard of hitherto, it cannot be desirable that he should know he had a right to command me ; and I cannot help beseeching you to consider this subject once more before you finally fix it.

As I am sending a courier to Sir David Baird, I have written this on the chance of an opportunity offering to forward it ; and in this manner I shall endeavour to keep you in the current of affairs here. I have sent Colonel Graham to Madrid to send me information of what is passing there. Lord Paget with the cavalry arrives at Zamora to-morrow, and next day I propose moving a corps with myself to Toro.

I know not if your Lordship has heard lately from General Charles Stuart ; he is in our front, and very well.

I have the honour to be, &c.

JOHN MOORE.

P. S. The Junta are gone to Badajos ; not a very good example for the people.

---

\* The disposition of the public mind is always bad ; our successes are never believed, but the country remains completely tranquil.

A A.

*Letter from Sir John Moore to Lord Castlereagh.*

MY LORD,                                    *Salamanca,* 10 *Dec.* 1808.

COLONEL Graham, whom I had sent to Madrid, returned to me last night. He could only get as far as Talavera de la Reina, where he found two members of the Supreme Junta, who informed him that Madrid had capitulated on the 3d. The Duke of Castelfranco and Mr. Morla, who were at the head of the Junta established at Madrid, are accused by the people of betraying them. Castellar, the Captain-General, and all the military officers of rank, refused to ratify the Treaty, and left the town with 16 pieces of cannon. The people refuse to give up their arms, but the French have the gates, the Retiro, and Prado. Saragossa stills holds out, and it is said, that on the 1st they repulsed the French, who had made a general attack. It is said that attempts are making to assemble a great force in the South; I dare say the force will be assembled, but the efforts it will make when assembled, I must think are very doubtful. I cannot believe that real enthusiasm is spread over any considerable portion of Spain. Had the people of Madrid been really determined, I do not see how Mr. de Morla and the Duke of Castelfranco could have given up the town. They accuse their leaders to cover their own want of spirit: this was the case with General St. Juan, who commanded when the pass of Somasierra was forced; it is thought his troops misbehaved, they have since accused him of treachery, and have murdered him. I certainly think the cause desperate, because I see no determined spirit any where, unless it be at Saragossa. There is however a chance; and whilst there is that, I think myself bound to run all risks to support it. I am now differently situated from what I was when Castanos was defeated : I have been joined by General Hope, the artillery, and all the cavalry (Lord Paget with 3 Regiments is at Toro) ; and my junction with Sir David Baird is secure, though I have not heard from him since I ordered him to return to Astorga. Madrid, though it has capitulated, must still engage a considerable part of the Enemy's force. Saragossa is also a considerable diversion ; and the collections forming in the South cannot be neglected ; all his force cannot thus be directed against me. The corps collecting under the Marquis of La Romana at Leon is, I am told by Sir David Baird, very bad. I shall however connect myself with it ; and I mean to move to Valladolid, where I shall order Baird to join me ; and to which neighbourhood I hope also that La Romana will advance.

This movement I shall begin to morrow, by sending two corps to join Lord Paget at Toro ; Generals Hope and Frazer, from Alva de Tormes and this place, shall move on Tordesillas. I hope on the 14th to be at Valladolid. My communication when there will become uncertain with Almeida and Portugal, from whence all my stores are not yet forwarded, but I must take my chance : I shall be in Fortune's way ; if she smiles, we may do some good ; if not, we shall still, I hope, have the merit of having done all we could. The army, for its number, is excellent; and is, I am confident, quite determined to do its duty. I have had a letter from Sir John Craddock from Corunna ; he was proceeding to Lisbon ; he has landed part of the money from the Lavinia there, and will land the rest at Oporto or Lisbon. I have begged of him to bring the two regiments from Gibraltar to the Tagus.

I understand that Mr. Murray is intended to relieve Mr. Erskine, and to supersede Mr. Kennedy. The latter has acted as Chief Commissary with this army since it reached Spain (Mr. Erskine is still at Lisbon), and has certainly acquired a degree of experience which is extremely useful : it is quite cruel for him to be thus superseded by an officer not previously of higher rank to himself, and who probably has much less experience, and not more ability : at any rate, a new man at the head of the Department would be very prejudicial at this moment ; Kennedy could not be expected to act under him. I have therefore begged Sir John Craddock to keep Mr. Murray at

Lisbon; and I hope, unless Mr. Murray's talents are known to be very superior, that he may not be permitted to supersede Mr. Kennedy with this army, who without money, and under many disadvantages, has hitherto supplied us well. I should hope that the rest of the cavalry your Lordship has mentioned, will be sent without delay.

The horses and harness of the waggon train will be useful, but their waggons are heavy and bad; those we get in the country are more convenient. I should therefore propose to leave the waggons at home, and send the rest of that establishment only.

Until affairs in Spain bear a more promising aspect, I should think your Lordship will approve of keeping at Corunna and Lisbon a sufficient quantity of transports for the re-embarkation of the army; and I think many reasons unite to make it desirable for us to be in possession of Cadiz. I mean to mention this to Mr. Frere. When it is agreed to, the two regiments from Gibraltar, as the most ready, could take possession, and garrison it.

I have the honour to be, &c.

JOHN MOORE.

## B B.

*Letter from Sir John Moore to Lord Castlereagh.*

MY LORD,                                   *Salamanca, 12 December,* 1808.

I LEAVE this place to-morrow; and I shall be at Valladolid on the 16th, with the troops I brought with me from Lisbon, with the addition of three regiments of cavalry from England, amounting to 1500. I have not heard from the Marquis of Romana, and must give up the co-operation of his corps for the present. Sir David Baird's will not be at Astorga for some days; but he will advance to Benavente when ready; and, as he will be in my rear, he can move up, or I can fall back upon him; but I do not think it advisable longer to delay moving forward. I shall threaten the French communications, and create a diversion, if the Spaniards can avail themselves of it; but the French have in the North of Spain from 80 to 90,000 men, and more are expected. Your Lordship may, therefore, judge what will be our situation if the Spaniards do not display a determination very different from any they have shewn hitherto. I have written to Sir John Craddock to keep whatever transports are not required for the embarkation of the troops in Portugal, ready to send to Vigo, if required. If I am forced to retreat, it will probably be on the Galicias. The road is good, and the country capable of being defended. In this case we shall want flour, as the country produces only cattle in any abundance. Whatever ships are sent from England, for the purpose of withdrawing the Army, should call at Corunna· for orders, and then rendezvous at Vigo. It is to Corunna also _that money, and every supply, should be forwarded. The communication from Lisbon and Oporto, through Portugal, is so very bad, that nothing can be forwarded in time; and, as I consider myself now united with Baird's corps, I shall certainly of the two, whether for retreat or communication, prefer Galicia to Portugal.

I fear that Mr. Frere is infinitely more sanguine upon the subject of Spain than I am. This is to be regretted, as it renders it more embarrassing for you to come to a decision upon the measure to be pursued. I have seen no ability with the Spanish Government, but much the reverse: none has been displayed by their officers in the command of the armies; no one officer has yet a chief direction of the military branch; the armies have shewn no resolution, the people no enthusiasm, nor no daring spirit; and that which has not been shewn hitherto, I know not why it should be expected to be displayed hereafter. I feel as if the British was the only efficient force in Spain. Your Lordship will consider with what view it was originally sent; whether in aid of an enthusiastic brave people, capable of fighting their own battles, or to contend alone with France, and retrieve the affairs of a beaten disorganized nation. We have had now some proof of the efforts of which Spain is capable; and we can judge by the resistance they have made, whether they have fought with that spirit and obstinacy of a people ardent for the independence of their country. It is certainly right for your Lordship to consider well these matters, that you may be able to estimate justly the aid which is to be expected in this struggle from the Spanish nation, and decide to what amount the British Army should be reinforced, or, if not reinforced, what measures it should follow. The French force in Spain may fairly be set down at 80,000 men *, besides what is in Catalonia; the British at 27 or 28,000, including the regiments coming from Portugal. The French expect considerable reinforcements. The armies which the Spaniards had formed have been beaten and dispersed, and are again collecting. This, my Lord, is, I believe, the true statement; and I leave your Lordship to throw into the scale what portion of enthusiasm, resolution, and ability, you think we have a right to expect from the specimen already given.

As this letter is private, I have written it with a freedom which otherwise I should not have used. It is my wish to give you every material upon which to found a just opinion; for certainly the situation of this Army is too critical to be long neglected; and unless a spirit is displayed by the Spaniards, of which we see no indication, it is impossible but they must be subdued.

I have the honour to be, &c.

John Moore.

---

* Sir J. Moore's intelligence, particularly that obtained through the Spanish Government, was often imperfect. Instead of 80,000, he should have said 150,000.

## C C.

Ex<sup>no</sup> S<sup>or</sup>,

AVIENDO apurado todos los medios, y reflexiones politicas militares, y convenientes p<sup>a</sup> q<sup>e</sup> V. Ex<sup>a</sup> desistiera del projecto derretirar sus tropas à Ciudad Rodrigo, y aun a Portugal, y las de Astorga à Galicia, diciendo V. Ex<sup>a</sup> de q<sup>e</sup> el Marques de la Romana solo havia podido juntar cinco mil hombres, determiné salir de Salamanca ayer manana, p<sup>a</sup> ir aencontrar la Junta Suprema de Govierno, considerando concluida mi comision, y oi me alcanzado un Posta con una carta del Marques de la Romana, cuya copia remito a V. Ex<sup>a</sup> p<sup>r</sup> sipuede hacer le mas fuerza q<sup>e</sup> mis reflexiones, y variar su plan, q<sup>e</sup> silleya averificarse, y no condesciende V. Ex<sup>a</sup> aq<sup>e</sup> se reuna todo su Exercito con el de Astorga, y el del Marques de la Romana en Zamora, ù otro punto, q<sup>e</sup> pueda imponer à los Enemigos, es inevitable la destruccion de España, y quiza V. Ex<sup>a</sup> mismo se verá obligado à embarcarse p<sup>a</sup> Ynglaterra, y si V. Ex<sup>a</sup> condocendiese en la reunion espresada, seria mui dable de q<sup>e</sup> los Enemigos desistieran de atacarce Madrid, y retroce dieran, loq<sup>e</sup> daria tiempo, aq<sup>e</sup> se reuniera el Exercito del Centro, y temar otras dispociones conducentes. Sp<sup>co</sup> a V. Ex<sup>a</sup> se sirva dar una contestacion alq<sup>e</sup> le entregue esta, p<sup>a</sup> q<sup>e</sup> mela embie por un expro, y si V. Ex<sup>a</sup> hariese la bondad de escrivir al Marques de la Rômana su ultima determinacion envista dela adjunta, seria mui conveniente.

Dios gue à V. Ex<sup>a</sup> m<sup>s</sup> a<sup>s</sup>. La Calzada de Ban'os 7 de Diciembre de 1808.

Ex<sup>mo</sup> Sen'or,

VENTURA ESCALANTE.

Ex<sup>mo</sup> S<sup>or</sup> Gen<sup>l</sup> More.

## D D.

*Letter from Sir John Moore to Lord Castlereagh.*

MY LORD,                                       *Toro,* 16 *Dec.* 1808.

        I HAD the honour to receive your Lordship's letter of the 3d Dec. with enclosures, forwarded to me by a King's Messenger, who reached me on the night of the 13th, at Alaejos, the head quarters of the Army, after its first march from Salamanca. I was to have proceeded, on the 15th, to Valladolid; which place I should have reached the next day, when I received the letter of which I send your Lordship a copy. It is from Berthier, Prince of Neufchatel, to Marshal Soult, Duke of Dalmatia. The officer who was charged with it was murdered by some peasants, near Valdestillos, between Segovia and Valladolid; who brought the letter to our advanced posts, to B. General Stewart. I was determined by the information it contained to prefer the speedy union of the Army to every other object; and therefore, instead of Valladolid, I marched to this place. I had already directed Sir David Baird to push on his corps, by brigades, to Benavente. The first arrived there yesterday, and the brigade of Guards will reach it this day. I shall march from this to-morrow, to some villages within two or three leagues of Benavente. I shall there be so close as to be able to protect Sir David's junction, and make it perfectly secure. It will be the 20th before all his corps are up. If then Marshal Soult is so good as to approach us, we shall be much obliged to him; but if not we shall march towards him. It will be very agreeable to give a wipe to such a corps; although, with respect to the cause generally, it will probably have no effect, Spain being in the state described in Berthier's letter. She has made no efforts for herself; our's come too late, and cannot at any rate be sufficient. The French seem to have been ill informed of our movements: they are, however, soon acquainted with them, as our advanced posts have met; and Gen. Charles Stuart, with a detachment of the 18th Dragoons, on the night of the 12th, surprised a detachment of their cavalry and infantry in the village of Rueda, killed and took prisoners the greatest part of them. The affair was trifling, but was managed by the B. General with much address, and was executed with spirit by the officers and men. It was a detachment from Valladolid, where Gen. Franceschi commanded, with 3 or 400 cavalry. He had no knowledge of our being so near, and would not believe one of the men, who escaped from the village in the dark, and carried to him the report of the surprise, and defeat, of the detachment. Whether, when Buonaparte hears that we have not retired to Lisbon, he will give to the corps on their march to Badajos a different direction, I cannot say; but whilst I march towards Soult I must take care not too much to uncover Astorga, and the passes into Galicia; from whence in future I must draw all my stores, and through which ultimately, if pressed, I alone can retreat. Should, therefore, on my approach, Soult retire towards Burgos to join Junot, who is on his march to that place with the 8th corps, I shall of course be forced to desist, and to return to this neighbourhood. In short, unless some great efforts, of which there is now but little probability, are made by the Spaniards, it is evident how the business must terminate. For, even if I beat Soult, unless the victory has the effect to rouse the Spaniards, and to give their leaders ability, it will be attended with no other advantage than the character it will attach to the British arms. I have apprised Sir John Craddock of Buonaparte's march to Badajos; which has since been confirmed to me, by a man who left Talavera, after his advanced guard had entered it. I have told him, that, in case of retreat, mine will be through Galicia; and I have begged him, after selecting the quantity of tonnage necessary for the embarkation of the troops in Portugal, to send the rest to Vigo, to wait my orders. The Lieutenant-General will communicate to your Lordship the quantity of tonnage he sends to Vigo, when you will be able to judge the quantity necessary to be sent there from England, should the re-embarkation of this Army become necessary. Your Lordship must see the probability of such an event; and will, I fancy, think it right to have the means upon the spot. Should this Army retire into Galicia, and remain in it any time, I understand from Sir David Baird that we shall want flour; which I should hope you will send from England. With respect to the propriety of sending reinforcements, I must leave your Lordship to determine. If at this moment I had 7 or 8000 cavalry, I should certainly do much. If we retire into the Galicias they would be an encumbrance. And, to enable us to keep our ground in Spain, the reinforcements of both cavalry, infantry, and artillery, must be considerable indeed. I shall endeavour to give your Lordship from time to time every information, and must then leave you to form your determination. It is a subject upon which you can form as good a judgment as the best military man. I shall ever be of opinion, that unless Spain herself makes greater efforts, and displays more ardour and energy in her own cause, the efforts of England can be of no avail.

I have the honour to be, &c.

JOHN MOORE.

P.S. I received a letter on the 13th from the Marquis of Romana, in which he says he will send an officer to me, as he does not choose to trust to paper, by a messenger, the subject he has to communicate. This officer has not yet come. The Marquis is still at Leon, he says, with 20,000 men, 3000 of whom have no arms; but from Sir David Baird's account they are in no state to be much depended upon; and he seems also to doubt their number. The fugitives from that and other armies are spread over the whole country. They have in general their arms, and will be troublesome subjects to the French. And we may expect to hear of continual insurrections, in different parts of Spain, of massacres, &c.; but there must be a great change in the conduct and character of this country before the people are brought to assemble in armies, and to act upon system.

J. M.

E E.

*Letter from Sir John Moore to Lord Castlereagh.*

MY LORD,                                          *Benavente, 28 Dec. 1808.*

        SINCE I had the honour to address you upon the 16th from Toro, the army has been almost constantly marching through snow, and with cold that has been very intense. The weather within these few days has turned to rain, which is much more uncomfortable than the cold, and has rendered the roads almost impassable. On the 21st the army reached Sahagun; it was necessary to halt there, in order to refresh the men, and on account of provisions. The information I received was, that Marshal Soult was at Saldana with about 16,000 men, with posts along the river from Guarda to Carrion.

    The army was ordered to march in two columns at eight o'clock on the night of the 23d to force the bridge at Carrion, and from thence proceed to Saldana. At six o'clock that evening I received information that considerable reinforcements had arrived at Carrion from Palencia; and a letter from the Marquis de la Romana informed me that the French were advancing from Madrid, either to Valladolid or Salamanca. It was evident that it was too late to prosecute the attempt upon Soult; that I must be satisfied with the diversion I had occasioned; and that I had no time to lose to secure my retreat. The next morning General Hope, with his own division and that of Lieutenant-General Fraser, marched to Mayorga. I sent Sir David Baird with his division to pass the river at Valencia; and I followed General Hope on the 25th with the reserve, and the light brigades, by Mayorga, Valderos, to Benavente; the cavalry, under Lord Paget, followed the reserve on the 26th; both the latter corps entered this place yesterday. We continue our march on Astorga: Generals Hope and Fraser are already gone on. Sir David Baird proceeds to-morrow from Valencia; and I shall leave this with the reserve at the same time. Lord Paget will remain with the cavalry, to give us notice of the approach of the Enemy. Hitherto their infantry have not come up, but they are near, and the cavalry is round us in great numbers; they are checked by our cavalry, which have obtained by their spirit and enterprize an ascendancy over that of the French which nothing but great superiority of numbers on their part will get the better of.

The diversion made by our march on Sahagun, though at a great risk to ourselves, has been complete; it remains to be seen what advantage the Spaniards in the South will be able to take of it. But the march of the French on Badajos was stopped when its advanced guard had reached Talavera de la Reina; and every thing disposable is now turned in this direction. The stores I had collected here are moving back to Astorga, and those at Astorga to Villafranca. The roads are very bad, and the means of carriage scanty. If I am pressed I must lose some of them; and I may be forced to fight a battle. This, however, I shall endeavour to avoid; for certainly, in the present state of things, it is more Buonaparte's game than mine. It is said that he comes himself with 10,000 of his guards. The force moving against us cannot be less than 50,000 men: we shall, when at Astorga, be about 27,000. The Marquis la Romana came forward to Mansilla with 6,000 to co-operate with me in the attack on Soult: I therefore conclude that he cannot have above 8,000 fit for action. The country about Astorga offers no advantage to an inferior army; I shall, therefore, not stop there longer than to secure the stores, and shall retreat to Villafranca, where, I understand, there is a position. But if the French pursue, I must hasten to the coast; for there is a road to Orense which leads more direct to Vigo, and which, of course, renders the position at Villafranca of no avail. Some time ago the Marquis la Romana intimated his intention of retiring into the Galicias by Astorga and Villafranca. I endeavoured to dissuade him from it; pointing out to him, that it was the only communication we had for our retreat or supplies, and begged that it might be left open to us. He stopped his retreat for the moment, but I much fear he will now prosecute it; in which case I know not how it will be possible for us to pass.

I had the honour to receive your Lordship's dispatches of the 10th by Captain Hardinge, yesterday morning. I shall be guided by circumstances; and shall not, you may rest assured, retreat an inch beyond what I am compelled to do. But I fear if once I am forced into the Mountains, that the want of the means of subsistence will make it necessary to proceed down to the coast, to be provisioned from the ships. I need hardly add, the necessity of sending immediately the means of transport to re-embark the army, at Vigo or Corunna.

The only part of the army which has hitherto been engaged with the Enemy, has been the cavalry; and it is impossible for me to say too much in their praise. I mentioned to your Lordship, in my Letter of the 16th, the success Brigadier-General Stuart had met with, in defeating a detachment of cavalry at Rueda; since that, few days have passed without his taking or killing different parties of the French, generally superior in force to those which attacked them. On the march to Sahagun Lord Paget had information of six or seven hundred cavalry being in that town. He marched on the night of the 20th from some villages where he was posted in front of the army at Mayorga, with the 10th and 15th Hussars. The 10th marched straight to the town, whilst Lord Paget with the 15th endeavoured to turn it. Unfortunately, he fell in with a patrole, one of whom escaped and gave the alarm; by this means the French had time to form on the outside of the town, before Lord Paget got round. He immediately charged them; beat them, and took from 140 to 150 prisoners, amongst whom were two lieutenant colonels and eleven officers; with the loss on our part of six or eight men, and, perhaps, twenty wounded. There have been taken by the cavalry from 400 to 500 French, besides a considerable number killed; this since we began our march from Salamanca. On his march from Sahagun on the 26th Lord Paget with two squadrons of the 10th attacked a detachment of cavalry at Mayorga, killed twenty, and took above one hundred prisoners. Our cavalry is very superior in quality to any the French have; and the right spirit has been infused into them by the example and instruction of their two leaders, Lord Paget and Brigadier-General Stuart.

I have the honour to be, &c.

JOHN MOORE.

---

### Sir John Moore to Lord Castlereagh.

MY LORD,                                                                  *Benavente, 28 Dec. 1808.*

I HAVE the honour to enclose some letters contained in a bag lately intercepted, the courier murdered, going from France to Buonaparte. Those I enclose were all that I thought in the least interesting. That from Champigni you will think particularly so.

I have the honour, &c.

JOHN MOORE.

---

### Sir John Moore to Lord Castlereagh.

MY LORD,                                                                   *Astorga, 31st Dec. 1808.*

I ARRIVED here yesterday; where, contrary to his promise, and to my expectation, I found the Marquis la Romana, with a great part of his troops. Nobody can describe his troops to be worse than he does;

and he complains as much as we do of the indifference of the inhabitants, and of his disappointment at their want of enthusiasm. He said to me, in direct terms, that, had he known how things were, he neither would have accepted the command, nor have returned to Spain. With all this, however, he talks of attacks and movements which are quite absurd, and then returns to the helpless state of his army and of the country.

He could not be persuaded to destroy the bridge at Mansilla. He posted some troops at it, who were forced and taken prisoners by the French, on their march from Mayorga. With respect to me, my Lord, and the British troops, it has come to that point which I have long foreseen. Abandoned from the beginning by every thing Spanish, we were equal to nothing by ourselves. From a desire to do what I could, I made the movement against Soult. As a diversion it has answered completely; but, as there is nothing to take advantage of it, I have risked the loss of the Army for no purpose. I have no option now but to fall down to the coast as fast as I am able. I found no provision here: the little which has been collected had been consumed by Sir David's corps in their passage; and there is not two days' bread to carry the Army to Villafranca. I have been forced to push on the troops by divisions, without stopping. General Fraser, with his division, will be at Villafranca this day, and will proceed on to Lugo. General Hope, with his division, stopped yesterday two leagues from this, and proceeds this morning, followed by Sir David Baird. The two flank brigades go by the road to Ponferada. I shall follow, with the reserve and cavalry, to Villafranca, either this night or to-morrow morning, according as I hear the approach of the French. There is no means of carriage: the people run away, the villages are deserted; and I have been obliged to destroy great part of the ammunition and military stores. For the same reason I am obliged to leave the sick. In short, my sole object is to save the Army. We must all make forced marches to the coast, from the scarcity of provisions, and to be before the Enemy; who, by roads upon our flanks, may otherwise intercept us; but, after a time, the same difficulty which affects us, must affect him; therefore, the rear once passed Villafranca, I do not expect to be molested.

I hope to find on the coast transports for the embarkation of the troops. If not, I hope to be able to take up some position, which I can maintain until they arrive.

It is not probable that we can be followed by the numbers which are now marching against us. And, once collected upon the coast, we shall certainly not allow ourselves to be molested by any thing like equal numbers. It is only whilst retreating that we are vulnerable. I have heard of some dispatches from your Lordship to me, entrusted to Lieut.-Col Chabot; but he has been sent into Portugal, and I have not received them.

The morning I marched from Benavente, some squadrons of Buonaparte's Guards passed the river at a ford above the bridge. They were attacked by B. General Stewart, at the head of the piquets of the 18th, and 3d German Light Dragoons, and driven across the Ford. Their Colonel, a General of Division, Lefebre, was taken, together with about 70 officers and men. The affair was well contested. The numbers with which Gen. Stewart attacked were inferior to the French. It is the corps of the greatest character in their army; but the superiority of the British was, I am told, very conspicuous. I enclose, for your Lordship's satisfaction, Lord Paget's report of it. This army, there cannot be a doubt, would have distinguished itself, had the Spaniards been able to offer any resistance; but, from the beginning, it was placed in situations in which, without the possibility of doing any good, it was itself constantly risked—and now it is good fortune alone that can save it. It is impossible to deny that its discipline has been affected by the late movements. The shoes and necessaries are destroyed; and, for some time after it reaches the coast, the men will be in the worst state.

I send the French General Lefebre to Corunna, to be forwarded to England. He is a young man; and, I should suppose, from the station he held, a personal favourite of Buonaparte.

I have the honour, &c.

JOHN MOORE.

R R

## F F.

*Letter from Sir John Moore to Lord Castlereagh \*.*

MY LORD,                                         *Corunna,* 13 *January,* 1809.

SITUATED as this army is at present, it is impossible for me to detail to your Lordship the events which have taken place, since I had the honour to address you from Astorga on the 31st December.  I have therefore determined to send to England Brigadier-General Charles Stewart, as the Officer best qualified to give you every information you can want, both with respect to our actual situation, and the events which have led to it.  From his connection with your Lordship, and with His Majesty's Ministers, whatever he relates is most likely to be believed.  He is a man in whose honour I have the most perfect reliance ; he is incapable of stating any thing but the truth, and it is the truth which at all times I wish to convey to your Lordship, and to the King's government.

Your Lordship knows that had I followed my own opinion as a military man, I should have retired with the army from Salamanca.  The Spanish

---

\* In this dispatch there are several omissions, owing to the following circumstance :

In the month of March last, the Secretary of State for the War Department sent for the Author, and informed him, that it was the intention of Administration to accede to laying this letter before Parliament; which, however, being a private letter, and not written in the usual manner of official dispatches, it was thought proper to omit some passages which his Lordship would point out.  The Author replied, that he could not presume to object to any omissions which did not affect his brother's reputation.  After this conversation it was judged improper to fill up the blanks.  One passage at the beginning, however, it was considered, might be restored, where mention is made of the Honourable Brigadier-General Stewart, brother to Lord Castlereagh.

armies were then beaten; there was no Spanish force to which we could
unite; and    .    &#42;    &#42;    &#42;    &#42;    &#42;    &#42;    &#42;
&#42;    &#42;    &#42;    &#42;    &#42;    &#42;    &#42;    &#42;    &#42;

I was satisfied that no efforts would be made to aid us, or favour the cause in
which they were engaged. I was sensible, however, that the apathy and indifference of the Spaniards would never have been believed; that, had the
British been withdrawn, the loss of the cause would have been imputed to
their retreat; and it was necessary to risk this army to convince the people
of England, as well as the rest of Europe, that the Spaniards had neither the
power, nor the inclination, to make any efforts for themselves.

It was for this reason that I marched to Sahagun. As a diversion it succeeded: I brought the whole disposable force of the French against this
army, and it has been allowed to follow it, without a single movement being
made    &#42;    &#42;    &#42;    &#42;    &#42;·    &#42;    &#42;
&#42;    &#42;    &#42;    to favour its retreat.
&#42;    &#42;    &#42;    &#42;    &#42;    &#42;    &#42;
&#42;    &#42;    &#42;    &#42;    &#42;    &#42;    The people of the Gallicias,
though armed, made no attempt to stop the passage of the French through
their mountains. They abandoned their dwellings at our approach, drove
away their carts, oxen, and every thing that could be of the smallest aid to the
army. The consequence has been, that our sick have been left behind; and
when our horses or mules failed, which on such marches and through such a
country was the case to a great extent, baggage, ammunition, stores, and
even money, were necessarily destroyed or abandoned.

I am sorry to say that the army, whose conduct I had such reason to extol
on its march through Portugal, and on its arrival in Spain, has totally changed
its character since it began to retreat.    &#42;    &#42;    &#42;    &#42;
&#42;    &#42;    &#42;    &#42;    &#42;    &#42;    &#42;    &#42;
&#42;    &#42;    &#42;    &#42;    &#42;    &#42;    &#42;    &#42;

I can say nothing in its favour, but that when there was a prospect of fighting the Enemy, the men were then orderly, and seemed pleased, and determined to do their duty. In front of Villafranca the French came up with

the reserve, with which I was covering the retreat of the army. They attacked it at Calcabalos. I retired, covered by the 95th regiment, and marched that night to Herrerias, and thence to Nogales and Lugo; where I had ordered the different divisions which preceded to halt and collect. At Lugo the French again came up with me; they attacked our advanced posts on the 6th and 7th, and were repulsed in both attempts with little loss on our side.

I heard from the prisoners taken, that three divisions of the French army commanded by Marshal Soult were come up: I therefore expected to be attacked on the morning of the 8th. It was my wish to come to that issue; I had perfect confidence in the valour of the troops, and it was only by crippling the Enemy that we could hope either to retreat or to embark unmolested. I made every preparation to receive the attack; and drew out the army in the morning to offer battle. This was not Marshal Soult's object: he either did not think himself sufficiently strong, or he wished to play a surer game by attacking us on our march, or during our embarkation. The country was intersected, and his position too strong for me to attack with an inferior force. The want of provisions would not enable me to wait longer. I marched that night; and in two forced marches, bivouacing for six or eight hours in the rain, I reached Betanzos on the 10th instant. *  *  *  *

*  *  *  *  *  *  *  *

*  *  *  *  *  *  *  *

*  *  *  *  *  *  *  *

At Lugo I was sensible of the impossibility of reaching Vigo, which was at too great a distance, and offered no advantages to embark in the face of an Enemy. My intention then was to have retreated to the peninsula of Betanzos; where I hoped to find a position to cover the embarkation of the army in Ares or Rodes Bays: but having sent an officer to reconnoitre it, by his report I was determined to prefer this place. I gave notice to the Admiral of my intention, and begged that the transports might be brought to Corunna. Had I found them here on my arrival on the 11th instant, the embarkation would easily have been effected; for I had gained several marches on the

French. They have now come up with us, the transports are not arrived. My position in front of this place is a very bad one; and this place, if I am forced to retire into it, is commanded within musket shot; and the harbour will be so commanded by cannon on the coast that no ship will be able to lay in it. In short, my Lord, General Stewart will inform you how critical our situation is. It has been recommended to me, to make a proposal to the Enemy to induce him to allow us to embark quietly; in which case, he gets us out of the country soon, and this place with its stores, &c. complete; that, otherwise, we have it in our power to make a long defence, which must ensure the destruction of the town. I am averse to make any such proposal; and am exceedingly doubtful if it would be attended with any good effect: but, whatever I resolve on this head, I hope your Lordship will rest assured, that I shall accept no terms that are in the least dishonourable to the Army, or to the Country. I find I have been led into greater length and more detail than I thought I should have had time for: I have written under interruptions, and with my mind much occupied with other matter. My letter written so carelessly can only be considered as private; when I have more leisure I shall write more correctly. In the mean time I rely on General Stewart for giving your Lordship the information and detail which I have omitted. I should regret his absence, for his services have been very distinguished: but the state of his eyes makes it impossible for him to serve, and this country is not one in which Cavalry can be of much use.

If I succeed in embarking the Army I shall send it to England — it is quite unfit for further service until it has been refitted, which can best be done there.      *      *      *      *      *      *
*      *      *      *      *      *      *      *

I have the honour to be, &c.

JOHN MOORE.

# TRANSLATIONS

OF

## LETTERS IN THE FRENCH LANGUAGE.

*From Mr. Frere to His Excellency Mr. De Garay.*  (See p. 56.)

SIR, *Aranjuez, 23 Nov. 1808.*

I HAVE thought it proper to address your Excellency, as a Member and Secretary of the Supreme Central Junta, a representation which appears to me too important not to be communicated to that Assembly through a person distinguished by their confidence, and by the important office he holds.

I have received letters from Sir John Moore, which renders it necessary for me to recapitulate the complaints which he has addressed to me, and which he regrets he is not able to make in person at Aranjuez.

He complains, in the first place, of the state of ignorance he is left in respecting the number and position of the Enemy's forces; and even of the plans and operations of the campaign, to such a degree (he writes) that, when the very unmilitary evacuation of Valladolid by General Pignatelli took place, that Officer did not think it his duty to inform him of it.

The particulars of the march, and of the effective strength of the army of Estremadura, were likewise for a long time unknown to him. The retreat of General Blake, and his subsequent retreat to Reynosa, he was also left ignorant of, until he learnt these events from Madrid. He continues in these words, " I am in no communication with any of the Spanish armies, " nor am I made acquainted with the plans either of the Government, or of " the Generals. Castanos, with whom I was put in correspondence, is dis- " missed from his command, at the moment I expected to hear from him ; " and Romana, with whom I suppose I now ought to correspond, is absent. " In the mean time the French, whose numbers I cannot learn, are only " four days' march distant from my army, which is only assembling. No " channel of information has been opened for me, and I have not been long " enough in the country to procure one for myself. I give you this infor- " mation, and I wish I could go myself to Aranjuez or Madrid, to make a " representation of it ; for, in truth, if things remain in this situation, the " ruin of the Spanish cause, and the defeat of their armies, is inevitable ; " and it will become my duty only to consider the safety of the British " Army, and to take measures to withdraw it from a situation where, " without the possibility of being useful, it is exposed to certain defeat."

In answer to those observations respecting General Castanos and the Marquis of Romana, your Excellency informed me, to my great surprise, that orders had been sent, ten days before, to the Marquis of Romana to come and take the command of the Army of the Centre; and to leave that of the North, and of the Asturias, under the command of General Blake.

It seems to me that a secret known to two-and-thirty persons (the number of the Junta) might have been trusted to the Minister of his Britannic Majesty, without any great additional risk of its being divulged; although there had been no question of a fact so interesting, that the knowledge of it was necessary for a correspondence, upon which might depend the safety of the English army.

It appeared to me that your Excellency was not insensible to the justice of this reflection ; to which I might have added, that the news of the entry of the French into Valladolid had been concealed from me; and, when I enquired if there was any foundation for the rumour which mentioned it, I was answered, that no official news had arrived that day, except a report respecting the moving some pieces of artillery, I believe, to Segovia. It was impossible for me to think, after such an answer, that authentic accounts had actually brought certain information of the event respecting which I was demanding an explanation; and that the fact was dissembled by an equivocation founded upon the non-arrival of the official dispatches from the Commandant.

The news of the defeat of General Blake, a piece of news which might have occasioned the total loss of the two divisions under General Moore and Sir David Baird, was undoubtedly communicated to me; but not until the evening of the day which followed the arrival of the courier. I am far from feeling myself the slightest ill-humour towards persons extremely respectable, and who, both in their answers and in their silence, only follow the system which has been traced out to them; but it is my duty to expostulate strongly against the continuation of a system which, without ensuring secrecy towards the Enemy, establishes distrust and mystery, instead of that confidence which should be the foundation of the united plans, on which the fate of the war must depend.

I have learned with much pleasure the news of recalling the disorganizing Commission which had been sent to the Army of the Centre; as well as that of nominating Mr. de Morla, with full powers to confer and conclude with our Officers, upon all business respecting an effective system of co-operation; and I hope that these powers will be further enlarged, both as to execution and deliberation.

The Courier which was sent to the Marquis of Romana will have undoubtedly carried an order to communicate freely with General Sir John Moore.

I cannot finish without thanking your Excellency for the attention with which, at a first conference, you listened to the particulars of a representation so extremely disagreeable.

I beg, &c. &c.

J. H. FRERE.

*From Sir John Moore to his Excellency the Marquis la Romana.*
(See p. 110.)

MY LORD MARQUIS,                                          *Salamanca, 8 Dec. 1808.*

     I TAKE the opportunity of writing to you through the means of an Officer, whom I am going to dispatch to Sir D. Baird. I have not yet received any certain information respecting Madrid; but I have reason to believe the people still hold out. A letter from the Junta of Toledo informs me, that it is their intention to assemble there a body of troops; and that the people are determined to die sword in hand.

General Castanos has received orders to retire upon Carolina, on the other side of the Sierra Morena.

The people in this part of Spain are too lethargic; they say they have no arms; they stand in need of a head, to excite them, to unite them, and to command them. I propose, on the 10th inst. to make a movement upon Zamora and Toro, that I may be nearer General Baird and you. When I am informed what progress you have made in the organisation of your Army, we shall be able to concert measures together; and I shall anxiously wait the reply to the letter which I had the honour to address to you on the 6th.

Two General Officers were here a few days ago, sent by the Supreme Junta. They did not appear to me to have either the authorities or the information necessary for concerting any operation. I thought I could explain myself more satisfactorily to you, General, and I refused to enter upon any discussion with them. They were the Generals Escalante and B. General Bueno.

     I have the honour to be, &c.

               JOHN MOORE.

*From the Marquis of Romana to Sir John Moore.* (See p. 120.)

SIR,                                        *Head Quarters, Leon, 11th Dec. 1808.*

YOUR Excellency's two letters of the 6th and 8th inst. have explained to me the cause of the retrograde movements which you had directed, of the divisions of the army under your Excellency's command; which I think very just and well-founded.

· I·shall not venture to reply to the subjects of your two letters till I can do it by means of an Officer, whom I will dispatch to-morrow to meet you at Zamora. In the mean while I shall prepare to effect the much-wished-for junction with Y. E.

I have the honour to renew to Y. E.

&c. &c. &c.

THE MARQUIS DE LA ROMANA.

––––––––

*To the Marshal Duke of Dalmatia, commanding the 2d Corps of the Army at Saldana. The Vice Constable Major General.*
(See p. 121.)

MARSHAL DUKE OF DALMATIA,          *Chamartin, Dec. 10, 1808.*

I READ to the Emperor your letter of the fourth of December, which was brought by one of your officers. His Majesty approves of all you have done. The 8th Regiment of Dragoons, the 22d of Chasseurs, the Regiment of Colonel Tascher, and the Hanoverian Regiment, form two brigades, commanded by the Generals Belle and Franceschi. These two brigades are under your orders, and you can manœuvre them as you think proper. The Emperor is of opinion, that, with the division Merle, and the Division Mouton, together with the four regiments of cavalry, nothing can resist you.

What are you to do? Take possession of Leon, drive back the enemy into Galicia, make yourself master of Benavente and Zamora. You can have no English in your front, for some of their regiments came to the Escurial and Salamanca, and every thing evinces that they are in full retreat. Our advanced guard is this day at Talavera de la Reyna, upon the road to Badajos, which it will reach soon. You clearly perceive that this movement must compel the English to hasten immediately to Lisbon, if they are not gone there already. The moment, Marshal, you are sure that the English have retreated, of which there is every presumption, move forward with rapidity. There are no Spaniards who can resist your two divisions. Order shoes and great-coats to be made at Leon, St. Andero, and Palencia. His Majesty grants every demand for improving your equipment. You may also require mules for your artillery, and horses to remount your cavalry; but let it all be done according to the regular forms of administration.

It is possible that, as soon as the Dragoons of General Millar shall arrive in Spain, the Emperor will send them to you; but this cannot happen these fifteen days. At the distance you are, Marshal Duke, you must direct yourself, and look upon all I write as only general instructions. His Majesty imagines that you will take every measure to reduce the country between the Duero, Galicia, and the Asturias; always preserving most attentively St. Andero. The 5th corps, commanded by the Marshal Duke of Trevise, has received an order to direct its march to Saragossa. The 8th corps, under the Duke of Abrantes, whose 1st division arrived at Vittoria on the 12th, will probably receive orders to unite at Burgos. Gun-boats and armed vessels of every kind have orders to sail to St. Andero. Load them with confiscated English merchandize, cotton, wool, artillery, and send all to France.

In short, hold Valladolid and Zamora in subjection. Valladolid is a good town, which has behaved well. It is thought to be very important to occupy Zamora. To conclude, the Emperor thinks that you can do what you please, as soon as the English retire to Lisbon.

Five divisions of Castanos' best troops have been routed, with even less difficulty than you found in beating the Andalusian * army at Burgos. The wreck of Castanos' army is pursued by Marshal Bessieres; who has cut them off from the road to Estremadura, and is pursuing them towards Valentia, several marches beyond the Tagus. The Emperor's head-quarters are at Chamartin, a little country-seat a league and a half from Madrid. His Majesty enjoys an excellent state of health.

The City of Madrid is quite tranquil; the shops are all open, the public amusements are resumed, and there is not the least appearance of the first proposals having been strengthened by 4000 cannon-balls.

THE PRINCE OF NEUFCHATEL,
Major-General.

I will send you to-morrow a Proclamation, and some decrees of the Emperor; in which you will recognise the style of him who was born to command the world.

------

*The Marquis of Romana to Sir John Moore.* (See p. 132.)

SIR, *Leon, Dec. 14th, 1808.*

FROM the forward movements which the army under Y. E.'s command is making, I am induced to dispatch my aide-de-camp, Mr. O'Niell, with this letter, which will inform you of the destination of

* Mistaken for the Estremaduran army.

my army, and of my designs. I have now 20 thousand men present under arms, whom I have begun to clothe and to organise; but much is still wanting to complete the work, and there are still at least two-thirds who are in want of clothing from head to foot.

Almost the whole army are without havre-sacks, cartouche-boxes, and shoes; and, notwithstanding all the exertions I have made to that effect, I have not been able to succeed, the country offering so few resources. I expect all these articles from day to day, but the distance which they are from this retards the execution of my orders. If the provinces were a little more zealous, I doubt not but the army would by this time be fit to act in concert with that of your Excellency. So much for the situation of my troops: I will now communicate to Y. E. my plans. If the Enemy were not in front of me, I should not a moment doubt the possibility of uniting my forces with your Excellency's, and of concerting a decisive attack upon the troops who now surround Madrid; but, according to the best information, there is a division, from about 8 to 10 thousand men, which extends from Sahagun to Almanza; and whose object, as far as I can judge, is to check my army, and to keep open the communication with the Mountains of Santander. Its position is along the little river of Cea, and it occupies the villages of Sahagun, which strengthen its left; its principal corps is at Saldana, and its advanced posts at Cea and Almanza. From this last place they push their reconnoitring parties as far as Pedrosa, at the entrance of Valdeburon; and they expect to harass my left. As long as this corps remains in this position I cannot abandon mine; both because I cannot expose nor abandon this country, from whence I draw large supplies of provisions, nor can I leave the Enemy a free passage to the Asturias, who would instantly take possession of this country, and threaten the passage into Galicia. As soon as I am able to manœuvre, I intend to push forward the corps which is in my front; and at the same time Sir David Baird can shew the heads of columns in advancing from Benavente upon the road to Palencia. This combined movement will oblige this division of the Enemy to fall back upon Reynosa, or even upon Burgos. If we were once clear of this party, I do not think it would be difficult for your Excellency to join us, as well as Sir

David Baird. I should very much wish to have an interview with Y. E. we might then smooth many difficulties. If I can effect it without committing any error here, I shall repair as soon as possible to Tordesillas, and I shall not fail to give you timely notice of it.

I have the honour to be,

&c. &c. &c. &c.

THE MARQUIS LA ROMANA.

---

*From the Marquis of Romana to Sir John Moore.* (See p. 144.)

SIR, *Leon, Dec.* 19*th,* 1808.

I HASTEN to reply to your Excellency's letter of yesterday, dated from Castronuero, to explain to you, that although I thought of making a retreat, it was only in consequence of the information which I received from Sir David Baird, and that otherwise it was far from my intention. I have placed my advanced posts so as to be able to retreat in good order; and, if Marshal Soult's corps does not receive more considerable reinforcements, I have nothing to fear from my position, which is but temporary, and solely to reorganise the army. I should wish to co-operate with Y. E. in the movement you are about to make upon Sahagun, and I shall only wait to learn when Y. E. proposes putting it into execution—to begin my march. I shall order a body of light troops to go round by the Mountains of Leon to Guardo, whilst the principal part of my troops will march upon Almanza; and from thence, coasting the river Cea, I shall move upon Saldana, where Marshal Soult's corps is expected to be; unless, as is reported, he has changed his position within these two days. The accounts say, that he has left only 1500 men at Saldana; and that he has filed off the rest towards Guardo, drawing nearer to the Mountains of Santander, which border upon Leon and the Asturias. After all, there is no great reliance to be placed upon the reports of the peasants, who are not very accurate in their observations; and are, besides, confounded by the continual marches and counter-marches of the Enemy.

I have the honour to acquaint Y. E. that the bridge and entrance of Sahagun are barricadoed with carts.

If your Excellency has formed any other plans I hope I shall be made acquainted with them, in the persuasion that I have no other wish than to act in concert with Y. E. in every thing, and to aid you, to my utmost, in all your operations. I think that, for the present, there should be no thoughts of a retreat; but that we should feel the pulse of the Enemy, and oblige them to retire from the Capital. If Y. E. thinks it advisable, we might have an interview at Benavente, and it would perhaps be easier then to concert a plan of operations.

I have this evening received letters from the Junta, dated from Merida, in Estremadura, on the 13th, in which they announce to me that the people at Madrid still hold out, that the French have been repulsed and beaten on their way to Saragossa, and that affairs are going on well in Catalonia.

I beg Y. E. to accept the homage,

&c. &c. &c.

MARQUIS DE LA ROMANA.

*From the Duke del Infantado to H. E. J. H. Frere.* (See p. 147.)

SIR, *Cuenca, Dec. 13th, 1808.*

I THINK it my duty to announce to you, as our very good and faithful Ally, that, having been sent to this Army of the Centre, to endeavour to hasten its arrival to the Capital, in order, if possible, to save it; but not having been able to succeed in my design, and preparing in consequence to join the Supreme Junta, I have found myself obliged by the Generals, and forced by circumstances, to take the command of the Army, till I receive the decision of the Junta. It was unfortunately the spirit of insurrection and discontent among the soldiery which placed me at the post I now occupy; and it is certainly a very disagreeable situation to have to correct inveterate evils, and to set out with the measures necessary to re-establish that order and discipline which have been totally neglected.

I cannot describe to you the state in which I found this body of famished troops, without shoes, most of them without uniforms, wanting ammunition, having lost the greatest part of their baggage, reduced to about 9 thousand infantry and two of cavalry, and, to crown all, having totally lost all confidence in their commanders. From these circumstances I thought it right to follow the plan adopted by my Predecessor, of coming to this mountainous country for a few days, in order to reorganise a little the troops; to give an opportunity to some stragglers and recruits to join me, to give shoes and repose to the men and horses, and then to set forward upon some new operations. But it is very important for their success, that these should be in concert with those of the other armies, especially of the English; and it would be, consequently, indispensably necessary, that we should mutually be made acquainted with each other's plans. Colonel Whittingham is ill at this moment, I should therefore wish that H. E. General Moore, the Commander-in-Chief, should send me an experienced and confidential officer, who can give me an account of the plan adopted by the General for this campaign, and inform him of what we shall have agreed upon together, relative to the part which this division of the Army can take in its execution. I shall be delighted if the choice should fall upon Colonel Graham, whom I had the honour of knowing at Mr. Stuart's.

I know not, Sir, when this letter will reach you, for I am still ignorant where the Junta has stopped, or established itself; and I believe that you are with it. My letter will not be less the testimony of my sincerest affection, as well as the assurance of my highest esteem,

With which I have the honour,

&c. &c. &c.

THE DUKE DEL INFANTADO.

--------

*The Marquis of Romana to Sir John Moore.* (See p. 157.)

SIR, *Leon, Dec. 21, 1808.*

I HAD the honour to write to you on the 19th, in reply to the letter which Y. E. remitted to me through my aide-de-camp, Mr. O'Niell; and, not having had any accounts since, I think it right to state, that I am desirous to co-operate in the attack which, it seems, it is Y. E.'s intention to make upon Saldana, that the success may be complete. The Enemy, when they have assembled all the forces which they have scattered about at all points in the surrounding parts, will have at the utmost, according to the best accounts I can obtain, from about 8 to 9 thousand infantry, and a thousand cavalry, with from 8 to 10 pieces of artillery. It would be of

T T

great importance to surround this corps, and to destroy it, before its junction with any other which Napoleon might send to reinforce it. If Y. E. determines upon this enterprise, I will make a movement with from 9 to 10 thousand men, of those which are best clothed and armed, all the rest being nearly naked, and very ill equipped.

If Y. E. gives me a speedy reply, I will set out to-morrow; but I have the honour to observe to you, that, when the blow is once struck, I must return to my winter-quarters, for want of clothing and equipments for my troops. However, it will be time enough to talk of this at our interview, as well as to concert the plan of operations which we are to follow.

I am persuaded that the Enemy is not strong, and that all the disasters we have witnessed are owing to the want of union in the operations of our armies. I have been informed by an Officer of Engineers, whom the Junta of Zamora have sent back to me from having some slight suspicions of his conduct, that the army of Palafox has received no check, as the Enemy give out; but that he has been obliged to fall back upon Saragossa, on account of Castanos' army having quitted Logrono, which he should not have abandoned. He gives very circumstantial details of the French army at Madrid, of the Emperor, of Junot's division, and, in short, of particulars which I think it very necessary to acquaint Y. E. with, and from which it appears to me that we must absolutely have an interview.

I have the honour,

&c. &c.

MARQUIS LA ROMANA.

*From the Marquis of Romana to Sir John Moore.* (See p. 162.)

(See p. 162.)

SIR, *Leon, 22d Dec. 1808.*

A CONFIDENTIAL person whom I had placed on the river Duero has written to me, on the 18th instant, that he is assured, that the Enemy's troops posted at the Escurial are moving in this direction.

He adds, that if the person who gave him this intelligence should not arrive the same day, he would go himself to Villacastin, twelve leagues from Madrid, to watch the two roads; the one of which leads to Zamora, and the other to Segovia.

I hasten to give this information to your Excellency, that you may judge what measures are requisite to be taken.

I have the honour, &c.

THE MARQUIS OF ROMANA.

---

*From the Marquis of Romana to Sir John Moore.* (See p. 163.)

(See p. 163.)

SIR, *Mansilla, 23d Dec. three o'clock in the evening.*

I HAVE the honour to inform you of my arrival here with the troops which I intend to employ as auxiliaries to your movement.

I have only been able to lead out 7000 infantry, 120 cavalry, and eight pieces of artillery. The troops are cantoned in the space of a league and a quarter round this town. The advanced posts are towards Saldana, except one corps, which I have sent to Villarmimio, three leagues distant from Cea.

I shall wait for your answer, and shall not begin to march until your Excellency has communicated to me your plan and intentions.

I request a positive answer, to enable me to send orders at an early hour to the troops.

I have the honour to be, &c.

THE MARQUIS OF ROMANA.

THE END.

ERRATUM.

P. 287, l. 19, *for* Lieut.-Col. Null *read* Lieut.-Col. Hull.

JOHN NICHOLS and SON, Printers,
Red Lion Passage, Fleet Street, London.

www.ingramcontent.com/pod-product-compliance
Lightning Source LLC
LaVergne TN
LVHW012205040326
832903LV00003B/134